Building Bridges

Through Sensory Integration

Third Edition

Therapy for Children with Autism and Other Pervasive Developmental Disorders

Ellen Yack, BSc, MEd, OT & Paula Aquilla, BSc, OT
& Shirley Sutton, BSc, OT

Foreword by Carol Stock Kranowitz, MA

Building Bridges Through Sensory Integration

All marketing and publishing rights guaranteed to and reserved by:

Phone: 817-277-0727 or 800-489-0727 (toll-free)
Fax: 817-277-2270
www.SensoryWorld.com

ISBN: 978-1935567455

BUILD ME A BRIDGE

I have known that you and I
have never been quite the same.
And I used to look up at the stars at night
and wonder which one was from where I came. Because you seem to be part of another world
and I will never know what it's made of
Unless you build me a bridge, build me a bridge, build me a bridge out of love.

I long for the day that you smile at me just because you realize
that there's a decent and intelligent person
buried deep in my kaleidoscope eyes.
For I have seen the way that people look at me
Though I have done nothing wrong. Build me a bridge, build me a bridge, And please don't take too long.

Living on the edge of fear.
Voices echo like thunder in my ear. See me hiding every day.
I'm just waiting for the fear to lift away.

I want so much to be a part of your world. I want so much to break through.
And all I need is to have a bridge, a bridge built from me to you.
And I will be together with you forever, and nothing can keep us apart.
If you build me a bridge, a tiny, little bridge
from my soul, down deep into your heart.

From *Soon Will Come the Light: A View from Inside the Autism Puzzle*
By Thomas McKean, 1994. Arlington, Texas: Future Horizons Inc.
(reprinted with permission from the author and publisher)

DEDICATION

This book is dedicated to the children and families that we have had the privilege of working with.

They continue to inspire us, teach us and challenge us.

Your tenacity, courage and strength of character are boundless.

ACKNOWLEDGEMENTS

We wish to thank our families for their endless support and the parents of the children we work with who gave us valuable feedback during the preparation of this book. Thanks to the Toronto Sensory Integration Study Group who believed in this project and provided a grant to assist in the publication of this book.

Finally, we would like to thank Dr. Jean Ayres and the other occupational therapists who have contributed to the evolution of the theory of sensory integration.

TABLE OF CONTENTS

Foreword xi

Letter to the Reader xiii

What Is in This Book? xv

PART 1 1

Chapter 1: What is ASD and Occupational Therapy? 3

Chapter 2: What Is Sensory Integration? 13

Chapter 3: What Are The Sensory Systems? 47

PART 2 63

Chapter 4: Identifying Problems with Sensory Integration 65

Chapter 5: Strategies for Challenging Behaviors 91

Chapter 6: Ideas for Self-care skills 121

Chapter 7: Adapting Home, School and Childcare Settings 151

Chapter 8: Activity Suggestions 193

Chapter 9: Equipment and Resources 245

References 273

About the Authors 283

Index 285

FOREWORD

Each time I open my copy of *Building Bridges through Sensory Integration* to reread, say, a suggestion for teaching a child with poor self-regulation, a definition of occupational therapy, or strategies for sitting in a circle, I thank Paula, Ellen and Shirley for writing this classic. The book is "just right" (as Dr. Ayres would say) because it has almost everything a parent, teacher, or professional needs to know about supporting children with sensory issues. Now that the book has been updated and reorganized, there is even more to applaud.

One very important point this revised book makes is that the explanations and sensory strategies are for all comers. The book is not exclusively for occupational therapists; it is intended for anyone eager to support a person with sensory difficulties. Another benefit is that the person with sensory difficulties need not be a child; the concepts apply to individuals of all ages. The strategies are suitable for those with ASD, as well as those with milder sensory challenges; for young children and older adults and everyone in between; and for home, school and clinical settings. Not only children but also grown-ups can improve their vestibular processing and self-regulation by bouncing on a therapy ball and pulling on a therapy band!

Part One of *Building Bridges* is a primer, dealing with Autism Spectrum Disorder (ASD), occupational therapy, sensory integration, and the sensory systems. Please read this introductory section to learn how thinking has evolved over the years about the topics that are the crux of the book.

A discussion of ASD reflects changes in the 5th edition of the *Diagnostic and Statistical Manual* (DSM-V). For instance, Pervasive Developmental Disorder and Asperger's Syndrome, which were previously considered distinct disorders, are now under the big umbrella of ASD. Atypical sensory processing, which earlier editions of the *Manual* ignored, is now included in the DSM-V as a characteristic of ASD. These and other modifications clarify our understanding of the body-brain-behavior connections and the benefits of sensory integration treatment.

The three authors' discussion of Occupational Therapy (OT) brings us up to date about their proud health profession. Recent research shows the value of OT in delivering services to children with ASD, helping them become "can-do" kids who participate more fully in life.

BUILDING BRIDGES THROUGH SENSORY INTEGRATION

Sensory integration (or sensory processing) and the sensory systems are also discussed in Part One. Examples of children with inefficient processing, scenarios for us to imagine ourselves in, and even poetry make these explanations interesting and worthwhile.

Part Two opens with a chapter about identifying sensory difficulties. A list of published questionnaires informs the reader about the various assessment tools that occupational therapists and other professionals may use. For non-OTs—like you and me and many other parents and teachers reading this book—the Building Bridges Sensory Screening is a great help for gauging whether a child has the disorder. It is important to remember that every behavior in this screening matters. Behavior tells us what cannot be easily expressed in words by a child, teenager, or adult who is confused, uncomfortable, and out of sync.

Then you can find strategies for challenging behaviors, including the Sensory Diet and other techniques; sensible ideas for self-care skills to help people with sensory difficulties make it through the day; and suggestions for accommodations to make at home, school, and early childhood settings.

My favorite chapter, Activity Suggestions, is whimsically illustrated and filled with hand-on, body-on, three-dimensional, ideas to try. Low-cost, easy-to-replicate, whimsically illustrated, fun and functional, the activities will please children as well as their grown-ups, and the benefits will begin to accumulate.

For example, children with over-responsivity to touch sensations may find many activities with the just-right amount of messiness, such as "Smelly Play-Dough" and "Drizzle Goo," to be quite appealing. Soon the children will look forward to coming to the table to participate in more tactile fun. And the more the children do, the more they want to do, and the more they can do.

Thank you, Paula, Ellen and Shirley, for putting your heads together to produce this wonderful, necessary book. This revised version is the best yet!

Carol Stock Kranowitz, MA, author of *The Out-of-Sync Child*

Bethesda, Maryland—Spring 2015

LETTER TO THE READER

Welcome!

In the summer of 1997, we three occupational therapists decided to write a book about how the knowledge and application of the theory of sensory integration can help children with autism spectrum disorders. The idea for this book evolved as we searched for resources to provide simple activity suggestions and accommodation strategies for children in our practices. The resources were limited, so we developed our own! Our collective years of experience working with children and adults in varied settings provided us with the opportunity to develop and evaluate the effectiveness of a wide range of ideas. We wanted the book to serve as a practical resource for parents, educators, occupational therapists and other professionals. We each had more than twenty years of experience working with children and wanted to share strategies that we had found to be successful. Thus we embarked on the challenging task of writing a book.

In November 1998, we self-published our book, *Building Bridges through Sensory Integration: Occupational Therapy for Children with Autism and other Pervasive Developmental Disorders*. The term "pervasive developmental disorders" was listed in the DSM-IV as the term to use when describing the range of autistic disorders. However, currently the term "autism spectrum disorders" (ASD) is used to describe this population. We will therefore use the term ASD throughout this book.

We chose the words "Building Bridges" from the poem titled "Build Me a Bridge" by Thomas McKean, from his book *Soon Will Come the Light* (1994). In this poem, McKean shares his insights about being a man with autism, and he implores the reader to build a bridge between his world and that of others. He believes that non-autistic individuals require a greater understanding of how people with autism spectrum disorders experience the world. He believes that greater understanding will allow for the creation of a "bridge" that will allow him and others to encounter greater participation in their communities. We believe that the theory of sensory integration can serve as one type of bridge. The theory can provide understanding of the sensory and motor differences that many individuals with ASD experience and how these differences can impact behavior and skill performance. We believe that the principles of sensory integration can help build a bridge that will support individuals to reach their full potential.

This book provides a practical resource for parents, educators, occupational therapists and other professionals. Our focus is on children who have a diagnosis of autism spectrum disorders (ASD) and who experience atypical sensory processing and impaired motor planning. Although this book is primarily directed at children and their parents, the majority of the content is applicable to adults. The strategies are not exclusively for those with an ASD diagnosis, but are useful for anyone with sensory challenges. We want to empower children, parents and service providers. We'll give you some new insights into behavior... and some strategies for increased success!

We have been astounded and very pleased at how well the book has been received. *Building Bridges* has been translated into Finnish, Korean, Polish and Complex Chinese. The book has been highlighted on recommended reading lists on many autism education and parent advocacy websites. It has been included in university curriculums and cited in many other publications. Furthermore, we are very proud that the book was awarded the 2008 15th Annual Teacher's Choice Award for best classroom resource in the United States. However, our greatest satisfaction has come from the positive feedback we continue to receive about the book from parents and professionals, who tell us that the book has been a parent-friendly and valuable resource. We have had repeated inquiries to write a third edition. Recently, we received a letter from a university professor who recommends our book for required reading in her class. Her plea for a third edition and that of many others motivated us to revisit our book to provide additional strategies and ensure that the reader receives current information. We each now have over thirty years of experience in the field and keep learning from each other, our clients and their families. We are proud to have completed this revised edition, and to have completed the original book with a collective of 8 small children underfoot.

WHAT IS IN THIS BOOK?

Part One explains the role of the occupational therapist with children with ASD and provides a detailed examination of the theory of sensory integration. To better understand the reasons for our recommendations, we encourage you to read this section of the book. Our goal was to make the theory easy to comprehend, and we hope that, when people are armed with knowledge, they will find it easier to adapt recommendations for the needs of individual children.

Part Two will offer readers methods of identifying sensory processing differences in children and provide a range of strategies and activity suggestions. General recommendations, specific strategies for dealing with challenging behaviors and accommodations for completion of certain tasks are presented. The Table of Contents and Index will help you navigate through this section.

We strongly recommend that, before implementing any recommendations contained in this book, you consult an occupational therapist.

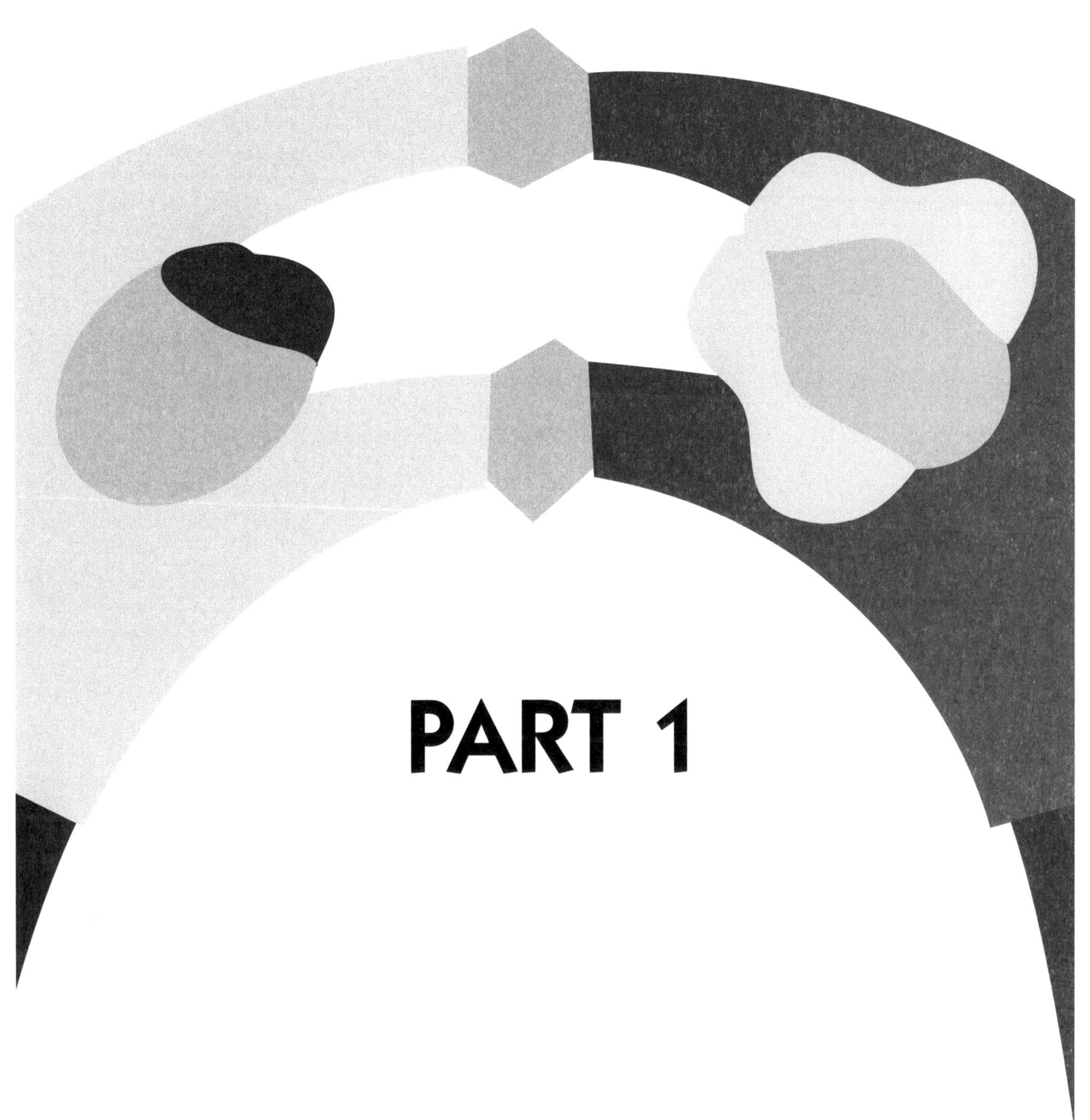

PART 1

CHAPTER 1

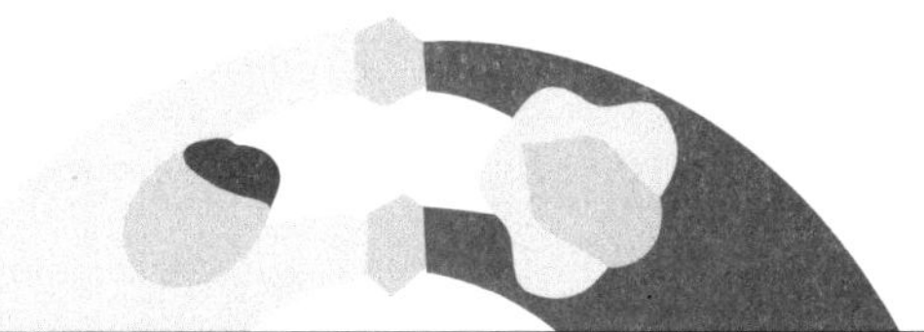

WHAT IS ASD AND OCCUPATIONAL THERAPY?

In this chapter, we define autism spectrum disorders and occupational therapy for our readers.

Classification of Autism Spectrum Disorders

Autism Spectrum Disorders (ASD) are defined in the Diagnostic and Statistical Manual V (DSM-V) as a class of developmental disabilities that are characterized by persistent deficits in social communication and social interaction and restricted, repetitive patterns of behaviors, interests or activities (APA, 2013). Symptoms present in early childhood and persist but may change throughout an individual's lifespan and impair everyday function (APA, 2013). Previous diagnostic labels including *Autistic Disorder, Asperger's Disorder* and *Pervasive Developmental Disorder: Not Otherwise Specified* are now included under the term ASD. Distinctions are now made according to three levels of severity that are based on the amount of supports required to manage the varying challenges. An additional change in the DSM-V, which is highly relevant to this book, is that atypical sensory processing is now listed as one of the possible characteristics of ASD. Hyper and hypo-reactivity to sensory input and/or unusual interest in the sensory aspects of an environment are now listed as a possible distinguishing characteristic.

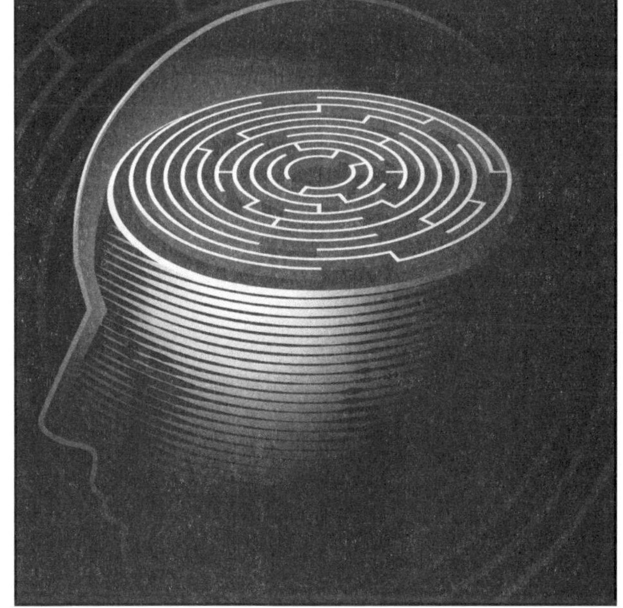

The new classification system has certainly led to some controversy and confusion. Many people with ASD and their advocates believe that it was beneficial to have sub-categories (e.g., Autistic Disorder, Asperger's Disorder) and strongly believe that the new system may negatively impact service delivery. Many clinicians and educators recognize that a new classification system exists but prefer to use the old terminology. Although we recognize the importance of differentiating between the subcategories or levels of severity, only the term ASD will be used throughout the book, as the information presented here can apply to all forms of the disorder. However, we do want to acknowledge that, when we review or reference other books or articles, many of these publications only use the term "autism."

The History of Autism Spectrum Disorders and Sensory Integration

In the 1940s, when Leo Kanner first coined the term "autism," he talked about a "biological impairment like physical or intellectual handicaps" (Kanner, 1943). He also discussed perceptual difficulties present in the children he was describing and commented on over-reaction to loud noises and moving objects. Unfortunately, in the '50s and '60s, this recognition of autism as a biological disorder seemed to lose its importance. During this time, autism was viewed as an emotionally based disorder resulting from parenting by a cold "refrigerator mother."

In the 1970s, we thankfully saw the move back to viewing autism as a neurological impairment. Books and articles began to focus on the nature of specific problem areas. Various literature focused on the social, communication, behavior and cognitive problems associated with the disorder. There also was a growing body of work that looked at the perceptual and sensory processing problems that people with PDD experience. Eric Schopler (1965) noted that many children with autism that he observed had abnormal responses to visual, vestibular or movement and auditory stimuli. Ornitz (1971) looked at childhood autism as a disorder of sensorimotor integration and later identified problems with the modulation of sensory input and motor output (Ornitz, 1973).

Carl Delacoto (1974), in his book, *The Ultimate Stranger*, put forth the hypothesis that autism resulted from a brain injury which caused perceptual dysfunction. He proposed that many of the behaviors exhibited by people with autism were attempts to normalize their nervous systems. He believed that if you could improve how the sensory systems worked, you could reduce abnormal behavior and increase your ability to attend to and complete tasks.

In the 1970s, A. Jean Ayres, an occupational therapist, published her two books, *Sensory Integration and Learning Disorders* and *Sensory Integration and the Child* (1972, 1979). Ayres (1979) defines sensory integration as the "organization of sensation for use" and discusses the effects on behavior and development when this process is impaired. In *Sensory Integration and the Child*, she offers a reader-friendly review of the theory and also addresses issues relevant to children with autism. The information Ayres presented supported the hypotheses that were proposed by Delacoto and Ornitz. Ayres described the behavioral problems associated with inadequate sensory integration. Many of these behaviors were consistent with Delacoto's and Orntiz's observations.

Knickerbocker (1980), another occupational therapist, also hypothesized that many behaviors exhibited by individuals with autism may be related to hyper- or hypo-reactions to sensory input. She suggested that planned sensory input provided through specific activities could help normalize reactions to sensory input and improve behavior.

Ornitz (1985, 1993) began to refine his hypotheses, and in his articles, he suggested that individuals with autism have difficulty registering, modulating and integrating sensory stimuli. He went on to suggest that these sensory processing differences may contribute to self-stimulatory behaviors and irregularities in arousal levels.

There are now autopsy studies that may lend support to these hypotheses. Developmental abnormalities have been found in the cerebellum and limbic regions of the brains of autistic individuals (Bauman & Kemper,1994). These regions play significant roles within the sensory integrative process, including the modulation of sensory input.

There are many books and articles which discuss the unusual responses to sensory stimuli that some children with ASD exhibit (Ayres & Tickle, 1980; Baranek & Bergson,1994; Cesaroni & Garber, 1991, Richard, 1997; Greenspan & Wieder, 1998). Recently, adults with autism have written accounts of their experiences and have reported aversive reactions and unusual sensitivities to certain stimuli (Grandin, 1986; Williams, 1992; Grandin & Scariano, 1992; McKean, 1994; Williams,1994; Grandin, 1995; Williams 1996). Many of these firsthand accounts have validated various aspects of sensory integration theory.

In 1985 and 1986, Temple Grandin, a woman with autistic disorder, published two books which include descriptions of her sensitivity to light, touch and sounds. She discusses how certain sensations, which would be harmless to others, would impact her behavior and emotions. For example, certain clothing textures would make her extremely anxious, distracted and fidgety. Certain sounds would cause her to scream and cover her ears.

Grandin discusses how she craved deep touch pressure and movement as a child and adolescent. She also tells how deep touch pressure helps to calm and organize her nervous system and reduces her hypersensitivity to touch. As a teenager, Grandin visited a farm and spotted a "cattle chute." This piece of equipment is used to contain cattle by exerting pressure against the sides of the body. She asked to go in the chute, believing that it would provide her with the pressure she always craved. She describes how she relaxed when in the chute and how better organized her thoughts became. Grandin subsequently built her own "squeeze" or "hug machine." The Emmy award-winning HBO movie, *Temple Grandin*, reviews her life and depicts her many sensory challenges and illustrates how she was helped by the deep pressure input that was provided by her "squeeze machine."

Grandin's experiences are consistent with Ayres' and Ornitz's hypotheses about the relationship between sensory processing and behavior. Her reported benefits of the squeeze or hug machine confirms the positive response to deep touch pressure, a calming and organizing strategy frequently proposed by occupational therapists. This strategy is also suggested by Donna Williams, another woman with autistic disorder, who describes the difficulties she has with sensory processing in her two books, *Nobody Nowhere* and *Somebody Somewhere* (1992 & 1994). In her book, *Autism: An Inside-Out Approach* (1996), Williams offers many strategies to assist individuals with PDD and suggests the use of deep touch pressure as a calming technique.

Individuals with ASD continue to offer insights into their challenges and gifts through their autobiographies. The following are some quotes from recent publications.

"High frequency and brassy, tin sounds clawed my nerves. Whistles, party noise makers, flutes and trumpets and any close relative of those sounds disarmed my calm and made my world very uninviting."

—*Pretending to be Normal*, Willey, 1999

"You don't know what it feels like to be me, when you can't sit still because your legs feel like they are on fire, or it feels like a hundred ants are crawling up your arms ... I want something that will put out the fire."

—*Carly's Voice: Breaking Through Autism*, Fleishman & Fleishman, 2012

"When I'm jumping, I can feel my body parts really well, too – my bounding legs and my clapping hands – and that makes me feel so, so good."

—*The Reason I Jump*, Naoki Higashida, 2013.

Autobiographical reports continue to share insights and provide firsthand accounts of how sensory differences can impact the behavior and quality of life. We also now have empirical evidence to support that there is a higher incidence of sensory challenges in individuals with ASD (Kientz & Dunn, 1997, Watling, Baranek et al., 2007), and atypical sensory processing is noted as a common feature of ASD in the DSM-V(APA, 2013).

What is Occupational Therapy?

This chapter illustrates the importance of having an occupational therapist on any team working with children with ASD.

Occupational therapy is a health profession concerned with how people function in their respective roles and how they perform activities.

The profession focuses on the promotion, restoration and maintenance of productivity in people with a wide range of abilities and disabilities.

The term *occupational therapist* can often be confusing. It carries the misconception that the profession's focus is on vocational counseling and job training. The word *occupation*, as defined in *Webster's Dictionary*, is "an activity in which one engages." Occupational therapists are involved in promoting skill development and independence in all daily activities. For an adult, this may mean looking at the areas of self-care, homemaking, leisure and work. The "occupations" of childhood may include playing in the park with friends, licking a popsicle, washing hands, going to the bathroom, cutting with scissors, writing at school, running, jumping, sitting at circle time and taking swimming lessons.

Occupational therapists graduate from universities with a baccalaureate or master's degree. They are educated in the behavioral and neurosciences and learn how to develop skills and promote independence through the use of meaningful activities. The occupational therapist (OT) may provide direct services to clients through assessment and treatment. They also provide indirect services to individual clients and organizations through consultation, mediator training, education, program development, case management and advocacy. The OT may provide these services in individual homes, child care centers, schools, hospitals, community and private agencies and clinics or industrial or residential facilities.

Occupational therapists are able to analyze all internal and external factors that are necessary for individuals to perform activities. Consider the grade one student who is learning to print. To learn this task, the student must have good hand skills, good sitting posture and balance, adequate joint stability and muscle strength, good body awareness and motor planning, mature visual perceptual and visual motor skills, good attending abilities and adequate sensory integration.

If sensory integration is impaired, the student could have difficulty printing because she may be uncomfortable with the touch of the paper against her arm and may have difficulty attending to the task as she is highly distracted by other activities that are occurring in the classroom. If the student has poor motor planning abilities, she may not be able to direct the movements of the pencil to appropriately form the required letter shapes. If the student has immature sitting balance, the height of the desk and chair will have to be analyzed and possibly altered to provide maximum stability.

Occupational therapists are concerned with:

Abilities:

- Balance and Postural Reactions
- Muscle Tone and Strength
- Body Awareness
- Fine Motor Abilities (pinches and grasps, manipulative skills, pencil and scissors use, handwriting)
- Gross Motor Abilities (running, jumping, climbing)
- Motor Planning (ability to plan, initiate and execute a motor act)
- Visual Perception (shape recognition, visual memory)
- Visual Motor Integration (copying shapes, copying block designs)
- Sensory Integration (response to sensory stimuli, discrimination of sensory input)
- Behavior (arousal level attention, problem-solving skills)

Skills:

- Self-Care Skills (eating, dressing, toileting, bathing)
- Community Living Skills (use of public transportation, money knowledge, shopping)
- Pre-academic Skills
- Play Skills (use of toys, types of play)
- Social Skills
- Pre-vocational and Vocational Skills

Environmental Factors:

- Physical Environment
- Family Situation
- Community Supports

Occupational Therapists provide consultation in the following areas:

- Early Intervention Programs
- Home, School and Vocational Settings
- Environmental and Equipment Adaptations
- Physical Aids and Assistive Devices
- Behavioral Strategies

Occupational Therapy and Children with ASD

Between the 1940s and early 1970s, the occupational therapy literature had few references to the profession's involvement with individuals with ASD. References include descriptions which focus on developing self-care and play skills and describe therapy practices that included the use of crafts, music therapy and behavior modification (Bloomer and Rose, 1989).

When Dr. A. Jean Ayres released her two books on the theory of sensory integration in 1972 and 1979, it had a significant impact on the practice of occupational therapy (Fisher et al., 1991). It provided a new framework for understanding factors that could interfere with an individual's ability to engage in activities. The theory of sensory integration also inspired the development of new assessment procedures and treatment strategies.

Occupational therapists began to look at how their clients responded to different types of sensations and if they could effectively organize and use sensory information. Sensory integration theory became a useful framework for occupational therapists working with clients who had ASD because so many of these clients had unusual responses to sensory stimulation.

The study and practice of occupational therapy utilizing a sensory integration frame of reference continued to evolve. In the 1970s, '80s and '90s, more and more articles in the occupational therapy literature began to address how impaired sensory integration may be contributing to many of the behaviors we see in individuals with ASD (Ayres & Heskett, 1972; Ayres & Tickle, 1980; Ayres & Mailloux,

1983; Becker, 1980; Chu 1991; Clarke,1983; Dunn & Fisher, 1983; Inamura et al., 1990; Williamson & Anzalone,1996). Specific books and articles were published which provide intervention strategies and methods to identify sensory integration problems which can be adapted for use with individuals with ASD (Kientz & Dunn, 1996; King 1991; Oetter, Richter & Frick 1995; Reisman, 1993; Reisman & Gross 1992; Reisman & Hanschu, 1992; Royeen, 1986; Slavik et al., 1984; Wilbarger, 1984; Wilbarger & Wilbarger 1991; Wilbarger, 1995; Zisserman, 1992).

The role of occupational therapy with individuals with ASD began gaining increased recognition in the 1990s. Many occupational therapy articles and books were written that explored the theory of sensory integration and its implications for individuals with ASD. Occupational therapists soon became frequent speakers at ASD workshops, conferences and association meetings. Many Internet sites were developed on which occupational therapy-related information began to be shared by parents and professionals. In addition to the publication of our book in 1998, several more books became available over the years which provided insights into sensory processing and ASD and offered practical supports (Anderson, 1998; Murray-Slutsky & Paris, 2000; Smith Myles et al., 2000; Bogdanisha, 2003; Miller & Kuhanek, 2004; Delaney, 2009).

The study by Miller-Kuhanek and Watling (2010) on occupational therapists who work with children with ASD revealed that sensory integration theory is utilized as the primary framework for intervention. In addition, it was noted that their primary focus of intervention was on sensory processing, attention, behavior and play. Intervention that utilizes a sensory integration frame of reference is a service that is increasingly sought after by parents. Studies report that this type of intervention is one of the top three services requested by parents of children with ASD (Goin-Kochel, Mackintosh & Myers, 2007: Green et al., 2006). Occupational therapists not only provide treatment to children but also play an important role in supporting families through education around the impact of atypical sensory processing on family dynamics and routines (Bagby, Dickie & Baranek, 2012).

Occupational therapists are increasingly recognized as having a pivotal role in the field and are beginning to assume leadership positions in autism research and practice (Schaaf, Imperatore Blanche,

2012). Occupational therapists are included as essential team members in currently recognized models of service delivery for children with ASD. These include but are not limited to the Denver Model of Intensive Therapy for Young Children with Autism (Rogers & Dawson, 2010), the SCERTS Model (Prizant & Wetherby, 2006), the Ziggaurat Model (Aspy & Grossman, 2007) and the DIR® Floor Time Approach (Greenspan & Weider, 1998, 2006). These models of service delivery recognize the important role that occupational therapists fulfill in contributing to this field with their knowledge of the links between atypical sensory processing and many challenges experienced by people with ASD. The occupational therapists' role in addressing sensory processing, praxis or motor planning and self-regulation is highlighted in each of these models of intervention.

Recent studies examining the effectiveness of occupational therapy treatment utilizing a sensory integration framework with children with ASD report positive results (Pfeiffer et al., 2011; Schaaf & Blanche, 2011; Schaaf et al., 2013,). Further research is needed to explore the effectiveness of different interventions and accommodations.

A likely consequence of the DSM-V now recognizing the prevalence of atypical sensory processing in ASD is that the occupational therapy role in provision of education, accommodations and treatment to manage sensory challenges will continue to expand.

Along with this expanded role, it is also critical that occupational therapists, educators and other professionals continue to collaborate and develop their expertise in this area.

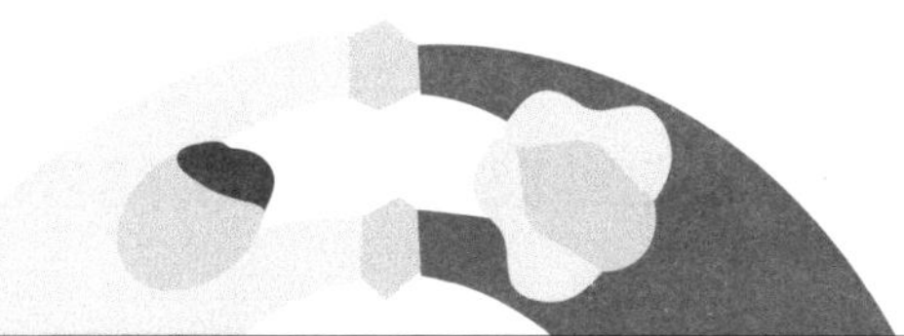

CHAPTER 2

WHAT IS SENSORY INTEGRATION?

In this chapter, we define sensory integration for our readers.

Picture yourself at a cottage. You are standing on the dock, about to climb into a canoe. You put your foot down into the canoe, and as you begin to step in, the canoe starts to rock. Automatically you adjust your body to keep yourself balanced and slowly sit down, placing yourself in the middle of the seat. This is *sensory integration.*

Our bodies and the environment send our brains information through our senses. This information is processed and organized so that we feel comfortable and secure, and we are able to respond appropriately to particular situations and environmental demands. This is sensory integration.

Sensory integration is a neurological process that occurs in all of us. We all take in sensory information from our bodies and the world around us. Our brains are programmed to organize or "integrate" this sensory information to make it meaningful to us. This integration allows us to respond automatically, efficiently and comfortably in response to the specific sensory input we receive.

Figure 1 illustrates how the process of sensory integration contributes to development.

attention
coordination
occular motor control
postural adjustments
eye-hand coordination
auditory/language skills
visual spacial perception
fine motor and gross motor skills
body scheme
motor planning
screening
postural security
awareness of two body sides
reflex maturation

SENSES: tacile, vestibular, proprioception, olfactory, gustatory, visual, auditory

Figure 1: Sensory integration as a Foundation for Learning (A. Jean Ayres PhD, OTR)

When stepping into that canoe, you receive information from various sensory channels. Your touch system tells you that your foot is on the bottom of the canoe. Your proprioceptive system tells you the position of your muscles and joints. Your vestibular system may be telling you that your centre of gravity is off and that you are on a moving surface. Your visual system determines that the canoe is lower than the dock.

If you have good sensory integration and efficiently receive and organize sensory information, you automatically adjust your body so that your transition to the canoe is successful. You do not become overly fearful when the boat moves because you are confident that you can maintain your balance. Unconsciously, you make fine adjustments and regain your centre of gravity. You can lower yourself to the seat because you judge the distance of the canoe from the dock and the size of the seat. You also have a good sense of where to sit and how much to move to centre yourself on the seat.

For the child who does not have good sensory integration, climbing into a canoe can be a disaster. One child may be quite fearful about the prospect of climbing into a boat because they are uncomfortable with or hypersensitive to the feeling of movement. They are terrified of anything that moves and do not have the confidence to maintain their balance. Another child may be overconfident and may not appreciate what can happen when trying to balance on a moving object. That child may climb into the canoe quickly, tipping the boat because they have poor body awareness and place all their weight on one side of the canoe.

In recent years, the terms "sensory integration" and "sensory processing" have sometimes been used interchangeably. Miller and Lane (2000) proposed that it is important to differentiate the theory of sensory integration from assessment and intervention practices. They suggested that the term "sensory integration" be used when referring to the guiding theoretical principles and that dysfunction in the processes involved in sensory integration be referred to as "sensory processing disorder," or SPD.

We have chosen to use the term "sensory integration" to reflect what happens in the nervous system when we receive and organize sensory information for use.

How Did the Theory of Sensory Integration Develop?

Occupational therapist Dr. A. Jean Ayres first proposed the theory of sensory integration (1972, 1979). She was practicing in a children's center during the late '50s and early '60s, and she developed a keen interest in how the brain works. Returning to college, Dr. Ayres obtained a doctoral degree and pursued postdoctoral work. During her studies, she formulated the theory of sensory integration based on established knowledge and theories found within the neuroscience field (Fisher, Murray & Bundy, 1991). In addition to her two books, Ayres also developed two test batteries to assist in identifying problems with sensory integration (Ayres, 1979, 1985).

The theory describes normal sensory integrative abilities and defines sensory integrative dysfunction and intervention programs which use sensory integrative techniques (Fisher et al., 1991). This theory continues to evolve (Bundy, Lane & Fisher, 2002) and provides a framework for intervention with children and adults with a variety of special needs (Smith Roley, Imperatore Blanche & Schaaf, 2001). Occupational therapists report that the theory of sensory integration was their primary frame of reference when working with children with ASD (Case-Smith & Miller, 1999, Watling et al., 1999, Miller-Kuhanek & Watling, 2010). Parents of children with ASD have noted in various studies that obtaining intervention utilizing a sensory integration approach is one of their priorities (Green et al., 2006, Goin-Kochel, Mackintosh & Myers 2007). The theory of sensory integration is not only an important frame of reference for the occupational therapy profession, but early on it also provided a valuable perspective for other disciplines (Windeck & Laurel,1989; Mora & Kasman, 1997).

How Does Sensory Integration Occur?

Williamson and Anzalone (1996) identify five interrelated components that help to understand how sensory integration occurs. These components are:

1. Sensory registration
2. Orientation
3. Interpretation
4. Organization of a response
5. Execution of a response

1. Sensory Registration

Sensory registration occurs when we first become aware of a sensory event. "Something is touching me" or "I hear something." We may not be aware of certain types of sensory input until they reach a certain threshold or intensity. Your sensory threshold varies throughout the day, depending on your previous sensory and emotional experiences, how alert or stressed you are and what you expect.

You may not be aware of a mosquito buzzing by the window, but when it is flying around your head, you are certainly aware that you hear something. You've experienced that sound before, and you expect the mosquito to land, creating a bite that will itch for days.

When you are highly aroused or anxious, your sensory threshold is lower, and you may register sensory input that may go ignored any other time. If you are awakened in the night by a loud bang, you may become highly aroused and hyper-vigilant. You may notice or "register" the sounds of creaking stairs and humming fixtures that you never pay attention to during the day.

Implications for ASD

As we reported earlier in this book, many children and adults with ASD over-register or are over-responsive to sensory stimulation. Some report hearing whispers from another room or trains that are miles away. Others report that certain clothing textures feel like sandpaper.

Kientz and Dunn (1997) compared performances of children with and without autism using The Sensory Profile questionnaire. They discovered that 85% of the items differentiated subjects with and without autism. Over-responsivity to touch and auditory stimulation were the most commonly cited items. Over-responsivity to touch and sound is also commonly cited by adults with autism (Grandin, 1986, 1995, McKean, 1994, Williams, 1992, Willey, 1999, Fleishman & Fleishman, 2012).

Children and adults with ASD may also under-register sensory information. They may not notice someone calling them, may not feel food on their faces, may not be aware of the position of their limbs in space and may only respond when sensory stimulation is highly exaggerated.

Greenspan and Weider (1998) reviewed the sensory processing patterns of 200 children with diagnoses of autism spectrum disorder. They found that 94% of the children exhibited unusual sensory processing patterns (39% were under-reactive, 19% were oversensitive and 36% exhibited a mix of over- and under-reactivity).

It is important to note that responses to sensory input may be highly inconsistent and vary on a daily basis. Also, some children who appear unresponsive to sensory input may in fact be highly sensitive to sensory stimulation. They may appear unresponsive because their nervous systems have "shut-down" to protect them from incoming sensory stimulation.

Examples of Over-responsivity:

- Distress with certain sounds
- Sensitivity to light
- Discomfort with certain textures
- Aversion to certain smells and tastes
- Irrational fear of heights and movement
- Frequent startle reactions

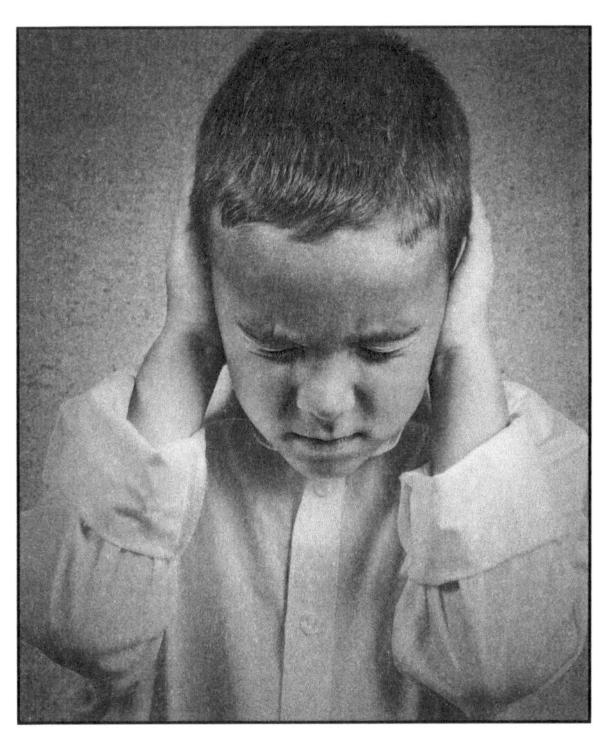

Examples of Under-responsivity:

- Lack of regard for sudden or loud sounds
- Unaware of painful bumps, bruises, cuts, etc.
- Unaware of food on face

- Lack of attention to environment, persons or things
- Does not become dizzy with excessive spinning
- Delayed responses

Please refer to Chapter Four for a more complete list of observations.

2. Orientation

Sensory orientation allows you to pay attention to new sensory information being received; "Something is touching my arm" or "I hear something buzzing around my head." We are able to determine which sensory information needs our attention and what information can be ignored. This happens through sensory modulation and the functions of inhibition and facilitation.

Our brains are programmed to modulate or balance incoming sensory information to function efficiently. We cannot possibly attend to all sensory stimuli in our environments. If all sensory input had equal importance, we could not select the relevant stimuli for the specific situation.

When talking on the phone, your brain decides that the voice in the receiver is important and needs your attention. It also decides that the television sounds, the feel of your clothing and jewelry and the placement of your hands are not as important.

Sensory modulation is necessary to regulate the brain's activity level and therefore our activity levels. Ayres (1979) compares the process of modulation to volume control. If the sensory information received is too loud, too intense or too insignificant, our brain can inhibit or "turn down" the flow of information. This neurological process of inhibition prevents us from attending to meaningless sensations. The process of inhibition lets us concentrate on the telephone conversation and ignore the voices coming from the television.

When we need to turn the "volume" up, we rely on facilitation. Sometimes we need help responding to meaningful sensations, and this is when the neurological process of facilitation is activated. When sitting in a lecture and our arousal levels are low, we may not properly attend to the voice of the professor. The process of facilitation helps us to pay attention to a voice and orient to the speaker.

Sensory modulation occurs unconsciously and takes place when there is a balance between inhibition and facilitation.

Implications for ASD:

Many children with ASD have poor sensory modulation. Atypical sensory registration and orientation can interfere with the processes of inhibition and facilitation. One child may not be able to follow verbal instructions or interact with others because they are attending to extraneous or irrelevant sensations of wind against their face or dust particles in the air. Another child may be overwhelmed and uncomfortable with certain sensations, displaying fear and anxiety.

Lucy Blackman (1999), in her autobiography, *Lucy's Story: Autism and other Adventures*, describes her difficulty with sensory modulation in the following quote: "Even today, continuous noise makes it impossible to interpret my environment or the people in it" (Blackman, 1999).

3. Interpretation

Our brains can interpret sensory information and describe its qualities. "I am being lightly touched on my arm by a piece of silk fabric." "I hear a loud, female voice telling me that it's time for dinner." The ability to interpret sensory information allows us to determine what to respond to and if it is threatening. We compare new sensory experiences with old ones. Our language, memory and emotional centers are involved with the interpretation process: "1 smell something. It smells like bread baking. I like that smell. It makes me feel happy. The smell reminds me of my childhood. It is okay for me to find out where the smell is coming from."

Your nervous system is also programmed to respond to sensory input to protect you from harm. Picture yourself at home alone, reading a book. Your husband isn't due back from his business trip until tomorrow. Suddenly, someone taps you lightly on the shoulder. Your heart immediately beats faster, your breath quickens, you are suddenly sweating and you jump out of the chair. Your body is ready to run or strike the person who touched you. When you realize it is your husband, your body relaxes, and your breathing and heart rate return to normal.

This is the nervous system's "fright, flight or fight" reaction that helps to protect the body from potential harm. This reaction immediately increases heart rate and respiration, diverting blood away from the digestive system to the muscles. Sometimes this reaction is appropriate. If the person tapping your shoulder was a burglar instead of your husband, you would want your body to instantly respond. If your heart rate and respiration increases and more blood flows to your muscles, you are better prepared to flee from the burglar.

Implications For ASD

Atypical language, memory and emotional development in individuals with ASD may interfere with the ability to interpret sensory information. Sensory experiences may not be adequately labeled or remembered. Familiar, pleasurable sensory experiences may not be connected with positive emotions. Individuals with ASD may also have problems with the stages of sensory registration and orientation subsequently hampering the interpretation process. It is difficult to interpret sensory information if our input is distorted, inconsistent, too strong or too weak.

Sensations may constantly be interpreted as new or unfamiliar. The world can seem like a confusing place when there is no sense of familiarity. One reason that children and adults with ASD may have difficulty with transitions and can become obsessed with order and set routines is because they strive for predictability in a world that bombards them with different sensations that are difficult to understand. As previously mentioned, individuals with ASD more frequently report over-responsiveness to sensory input.

The term *sensory defensiveness* describes the tendency to react negatively or with alarm to sensations that are generally considered inoffensive (Wilbarger & Wilbarger, 1991). Children may be defensive to all types of sensory input or one specific sensation. Defensive responses may be highly variable and inconsistent. Wilbarger and Wilbarger (1991) suggest that 15% of the general population likely have mild, moderate or severe forms of sensory defensiveness. The percentage of individuals with ASD who are sensory defensive is not known, but the numbers are likely significant, and its effect on behavior is easily observable.

Examples of Sensory Defensive Behaviors:

- Touch or Tactile Defensive – avoids touch from others; dislikes messy play; is irritated by certain clothing textures and labels.
- Gravitational Insecurity – fear and dislike of movement and changes in body position; discomfort with changes in head positions; fear of having feet off the ground.
- Auditory Defensiveness – over sensitivity to loud, unexpected or specific sounds; fearful of appliances such as vacuum cleaners or hair dryers.
- Visual Defensiveness – over sensitivity to strong or different types of light; avoids or squints in sunlight; avoids eye contact; dislikes glare from televisions and computers.
- Oral Defensiveness – a combination of over sensitivity to touch, smell and taste; includes dislike of certain food textures and types; has difficulty with tooth brushing and face washing.
- Other – may be over sensitive to smells and tastes; awareness of smell of objects and people; some children may gag with certain smells; can identify specific brands of food by taste.

Children who are sensory defensive operate under high levels of anxiety as they are bombarded by sensations that they do not like, and this may encourage "fright, flight or fight" reactions. As they are often in a hyper-aroused state, they become hyper-vigilant and have lower sensory thresholds which makes them even more responsive to sensory input. These children are not just more responsive to sensory input, they feel that they are being threatened or attacked by the sensory input and they need to defend themselves from the attack. John Elder Robinson, a man with Asperger's Syndrome, expressed this idea in a chapter of his book, *Be Different* (Robinson, 2011), titled "Underwear with Teeth." In this chapter, Robinson describes his over-responsiveness to touch input, particularly related to clothing. The following quote illustrates how some people may feel under attack by sensory input: "I still have to endure the constant assault from seams and labels on clothing." (Robinson, 2011).

Children who are sensory defensive may avoid sensations to prevent negative reactions but may also seek out certain sensations as a coping strategy. Certain types of sensory input, such as deep-touch pressure, can help decrease hyper-reactive responses to sensory input. Bumping into objects and bouncing and squeezing between pillows and furniture may be a calming or organizing strategy that the child finds successful. Some children may engage in certain types of sensory-seeking behaviors to screen out uncomfortable sensations. For example, some children create an excessive amount of noise through humming or babbling to screen out irritating or unexpected noises. Blackman (1999) describes the following strategies that she created to manage sounds that were distressing: "…so I relied on activities such as swaying, humming and running in circles, which defended me against uninterrupted exposure to my sound-environment" (Blackman, 1999).

4. Organization of a Response

Our brains determine if a response to a sensory message is necessary and we choose the response. Messages can be physical, emotional or cognitive. Remember our example regarding the mosquito landing on your body? You can choose to respond to that sensory event in different ways:

Physical Response - *I will hit the mosquito.*

Emotional Response - *I am anxious. I do not want the mosquito to bite me.*

Cognitive Response - *I choose to ignore the mosquito.*

Implications for ASD

Difficulties with registration, orientation and/or interpretation affect the ability to organize a response to sensory input. Appropriate responses to sensory input cannot be organized if the nature and meaning of the input is unclear. For some, the response may be exaggerated if the input is interpreted as being harmful. The "fright, flight or fight" response may be activated. For others, there may be no input response because the input did not register.

Atypical cognitive and emotional development in individuals with ASD further interferes with their ability to organize a response. Their emotional reactions may be exaggerated or minimized, and they may experience problems maintaining attention, formulating and comparing choices and initiating plans of action.

5. Execution of a Response

The execution of the motor, cognitive or emotional response to the sensory message is the final stage of the sensory integration process. However, if there is a motor response (i.e. hitting the mosquito), that action generates a new sensory experience as the brain receives information about body movement and touch – and the process begins again.

The ability to execute an appropriate response is dependent on the previous components and adequate motor planning abilities. Motor planning is the ability to perform purposeful activities and will be further discussed in this chapter.

Implications for ASD:

Impaired motor planning ability is increasingly recognized as a feature of ASD. Greenspan and Wieder (1998), in their review of 200 cases of children diagnosed with autism spectrum disorder, reported that 100% of the children experienced some kind of motor planning problem. Impaired motor planning significantly interferes with the ability to plan and execute motor responses.

Hill and Leary (1993) and Leary and Donnellan (2012) offer valuable insight into many behaviors observed in individuals with ASD. They suggest a strong association between certain behaviors and specific types of motor or movement disturbances. They identify similar movement disturbances in other neurological conditions, including parkinsonism, Tourette's syndrome and catatonia. They suggest that the movement disturbance relates to impaired motor planning and is reflected in difficulty with starting, executing, stopping, combining and switching motor acts. Therefore, the child who appears non-compliant when given motor-related instructions or the child who engages in perseverative or self-stimulatory behavior may have difficulty starting, switching or stopping motor acts.

Impaired sensory integration may cause or contribute to these motor planning difficulties, as adequate processing of sensory information from the body and the environment is necessary to efficiently execute, regulate and change motor activity.

Additional Differences in Sensory Experiences

In this edition and in our original book, we address differences in sensory processing or sensory integration experienced by children with ASD with a specific focus on sensory modulation difficulties. However, we want to acknowledge that there are many other sensory-related differences experienced by this group. Bogdanisha (2003) describes some of these additional sensory as well as perceptual differences, including:

- Monosensory processing – difficulty processing sensory information from more than one sensory system at a time
- Synaesthesia – stimulation of one sensory system can trigger perception of the stimulus by a different system (e.g., experience of sound as colors)
- Delayed processing
- Distorted perceptions – (e.g., distortions perceived in size, shape)
- Fragmented perceptions – ability only to process small units of the sensory environment at a time

Mukhopadhyay (2008) not only demonstrates the complexity of sensory differences but also addresses how these differences can offer unique perspectives. He refers to synaesthesia in his chapter, "The Color of My Scream." He also describes delayed processing and fragmented perceptions. Mukhopadhyay's writings are filled with symbolic prose and poetry that is reflective of his unique sensory experiences and perceptions.

There was Mother's voice,
Trickling down with drops of a tune.
There was the floating depth
Of some thought-filled dark.
Lit with voices of dreams.
As I saw them all
With the color of my scream.
(Mukhopadhyay, 2008)

Sensory Gifts vs. Sensory Challenges

"Autism is about a different development of sensory perception that brings a different development of cognitive mechanisms… not all the differences in perception are dysfunctional and sensory differences are not necessarily problems/difficulties" (Bogdanisha, 2006).

We would like to take this opportunity in our third edition to note that many sensory differences experienced by children and adults with ASD do not necessarily lead to challenges or barriers but can actually enhance quality of life. Heightened registration of sounds and images contribute to the success that many individuals with ASD have as musicians, artists and photographers. Unique sensory differences can lead to vocational or recreational interests. Temple Grandin's heightened registration of visual input and strong visual memory supports her ability in her career to design animal slaughter plants: "Every design problem I have ever solved started with my ability to visualize and see the world in pictures" (Grandin, 1996).

As parents, educators and therapists, we often focus on the challenges presented by differences. We wrote this book to provide strategies to support sensory challenges, but we also want to encourage readers to also be aware that certain sensory differences can be not only welcomed and encouraged but also celebrated.

What are the Results of Sensory Integration?

Sensory integration contributes to the development of self-regulation, comfort in the environment, motor planning, motor skills, attention and readiness to learn. We will take a closer look at two areas that may not be familiar—self-regulation and motor planning.

Self-regulation

There has been a literary explosion of books and articles on self-regulation in the educational and developmental literature since the publication of our first book. Shanker (2013) proposes a model of self-regulation that identifies biological, emotional, cognitive, social and moral domains. Occupational therapists, when addressing self-regulation, primarily focus on the biological or physiological ability to self-regulate arousal levels. For the purposes of our discussion, we use the definition of self-regulation as the nervous system's ability to attain, maintain and change levels of arousal or alertness (Williams & Shellenberger, 1994). These levels change depending on the needs of specific situations and activities.

Arousal is our level of alertness. The ability to maintain appropriate states of arousal develops from our ability to balance (regulate or modulate) sensory input from our environment. A normal state of arousal is essential for the development of executive functions, which include the following abilities:

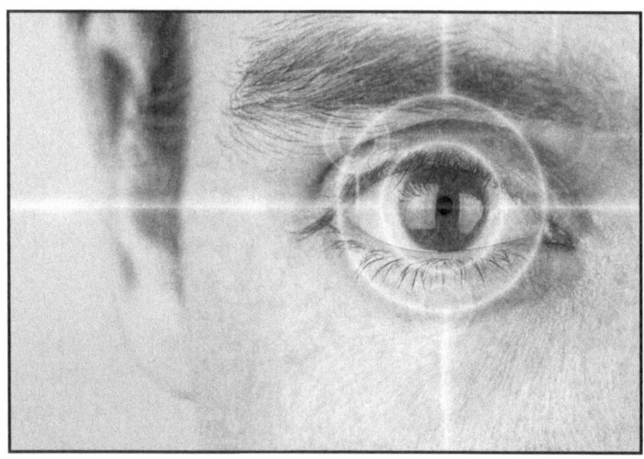

- Planning and organization
- Inhibition and impulse control
- Attending behaviors (shifting and focus)
- Working memory
- Task initiation
- Self-monitoring
- Emotional control

Our state of arousal varies throughout the day. We all use various strategies to regulate our levels of arousal. For most of us, our state of arousal is fairly low when we wake up and start our morning routines. For some people, their state of arousal increases after a quick shower; some may need the caffeine boost of a first cup of coffee; some people feel more awake after an early morning jog.

You are on your way to work. Your level of alertness may be reduced if you are lulled by the slow rocking of the subway train and may increase again as you step outside and are bombarded by the traffic's screeching brakes and blaring horns. After working at your desk for a couple of hours, you may experience trouble concentrating and instinctively know that a body stretch or quick walk to the water cooler will increase your state of arousal and increase your ability to concentrate on your work.

It is 2:30p.m. and you are in a meeting. The person speaking has a low voice with little animation. He's been droning on for an hour. Your boss is present and you are starting to fall asleep. You begin using familiar strategies to keep awake—shifting slightly in your chair, popping a mint into your mouth or fiddling with your hair.

Strategies to enhance self-regulation take into consideration the effect that different sensations can have on the nervous system. Remember that certain types of sensations can excite the nervous system, and other types of sensations can relax the nervous system.

Children with sensory integration problems often have difficulty achieving and maintaining normal levels of arousal. Normal levels of arousal are dependent on adequate sensory modulation. It is difficult to develop strategies to change arousal levels when an individual does not respond appropriately to sensory information. Arousal levels can be directly affected by reactivity to sensory input. Hyper-reactivity can increase arousal, and hypo-reactivity can create insufficient arousal levels.

Joey is a 5-year-old boy who has Asperger's Disorder. His kindergarten class just came inside from the playground, and now it is circle time. Joey is highly aroused from his high level of activity outside, but now he has to sit and attend to a story. The other children are initially slightly restless but they soon settle down and listen to the story. Some children calm themselves down by sitting in a teacher's lap, sucking their thumb or twirling their hair. Joey is not able to settle down. He remains highly aroused. He is distracted by all of the toys he sees in the classroom. He hears the teacher's aide preparing snack at the back of the room. He wonders what smells so good and wants to see what he is having for snack. Joey wants to hear the story but he frequently gets up from the circle, he bumps into the children sitting beside him, he continually adjusts his posture and he frequently speaks out loud.

Joey has poor sensory modulation. He cannot balance incoming sensory information. He cannot decide what sensory information is important and needs his attention. Joey is not able to determine what strategy he can use to improve his ability to sit in the circle and listen to the story. To assist Joey with self-regulation, specific strategies that offer deep touch pressure can be incorporated into his routine. For example, Joey may benefit from playing tug of war when coming in from outside, and he may be able to attend better during circle time if he has a weighted pad in his lap. Williams and Shellenberger—in their book *How Does Your Engine Run? A Leader's Guide to the Alert Program for Self-Regulation*

(1994)—describe the excellent program that they developed to teach self-regulation strategies. The program teaches children and adults how to recognize their own varying levels of arousal or alertness and how these levels impact learning, behavior and attention. Williams and Shellenberger provide a range of strategies that can be easily taught to children that can help to increase or decrease arousal. For additional information on the subject, another book that integrates sensory strategies with cognitive behavior therapy is *The Zones of Regulation: A Curriculum Designed to Foster Self-Regulation and Emotional Control* (Kuypers, 2011).

Implications for ASD

Many children and adults with ASD appear to have difficulty with self-regulation (Siegel, 1996). Problems with self-regulation may contribute to many of the behaviors observed in individuals with ASD. These behaviors include disregard for or exaggerated responses to sensory stimulation, inconsistent ability to attend to tasks, distractibility, poor impulse control, limited frustration tolerance and fluctuating emotional reactions. Many children and adults with ASD also operate under high levels of anxiety that increases arousal. With increased arousal, sensory thresholds are lower, and there is registration of an excessive amount of sensory input. It is important to try and determine if observable behaviors are related to sensory defensiveness or pre-existing anxiety. However, similar calming strategies may be useful in reducing anxiety and limiting sensory defensive responses.

The child with poor self-regulation has difficulty maintaining a calm, alert state which is necessary for optimal learning and participation in everyday activities and routines. Children with ASD often have days that are filled with classroom learning as well as appointments with speech and language pathologists, occupational therapists and ABA providers and participation in floor-time sessions or social skills groups. It is critical that, in all of these settings, efforts be included to support self-regulation. There are a number of new resources available that provide strategies to encourage self-regulation (Moyes, 2010, Shankar, 2012, Hyche & Maetrz, 2014, Garlard, 2014).

Children with ASD, whether verbal or nonverbal, can learn various strategies to assist with self-regulation. These strategies are presented throughout Part Two of this book.

Motor Planning

Motor planning or "praxis," is the process of deciding what your body has to do and then doing it. Praxis comes from the Greek word for action. Both motor planning and praxis refer to the same process that includes conceiving, planning, sequencing and executing actions. Motor planning assists with the sensory integration processes of organizing and executing responses to sensory input. Motor planning relies on sensory feedback from the body and environment as well as on language, memory and cognitive or thinking skills. It is a very complex process that involves many parts and functions of the brain. The steps involved in motor planning include:

- Creating an idea or ideation
- Using sensory feedback to determine the starting position of the body
- Initiating the action
- Sequencing the steps required in the action
- Adjusting actions accordingly
- Stopping the action

Robbie sees his Barney doll sitting on the shelf. He decides he wants to give Barney a ride in his wagon. He must stand on the tips of his toes and fully extend his arms to reach Barney. Then he must walk a short distance while he carries Barney and place him in the wagon. The wagon is quite heavy for a three-year-old boy, so Robbie must use all of his strength to pull the wagon around the room. He moves quickly, but he is very careful and slows down when near a corner of the room so the wagon won't scratch the walls. Soon, he begins to tire and becomes bored with this game. Robbie relaxes his muscles, stops pulling the wagon and goes to look for Mickey Mouse.

Robbie's actions appear simple, but the processes that allow him to participate in this type of activity are very complex. He first had to come up with the idea of pulling Barney in the wagon. He knew that Barney and the wagon were toys, and he remembered experiencing pleasure when playing with Barney. He knew that he could physically remove Barney from the shelf, and he understood the functions of the wagon. This process is called ideation and involves language, cognitive, memory and emotional components.

Motor planning also relies on the process of sensory integration. Sensory integration provides us with information from our bodies and the environment that is necessary to help us plan, execute, monitor and adjust our movements.

Imitation is an early form of motor planning. The infant's ability to mirror gestures and facial expressions is an important milestone in child development. It is also important for motor development as well as communication and bonding between babies and parents (Trott et al., 1993).

As infants and toddlers move and explore their world, they are bombarded by sensations. They learn how their bodies relate to objects, people and the earth's gravity. Through these sensations, they develop a body map or body scheme. Movement experiences create memories that can be relied on in the future when similar movement patterns need to be repeated. This allows us to generalize skills so we can perform similar actions in different settings. We can also borrow from pre-existing motor plans to build new or expanded actions.

Toddlers climb up and down the stairs hundreds of times to learn about the position of their body in relation to the steps. They learn how high to lift or lower their legs. They learn what sounds the stairs make and how they feel when their foot hits the step. Initially, they proceed slowly and are always looking down at their feet to be sure that their legs are moving appropriately. Soon they can negotiate stairs quickly and can climb the steps at day care, at grandma's house and on the playground.

Children also develop constructional abilities, which is another form of motor planning. This includes building with blocks to create towers, stringing beads and arranging furniture to build a fort. Successful accomplishment of these tasks requires feedback from our bodies in relation to objects and the ability to perceive and identify the characteristics of different objects. The feedforward and feedback components of motor planning help us to determine *what will happen* and *what did happen* when we move. With feedforward, we can anticipate the necessary steps, strength and speed required to complete a motor act. This process helps us prepare to lift a heavy suitcase or grocery bag. Feedback is the information we receive while performing a motor act that allows us to monitor and adjust our movements as needed.

When you learn a new skill like knitting, tennis, driving or skiing, you initially have to exert a high degree of energy and concentration to perform the required movements. You fatigue easily, your frustration tolerance is limited and you cannot casually engage in conversation because all of your attention needs to be directed to the task. If you have good motor planning, you sail through this learning phase quickly. You do not always have to consciously think about and plan all of your movements. You can engage in the activity for extended periods while carrying on a serious conversation. Writing with your non-dominant hand can illustrate how much harder you have to concentrate when completing an unfamiliar task.

Good motor planning is very time and energy efficient. It enables us to complete familiar tasks without having to think through each step. Many of us can drive home from work while planning the evening's activities and then arrive home not having remembered what streets were taken to avoid traffic. We are able to go on "automatic pilot" while we put our energy into other thought processes.

Dyspraxia or Impaired Motor Planning

The term *dyspraxia* refers to a difficulty in motor planning. Motor planning is a very complex process, and there are many areas in which the process can break down.

The type of motor planning problem that sensory integration theory can address involves inefficient processing of information from the tactile, vestibular or proprioceptive systems. Children with this type of motor planning problem have difficulty learning new motor tasks, but with repeated practice, their competence can improve. However, their competence often remains restricted to the particular task they practiced and does not generalize to similar activities (Fisher et al., 1991). An excessive amount of energy and concentration must be exerted to perform motor tasks due to limited body scheme and inadequate memories for movement experiences.

Motor planning difficulties can be very frustrating and confusing. Often the child knows what he or she wants to do and understands the demand, but cannot access the motor plans necessary to accomplish the task.

> *It was Karen's first day at Kinder-Gym. The instructor started showing the children warm-up exercises. Karen had trouble imitating the instructor's movements. Then the children were asked to skip around the gym, and Karen had difficulty keeping up with the group. She tried to skip, but was unable to alternately lift her legs. Next the group did somersaults which Karen was able to perform. This was one of her favorite activities that she repeatedly practiced at home. At the end of class, the children sat in a circle, and the instructor demonstrated some action songs. Karen couldn't do the actions for the Itsy Bitsy Spider or the Wheels on the Bus, and she was slower than the other children when playing Head and Shoulders. Karen went home frustrated and unhappy.*

Motor performance in children with motor planning problems is often very inconsistent. They may easily perform some complex actions (like a somersault) and have difficulty with seemingly simpler actions (like playing Head and Shoulders). Their motor abilities are significantly affected by practice, level of fatigue and their ability to concentrate. Motor performance can vary from day to day or minute to minute. A child's inability to complete a requested task is often mistaken as poor cooperation.

Parents and teachers are often confused by the inconsistencies in motor performance exhibited by children with motor planning problems. Some children can create intricate Lego buildings but cannot imitate simple block designs. Other children are able to paint very intricate pictures but have great difficulty learning how to print. These are examples of problems with the constructional components of motor planning. Sometimes it is easier to construct buildings or draw when it is self-directed. This is true for other aspects of motor planning. For many of us, it's easier to dance when we are leading and in control of the steps we make.

Motor planning problems affect the ability to sequence, time and grade motor activities. The feedforward and feedback processes of motor planning are significantly compromised when there is a sensory integration problem. Poor body awareness does not provide the information necessary to anticipate motor demands or adjust movements once executed.

Motor planning problems interfere with the performance of self-care skills, as a child may have difficulty performing or sequencing actions needed to complete tasks, like dressing, independently. Speech production can be affected by poor motor planning by interfering with the movements of the lips, tongue and jaw that are necessary to form and sequence sounds and words. Motor planning problems can even spill over into academic work, as manifested in organizational difficulties.

Children with motor planning problems can demonstrate a range of behavioral responses. Many can become easily frustrated and avoid motor activities. Others will persevere with activities and will develop compensatory strategies to complete the tasks. For example, some children will talk themselves through a task, and others will use visual cues. Some children are highly impulsive and try to complete tasks as quickly as possible. Others may appear inflexible as they try to direct their own actions and control the actions of others.

Children with motor planning problems may experience a sense of bewilderment. They do not have a physical disability that restricts their movement, yet they know something is different. They are not sure if they can complete tasks, even tasks they have completed successfully the previous day.

Implications for ASD

There appears to be a significant percentage of children with ASD who have some form of a motor planning problem (Greenspan & Weider). Kanner (1943), in his first descriptions of autism, reported the presence of motor problems. Hill and Leary (1993), Attwood (1993) and Leary and Donnellan (2012) note that some of the movement problems experienced by individuals with ASD are similar to difficulties experienced by people with Parkinson's disease. These problems include delayed initiation of motor actions, problems stopping or changing movements, difficulty combining motor acts and general difficulty with the execution of movement. In their autobiographies, Mukhopadyhayy (2011) and Blackman (1999) share many examples of how impaired motor planning abilities have impacted their lives.

The cause of motor planning problems in children with ASD is likely quite varied and difficult to identify definitively. Contributing factors may include impairments in cognitive, language and memory functions. For those children who exhibit impaired motor planning along with unusual responses to sensory stimulation, one of the contributing causes may be faulty sensory integration. They may not be developing the appropriate body awareness and memories for movement experiences that are so necessary for motor planning.

A problem with motor planning may also be a factor in some of the unusual behaviors exhibited by children with ASD. New actions require a lot of energy and concentration to learn, and children may become "stuck" in old motor plans. Some children may have difficulty stopping one action to start another action. This may help to explain some of the perseverative behaviors observed in children with ASD. If a child is only capable of a few motor plans, then their choices for activities may be limited.

Interest and use of toys may be complicated by the inability to effectively manipulate the toys. Some children may not be capable of sequencing the actions of the toys that are sometimes necessary for imaginative play. Children may prefer unstructured gross motor activities, like rough-and-tumble play and games that require specific or sequenced movements, like games with balls and sticks.

> *Sam was involved in an applied behavioral analysis program in which he made significant gains in color and shape matching but made limited progress in verbal or motor imitation. Sam loved to play with cars, but all he did was bang the cars on the floor. He did not put the cars on the race track or place figures inside the cars. He sometimes was able to push the buttons on his battery-operated cars, getting them to move, but he couldn't do this consistently. He sometimes had difficulty isolating his pointer finger to touch the start button, and sometimes he was not able to exert enough pressure on the button to activate the engine.*

Any evaluation procedures or treatment approaches for children with ASD must consider that these children may be experiencing motor planning problems. An experienced occupational therapist can help determine if motor planning impairments are related to impaired sensory processing. They can provide necessary treatment and develop strategies to accommodate or compensate for impaired motor planning.

What is Sensory Integration Dysfunction or Sensory Processing Disorder (SPD)?

Ayres (1972) originally labeled the existence of impaired sensory processing as "sensory integration dysfunction." As the theory of sensory integration evolved and OT practice guided by this theoretical concept expanded, efforts have been made to develop new terminology and classification systems. Miller and Lane (2000) proposed that it was important to differentiate the theory of sensory integration from the disorder as well as from assessment and treatment procedures. Miller and Lane (2000), among others, began to use the term "sensory processing disorder" instead of the previous designation of "sensory integration dysfunction."

Miller (2006) and Dunn (1997) proposed classification systems to differentiate the different types of sensory processing disorder. Although there is no consensus yet regarding terminology, these classification systems are appearing in occupational therapy publications with increasing frequency.

The Dunn Model focuses on the threshold of the nervous system to register a sensory event and the self-regulation strategies the individual uses to manage his or her responses to sensory input. These strategies are perceived as either active or passive.

Dunn Model

Hypo-responsive/High Threshold	Hyper-responsive/Low Threshold
• Low Registration	• Sensory Sensitivity
• Sensory Seeking	• Sensory Avoiding

An individual with a high threshold requires more intense sensory input to register that the event has occurred and therefore presents as hypo-responsive to input that most others register immediately. Individuals who are "sensory seeking" respond to that state with an active strategy and need to seek additional sensory input. Others who are passive responders do not require additional sensory input and are characterized as "low registration."

An individual with a low threshold will orient to the slightest sensory event and therefore present as hyper-responsive to sensory input. "Sensory sensitivity" is used to described those individuals as they do not actively try and avoid the input. Individuals who physically avoid certain types of sensory input and create rituals or routines to ensure avoidance of specific sensations use a "sensory avoidance" strategy.

The Miller taxonomy attempts to classify sensory challenges into separate categories and acknowledges that there can be some overlap between categories. This taxonomy will likely evolve over time as research and clinical practice continues to reveal and refine our understanding of sensory integration.

Sensory Modulation Disorders

- Over/Under-Responsivity
- Sensory Seeking

Sensory Discrimination Disorder

Sensory-Based Motor Disorder

- Postural Disorders
- Dyspraxia

Classification systems of sensory processing disorders also exist outside of the occupational therapy literature. SPD is recognized in the *Diagnostic Classification of Mental Health and Developmental Disorders of Infancy and Childhood, Revised* (Zero-Three, 2005) and the *Diagnostic Manual for Infancy and Early Childhood* (ICDL, 2005). Unfortunately, despite excellent and well-coordinated efforts to have SPD included in the *Diagnostic and Statistical Manual of Mental Health Disorders V* (APA, 2013), the attempt was not successful. The group of experts that led this charge was spearheaded by Lucy Miller and the

SPD Foundation. It is hoped that, through their continued efforts and that of others, SPD may eventually be included in the DSM-VI.

For the purposes of this book, we will use the term "sensory processing disorder," or SPD, as it is the term that is now most currently recognized to describe the combination of challenges experienced by people who have impaired processing and integration of sensory input.

Regardless of the terminology or classification systems used, there is consensus regarding the main components of SPD.

Generalized Signs of SPD

- Inappropriate and inconsistent responses to sensory stimulation
- Difficulty organizing and analyzing information from the senses
- Reduced ability to connect or "integrate" information from the senses
- Limited ability to respond to sensory information in a meaningful and appropriate manner
- Difficulty using sensory information to plan and execute actions

Checklists to identify sensory integration problems are provided in chapter four.

Let's briefly review some of the observable signs of SPD:

- Over-responsivity or under-responsivity or mixed responses to sensory stimulation
- Avoidance of sensory input
- Seeking of sensory input
- Unsurety of body position
- Poor motor planning
- Poor coordination, inconsistent motor performance, difficulty learning new motor tasks
- Easy distraction, limited attending skills
- Over arousal, high activity level, hyper-vigilance
- Under arousal, low activity level, self-absorbed manner, passiveness

Incidence and Cause of SPD

When you consider the general population, the efficiency of the process of sensory integration can be viewed on a continuum. Some of us are natural athletes, have excellent body awareness, are comfortable in our environments, adapt easily to change and learn new skills quickly . Others may not keep up in aerobics classes, may bump into people and objects, dislike the feel of labels in their clothing, do not cope well with change and have difficulty learning new tasks. Some people smell dirty diapers before others, and others are oblivious to noxious smells. We all have certain types of sensations that we dislike and certain sensations that we crave, making us all unique.

Ayres (1979) estimated that five to ten percent of "normal" children experience sensory integration problems that require intervention. Intervention is required when sensory integration problems prevent children from adequately performing and participating in the activities of childhood. Recent studies have provided information regarding the incidence of SPD in the general population. Ayn, Miller, Milberger and McIntosh (2004) identified that 5.3% of the 702 kindergarten children surveyed met the criteria for a sensory processing disorder. Ben-Sasson, Carter and Briggs-Gowan (2009) surveyed the parents of 925 children between 7 and 11 years old and reported that 16% showed sensory over-responsivity to tactile and auditory input. Incidence of sensory processing challenges is much higher among the ASD population. In the Tomchek and Dunn (2007) study, 95% of children with autism in a sample of 281 demonstrated some degree of sensory processing dysfunction.

The etiology of sensory processing disorders is not clear, but neuroscience research is beginning to identify possible neuroanatomical differences that may be contributing factors. Koziol, Budding and Chidekel (2011) identified abnormal structure and/or neurochemistry within the basal ganglia and/or cerebellum, and Owen et al. (2013) identified reduction in white matter microstructure (posterior cerebral tracts).

What Does Sensory Integration Theory Offer Children With ASD?

1. Sensory Integration Increases Understanding

Sensory integration theory provides a useful framework for understanding many behaviors exhibited by children with different forms of ASD. Problems may contribute to high levels of anxiety, avoidance of people, lack of interest in the environment, difficulty with transitions and many other behaviors. For example, if a child is over-responsive to light touch and sounds, they may avoid people and toys as a way of protecting themselves from receiving uncomfortable sensory stimulation.

Sensory integration theory can provide a framework for understanding some forms of stereotypic or self-stimulatory behavior exhibited by many children with ASD. This framework hypothesizes that some self-stimulatory behavior is the expression of a sensory need (King, 1991). For example, rocking, spinning, banging, jumping, scratching or mouthing behaviors may be a reflection of an individual need for stimulation of the vestibular (movement), proprioceptive (deep pressure) or touch systems.

All of us use various types of self-stimulatory behaviors to maintain attention and relax our nervous systems (i.e. twirling hair, mouthing pencils, tapping feet, rocking in rocking chairs, bending paper clips). In children with ASD, these behaviors are usually more extreme and can interfere with function. The analysis of self-stimulatory behaviors can reveal what sensations are being sought and under what circumstances.

Often more appropriate, alternate behaviors which do not interfere with function and offer the same sensory input can be substituted. Sensory opportunities can be provided throughout the day in structured home and school programs and informally through sensory stimuli provided during normal activities of daily living. It is hypothesized that, through provision of a "sensory diet," the need for these behaviors may decrease.

1. Sensory Integration Helps Guide Intervention

Intervention strategies based on sensory integration theory can help an individual to:

- Regulate arousal levels
- Increase ability to attend and decrease distractibility

- Decrease anxiety
- Increase comfort in the environment
- Decrease stereotypic or self-stimulatory behaviors
- Develop internal motivation
- Facilitate positive interactions with peers and adults
- Promote communication
- Improve performance of a variety of skills and increase independence

An important goal of sensory integration intervention is to assist children in achieving a state of calm alertness. Once arousal levels are regulated, interventions that focus on communication, socialization and skill development have a better chance for success. Many children with ASD have difficulty attending to tasks and learning new skills because they operate at high levels of arousal and anxiety, since they over-react to sensory stimuli. Other children do not respond because they are under responsive to stimuli or overly selective of stimuli.

A regime of sensory-based activities (sensory diet; see chapter five) can be effective in regulating arousal levels. Following close observation and history taking, this individualized schedule of sensory activities can be incorporated into daily life and help to improve responses to sensory stimuli.

Effective calming strategies for children with ASD are deep touch pressure and rhythmic vestibular (movement) stimulation. Techniques can be introduced into the home and the classroom with the use of rocking chairs, swings, weighted vests and collars, lycra body suits, anti-stress squeeze balls or padded chairs.

Regular treatment sessions with an occupational therapist may also be recommended to further assist in facilitating more normalized responses to sensory stimuli and to enhance the organization of sensory information. The goal of therapy is to provide and control sensory input so the child can spontaneously and appropriately form responses that require integration of those sensations (Ayres, 1979).

Emphasis in treatment is not on specific skill development but on enhancing sensory integrative functions. Sensory-based activities, whether provided during treatment sessions or through home and school programs, are always purposeful and require the active participation of the child.

Another goal of treatment is to assist in the development of motor skills. Many children with ASD have motor planning difficulties because of inadequate knowledge about their bodies, how they move and where they are in space. Development of fine and gross motor skills may be delayed due to impaired motor planning, limited attending skills, reduced motivation to complete tasks, fear of and discomfort while exploring the environment and an over-involvement in stereotypic behaviors.

2. Sensory Integration Assists Parents And Professionals

Sensory integration theory offers:

- A different perspective for understanding behavior
- Solutions to improve behavior
- Strategies to increase attention, motivation, communication and interaction
- Physical and environmental accommodations
- Programming strategies

Sensory integration theory offers important insights and tools to help children with ASD perform everyday activities. Together with parents, occupational therapists can develop a variety of activity suggestions and modifications to self-care routines for a child, which can improve comfort, compliance and independence.

For example, the modification of eating utensils may be helpful for the child who over-reacts to touch, proper chair and table heights are important for the child who is uncomfortable when his or her feet are off the ground, the use of deep pressure can be applied as a calming strategy prior to bedtime, and sleeping in a sleeping bag with a body pillow may help prepare the child for sleep and encourage sleeping through the night.

Sensory integration theory can assist other professionals in their work with individuals with ASD. Speech-language pathologists and behavioral psychologists can maximize the outcomes of their interventions with strategies that reduce their clients' anxiety levels and optimize their attention. For example, swinging on a platform swing can often reduce anxiety, increase eye contact and improve attention to tasks. The vestibular or movement stimulation provided by the swing may have an organizing effect on the nervous system and may facilitate communication.

Introduction of communication programs while swinging on a platform swing can be a useful strategy for children who are not succeeding during traditional speech-language therapy sessions. The combination of sensory integration and communication strategies is a growing theme, evident in the literature and at conferences on ASD (Cimorelli et al., 1996; Mora & Kashman, 1997).

The "floor time" approach developed by Stanley Greenspan and Serena Wieder (1998) recognizes the importance of attention to individual sensory and motor needs in both the assessment and programming phases of intervention. This approach involves techniques to encourage playful interactions with a goal of developing new emotional and intellectual capacities (Greenspan and Wieder, 1998).

Some children involved in programs based on applied behavioral analysis (ABA) may achieve longer periods of compliance and increased attention to tasks if their sensory needs are considered when engaging in structured activities. Movement breaks, which focus on specific types of sensory stimulation, and the use of weighted vests, padded chairs or lycra body suits can help to reduce anxiety and increase attention, thereby maximizing a child's participation in discrete trial training sessions.

Consultation with educators can help maximize participation in the learning process at school. Sensory activities can be incorporated into classroom routines and are particularly useful during transition times. For example, when children arrive at school or after recess or lunch, calming and pleasurable activities can be offered to achieve a level of calm alertness.

What Does Sensory Integration Theory Not Offer?

Sensory integration theory does not provide all the answers and does not offer a cure. It can help to explain some behaviors and offers strategies for intervention.

Please recognize that this framework provides an understanding for only one piece of the ASD puzzle. Behaviors that initially appear sensory related may be caused by several other issues. Repetitive movements may represent a sensory-seeking behavior designed to reduce anxiety, or they may be involuntary tics or a reflection of obsessive compulsive tendencies. Some sensory motor behaviors may be used by children to communicate, to protest, to avoid/escape or to gain attention. The Murray-Slutsky and Paris book, *Is It Sensory or Behavior?* (2005), is an excellent resource that provides materials to help determine the function of many behaviors seen in children with ASD.

Children with ASD have a multi-system disorder that affects all areas of development. Knowledge of cognitive, language, behavior and emotional development is equally important when devising programs for children with ASD.

What about Research?

A growing body of research exists today related to the application of sensory integration theoretical principles to intervention with children with ASD.

Early studies demonstrated some promising results. Wolkowicz et al. (1977) reported improved behavior and social skills in four children diagnosed with autism following four months of occupational therapy treatment utilizing a sensory integrative approach. Ayres and Tickle (1980) studied 10 children with autism reporting that the children who were hyper-reactive to sensory input responded better to treatment utilizing sensory integration techniques. Improvement was noted in behavior, socialization and communication. However, sample sizes for these studies were quite small, and the methodology had areas for improvement.

Some individual case studies demonstrate the effectiveness of sensory integration strategies (Ayres & Mailloux, 1983, Grandin, 1992, Larrington, 1987). Other studies report on the use of sensory integration on language development (Benaroya, Klein & Monroe 1977; Cimorelli et al., 1996) and on decreasing self-stimulatory behaviors (Bonadonna, 1981, Bright et al., 1981, Brocklehurst-Woods, 1990, Duker & Rasing, 1989, Iwasaki & Holm, 1989).

Early studies yielded inconsistent results and were highly criticized for the methods that were used to evaluate effectiveness of treatment. Two studies published in the early 1990s utilized improved methodology to study the effectiveness of OT-SI treatment (Humphries et al., 1990, 1992; Polatajko et al, 1991). These were randomized, controlled clinical trials that evaluated the effectiveness of OT-SI treatment compared with more traditional perceptual motor training. The population they studied were children with learning disabilities. The results indicated little difference between the two groups in motor outcomes and no gains in academic, cognitive or language skills in either group compared to the control group. These studies are often referred to in the literature to indicate that OT-SI treatment is not a useful approach for treatment of children with any presenting diagnosis. However, when the methodology used in these studies is further explored, it is clear that they were not accurate evaluations of how OT-SI treatment was typically conducted in clinical settings. Two of the authors of this book participated in these studies as clinicians providing treatment to study participants. Treatment protocols had been developed by the researchers to differentiate between the two treatment groups. For example, the SI group could swing in a hammock but could not swing while tossing a bean bag at a target, which was an activity used in the perceptual motor protocol. This approach to treatment severely diminished the impact of the OT-SI treatment as it was not an accurate reflection of what occurred in clinical settings. SI treatment is not characterized by sensory stimulation alone but the intent is to provide controlled sensory input to enhance adaptive responses while the child is engaged in purposeful activity (e.g., throwing a bean bag at a target while swinging). At the time of publication, there were no published treatment fidelity measures that guided practice. In 2007, Parham et al. established guidelines that should be followed when providing OT-SI treatment. The 1991 studies did not meet basic standards for treatment but also were lacking in training and supervision of clinicians. The significance of the results of these studies therefore needs to be reconsidered with these limitations in mind.

A recent well-designed, randomized controlled study (Schaaf et al., 2013) that evaluated the impact of occupational therapy using a sensory integration approach yielded very positive results. Children between 4 and 8 years with an autism diagnosis showed significant improvement after 30 treatment sessions compared to a control group. Gains were made related to specific Goal Attainment Scales as well as in performance of self-care routines and socialization.

Every day, we see the value and effectiveness of the strategies contained in this book. Clinical judgment and clinical expertise are in fact components of evidence-based practice. We hope that future research will further validate this approach, but scientific evidence may be challenging to obtain. It is very difficult to conduct scientific research on children with ASD, as causes are not known, the nervous system differences are not yet fully appreciated and the diagnosis is based on behavioral characteristics.

Even within the same subcategories of ASD, presenting behaviors are highly variable, and we do not know exactly what happens in the brain to cause these behaviors. Interventions that are effective for one child may not be effective for another, even though their behaviors may be very similar.

To parents and professionals, please take the information presented in this book and see if it makes sense for the individual child you are living or working with. Try some strategies and look for changes. Sometimes no changes will be observed because the approach did not meet the needs of a specific child. Sometimes the approach directly addresses the child's needs and can provide bridges for facilitating understanding and change. For some children, the changes are subtle, and for others they can be very dramatic and significantly improve the child's and family's quality of life.

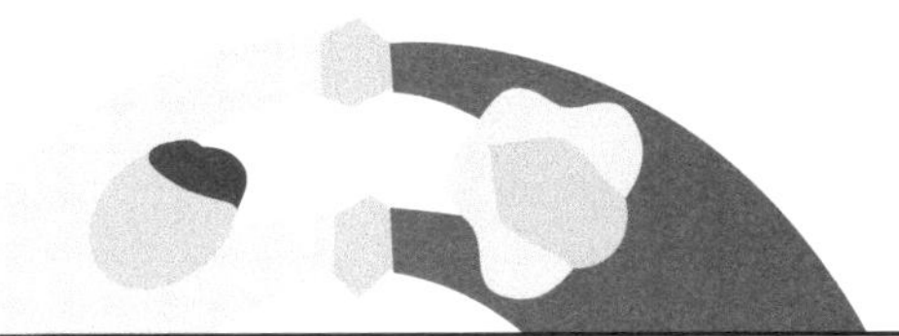

CHAPTER 3

WHAT ARE THE SENSORY SYSTEMS?

Sensory integration theory addresses all of the sensory systems but focuses primarily on the vestibular, tactile and proprioceptive systems.

Let's explore these systems and briefly review what happens when sensory integration functions efficiently and what happens when a child's sensory integration is inefficient.

Children with or without a diagnosis of ASD can experience problems with the tactile, vestibular or proprioceptive systems and can exhibit similar responses and behaviors. However, children with ASD have other impairments that may contribute to their sensory problems.

The Tactile System

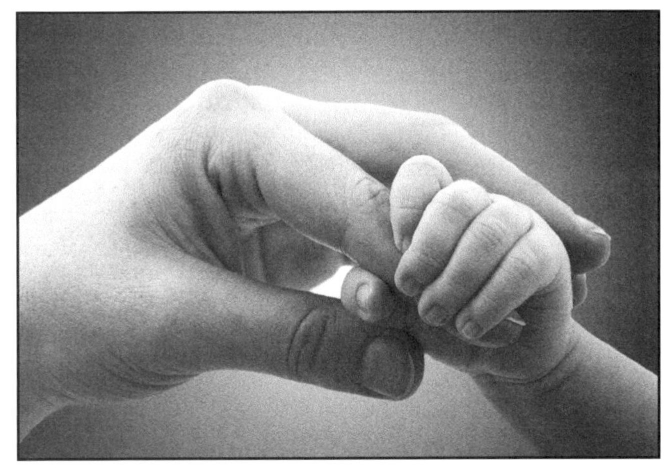

The mother feels her unborn child kick against her tummy. She quickly summons her older children to come and feel her unborn baby kick. Everyone experiences a sense of wonder and amazement as the tiny kicks push against their hands. They have all experienced the miracle of life through their sense of touch. Even the unborn infant has experienced the sensation of amniotic fluid swishing around the body and the vibrations of the mother's digestive system.

The tactile system provides us with our sense of touch. It is the first sensory system to operate in the uterus (Fisher et al., 1991), and it is important that this sense works efficiently from birth. Newborn infants have reflexes necessary for survival which can be stimulated through touch. The sense of touch enables them to turn their faces to nipples bearing milk, start bonding with their parents and feel calmed by warm, soft blankets when falling asleep. The sense of touch is important to growth and development as well as survival. Premature infants who are regularly massaged are more alert, active and calm and have increased weight gain and better orienting responses (Ackerman, 1991).

> *Katie was two weeks old and cried whenever she was hungry. Her mother picked her up and nestled her against her breast. Katie felt the nipple touch her cheek. This touch stimulated the rooting reflex that automatically turned Katie's head in search of food. As soon as Katie felt the nipple touch her lips, she would latch on and begin to suck. Initially, Katie needed to feel the nipple against her cheek in order to know which direction to turn her head and needed to feel the nipple in her mouth in order to begin sucking.*

The tactile system receives information about touch from receptor cells in the skin. These receptors are all over our bodies, providing information about light touch, pressure, vibration, temperature and pain. Feedback from the tactile system contributes to the development of body awareness and motor planning abilities. Every activity of daily life, including dressing, hair and teeth brushing, eating, toileting, household chores, school work and job tasks are dependent upon a functional tactile system. As with all sensory systems, the tactile system has both protective and discriminative abilities which complement each other throughout our lives.

The protective system is more primitive. It alerts us when we are in contact with something that may be dangerous and triggers our bodies to react against potential harm. Carol Kranowitz, in her book *The Out-of-Sync Child: Recognizing and Coping with Sensory Integration Dysfunction* (2006), labels the protective system as the "Uh-oh!" system. This very suitable label illustrates the response that the protective system can generate. Sometimes the nervous system is gently alerted, and other times the "fright, flight or fight" response is activated.

You're sitting around a campfire. A mosquito lands on your leg. The light touch alerts you to potential harm, and you slap your leg in effort to prevent the mosquito's bite.

The discriminative system enables us to feel the quality of the item we are touching. The ability to feel the soft touch of a parent, the fuzzy skin of a peach, the bumpy surface of a strawberry and the piano keys under our fingers are all dependent upon the discriminative system. Kranowitz (1998) refers to the discriminative system as the "Aha!" system, because it provides us with the details about touch.

Lia reached into her handbag for her keys. It was late and she didn't want to turn on the light and disturb her family. Her fingers found one set of keys on a plastic key ring. She immediately let this go, as she knew it was the keys to her car. Her fingers then touched the hard, metal surface of her house keys and she immediately retrieved them from her purse, opening the door without disturbing her family.

Initially, our protective system is dominant, but as the nervous system matures, we begin to increasingly rely on the discriminative system. Newborn infants are more easily irritated by light touch, and their ability to use their sense of touch to explore the environment is limited. As the infant matures, this ability increases and becomes necessary for learning and brain development. The discriminative system becomes a vital transmitter of information, and the protective system remains ready to respond to any potential threats.

Successful function of the tactile system depends on the balance between both the protective and discriminative systems. When the sensory integrative processes of registration, orientation, interpretation and sensory modulation are intact, we automatically know which touch is alarming, which touch is pleasurable, which touch can be ignored and which touch needs to be explored.

Tactile Dysfunction

Children with a dysfunctional tactile system may be under- or over-responsive to touch or may have problems with tactile discrimination.

Some children may excessively register and orient to touch input. They may have problems with sensory modulation and may be unable to inhibit or screen out touch sensations. Consequently, they are always aware of the feel of their clothes against their skin, their hair against their necks and their glasses resting against their noses. They may have difficulty shifting attention to other sensations like the sound of a human voice because they are so overwhelmed by the messages about touch.

Some children interpret and react to harmless light touch as being potentially dangerous. They are often described as being tactile defensive, with their protective systems working overtime. Many touch sensations are regarded as threatening and something to be avoided. They may have no difficulty touching objects or people but cannot tolerate receiving touch that is not self-directed. Behaviorally, these children may appear anxious, controlling, aggressive, unwilling to participate in home and school activities and inflexible in order to control the touch input received from the environment. The constant feeling of being vigilant or on guard and the frequent experience of the fight, flight or fright response consumes a lot of energy. Subsequently, there is less energy and attention for learning and interacting.

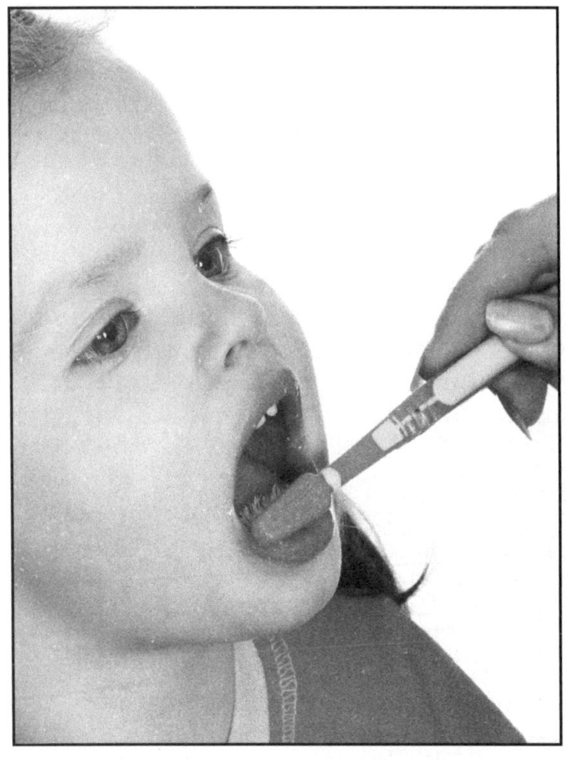

Every time Sarah's mother tried to brush her teeth, Sarah became upset and screamed. Her mom had to restrain her on her lap and hold her jaw still in order to get the toothbrush into Sarah's mouth. Brushing had to be done quickly and with a great deal of pressure or Sarah would bite the toothbrush and try to run away. Sarah responds similarly to nail cutting and hair brushing and washing. Sarah refuses to learn to do these activities independently. Her mother cannot understand why these activities create so much distress.

Other children are under-responsive to touch. They may have low arousal levels and may not register or orient to touch sensations unless they are very intense. These children do not get appropriate feedback about where they are being touched, significantly interfering with the development of body awareness and motor planning. For example, feeding and speech problems may be related to hypo-responsive touch systems. It is difficult for the tongue to move food or form sounds if there is a lack of awareness of the parts of the mouth. Consider what it feels like for a few hours after your mouth is numbed at the dentist. You often slur your words and food drips out of your mouth when eating.

Some children may experience poor tactile discrimination. They register touch but seem unable to determine the features of what they are touching. They have difficulty discriminating between textures, face problems using their sense of touch to search for objects in a drawer or a purse and do not develop memories for touch experiences. Knowledge of how things feel contributes to our ability to manipulate objects. Poor tactile discrimination can contribute to problems with body awareness and motor planning. Think about how difficult it is to manipulate objects when you are wearing thick woolen gloves.

> *Max's fine motor skills were developing slowly. He had difficulty doing up buttons and zippers. He couldn't learn how to tie his shoes as the laces kept falling out of his hands. He had a limited attention span for fine motor activities, as he consumed a lot of energy using his vision to confirm where objects were in his hand.*

Some children who are under-responsive to touch may also have a delayed reaction to touch. For example, pain from a cut or a burn may be felt hours after it has occurred and not at the time it happened. This is a real safety concern. For most of us, if an action harms us, we immediately feel pain and discontinue the activity. If a child is unable to immediately experience discomfort or pain, the activity may be continued, producing increased injury.

> *Michael and his class went to a conservation area for a class trip. They decided to walk through a stream in bare feet to cool off. Immediately after entering the stream, screams could be heard from Michael's classmates who quickly scrambled on to the*

grass. There were sharp stones in the stream that had cut the children's feet. Michael was enjoying the swish of the water around his feet and continued to walk in the stream. When his teacher asked him to come out of the water to check his feet, Michael was surprised to see the cuts on his feet. Later, at home, Michael would not let his mom wash his feet because they hurt.

Some children seem to seek out excessive amounts of touch sensations. Their arousal levels may be turned on low, and they crave touch in order to provide necessary input to their nervous systems. These children may touch everything, including repeatedly stroking mom's hair, rubbing the teacher's pantyhose and touching the fancy knick-knacks on grandma's bookshelf. Safety can also be an issue for these children. Often the desire for touch causes them to be impulsive in their pursuit of touch, and they do not take the time to ask themselves, "Is this harmful?" or "Do I need permission?"

The importance of touch in a child's life cannot be overstated. The inability to respond appropriately to touch sensations can seriously interfere with the ability to develop many skills. For those children who react uncomfortably to touch, the impact on social and emotional development is disastrous.

The Vestibular System

The baby's cries awakened his parents at three AM, and the father went to his son's room, gently picking up the baby. Immediately, the baby's cries changed from screams to sobs. The father held his son and sat in the rocking chair, rocking slowly as the sobs subsided. The baby soon fell back to sleep. Later that day, while in a long line at the bank, the father noted that he had only five minutes to get back to work. He felt the anxiety that we all have felt, with so much to do and so little time. The father started to rock his body back and forth while standing in line. He smiled to himself as he recognized that he was calming his nervous system in the same way he had calmed his son's nerves the night before.

The vestibular system provides information about movement, gravity and changing head positions. It tells us that we are moving or remaining still as well as the direction and speed of our movement.

It helps to stabilize our eyes when we are moving and tells us if objects around us are moving or remaining still. We develop our relationship to the earth through the vestibular system. Even without our eyes, we are able to determine if we are vertical or horizontal.

The vestibular system is fundamental to all our actions. Ayres (1979) suggests that the vestibular system plays a critical role in the modulation of all other sensory systems. She noted that the vestibular system assists with the processes of inhibition and facilitation (see Chapter Two). Remember, this is the process described as "volume control", in which sensory information is turned up or down depending on specific needs and situations. This ability to balance incoming sensations assists with self-regulation and allows us to maintain appropriate levels of arousal.

We need to accurately process vestibular information to properly use our vision, prepare our posture, maintain balance, plan our actions, move, calm ourselves down and regulate our behavior. The vestibular system develops before we are born, and feedback from this system continues to be utilized and refined throughout our lives. The receptors for the vestibular system are located within the structures of our ears (the semi-circular canals, the utricle and the saccule). As fluid moves in the ear, it displaces strategically placed hair cells in these structures which can detect changes in gravity and different types of movement.

The vestibular system has a very strong relationship with the auditory system. Both systems respond to vibration. In primitive animals, these two systems were anatomically and functionally connected. Auditory or hearing receptors evolved out of gravity receptors, and there remains some neural connections in humans today (Ayres, 1979). Parents and occupational therapists frequently observe increased vocalization and expressive language when a child is engaged in movement activity. Babies often babble more when they are swinging, and children with language delays often are able to produce more words when jumping, running or tumbling. Ayres (1979) suggests that this occurs because of the links between the auditory and vestibular systems.

The visual system and the vestibular system also have a close relationship. The vestibular system has an important influence in the development of eye movements, including tracking and focusing. The vestibular and visual systems together help the body maintain an upright posture.

Information from the vestibular system is necessary for muscle tone, or the readiness of a muscle to perform work. Muscle tone is necessary for posture and movement, and the ability to generate muscle tone is essential for doing activities that require more strength.

The vestibular system has both protective and discriminative functions. For a newborn, movement can stimulate reflexes designed to prevent falling. As the brain develops, there are more mature reactions designed to protect the body from harm. Toddlers who are learning to walk and are frequently tripping can register the pull of gravity and sense when they are falling. Automatically, they extend their arms to protect their head and bodies from the fall. An adult who is standing in a canoe registers that the boat is unsteady and can automatically gain stability by moving his or her feet further apart and raising the arms to lower his or her centre of gravity.

The vestibular system can discriminate between acceleration, deceleration and rotary movements. It can detect movements that are slow, fast or rhythmic. Some vestibular sensations, like slow rocking, can be calming. Other vestibular sensations like quick movements can excite the nervous system.

Vestibular Dysfunction

Some children experience difficulty processing information from the vestibular system. These children can be under over-responsive to vestibular sensations or have mixed sensitivities.

Children who over-respond to vestibular sensations are fearful with any changes in gravity and position. They interpret these changes as being potentially harmful and are often referred to as being gravitationally insecure. They do not like heights or when their feet are off the ground, and they do not like when their centre of gravity is displaced. These situations can trigger a sensory defensive response and activate the fright, flight or fight reaction. Some children are so sensitive to changes in gravitational demands that they will get down on their hands and knees to go through a doorway, manage a change in floor surfaces or negotiate stairs. The fear they experience is very real. They avoid stairs, bicycles and playground equipment. Some children cannot even tolerate changes in head position, particularly when tipped back.

> *Saied quietly sat in the bathtub watching his rubber ducky bobbing in the water. Grandpa was about to wash Saied's hair and he began to tip Saied backwards to put his head in the water. Saied screamed in terror! Grandpas eyes widened in alarm! What had he done to hurt his grandchild? He tried again, reassuring Saied and moving slower. Saied screamed again. Grandpa decided to wash Saied's hair by putting a facecloth over his eyes and pouring water over his head while he was sitting. Saied didn't like it, but he preferred it to leaning back in the water.*

Some children feel discomfort with certain types of movement but do not feel threatened. These children can become dizzy or nauseated with movement. They may become sick or uncomfortable with the movement of cars, elevators, swings or carnival rides.

Over-responsive reactions to movement and changes in gravitational demands have a negative impact on development. Common childhood activities including climbing trees, gym skills, midway rides, boat rides and rollerblading cause a great deal of anxiety and tend to be avoided. The desire to avoid movement has a negative effect on physical exploration of the environment. When a child does not explore the environment, gross and fine motor skills are not practiced and can become delayed. When actions are not practiced, they cannot be committed to memory, thus negatively affecting the development of motor planning. Children with gravitational insecurity often prefer and are more skilled when doing fine motor activities because they can be practiced in a stable, movement-free position.

When movement is interpreted as scary or uncomfortable, children become invested in preventing movement. They may become anxious and insecure. Controlling, inflexible behavior is often the strategy used to prevent unpredictable movement. Children may resist participating in many activities at home and school. Interactions and social skill practice in the playground and schoolyard become limited as they avoid physical activity, creating self-imposed isolation. Vestibular sensations, such as rocking or rhythmical movement, which is so calming and organizing for the child with a functional nervous system, can be terrifying and disorganizing for a child who is hypersensitive to movement.

At the opposite end of the spectrum is the child who craves movement. This child is always on the go and does not seem able to sit still. Climbing, bumping, jumping, falling and tumbling are common activities engaged by these children. They may not appropriately register movement, or their nervous systems may require an excessive amount of movement to stay alert and organized. Children may be so motivated to move that it is very hard for them to maintain attention for any length of time. They have

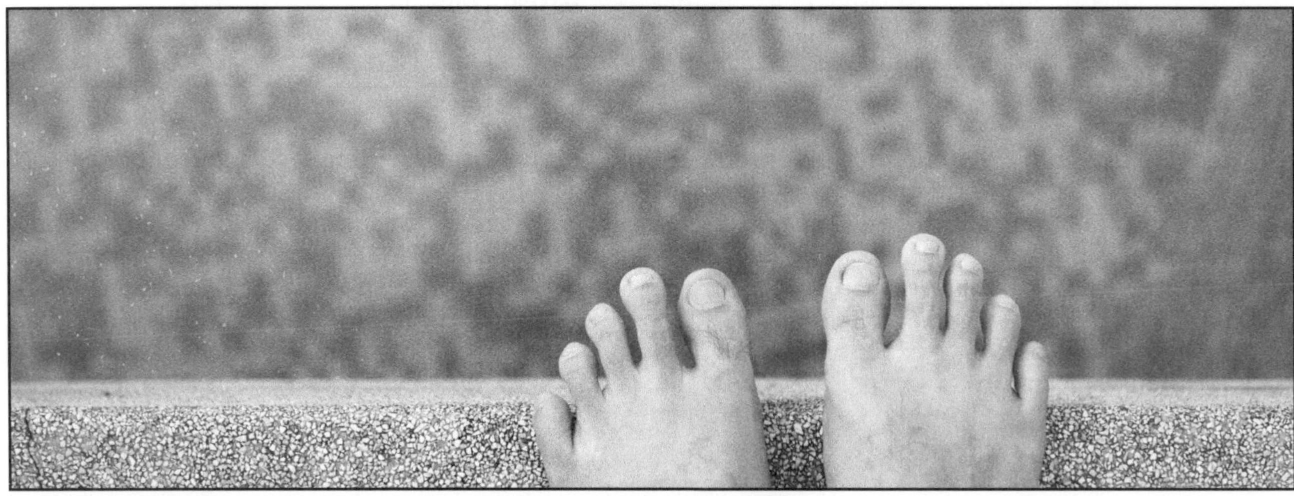

difficulty staying at the dinner table, sitting in a circle for a story or completing work at their desk. Their desire to move compromises their ability to attend to and learn new skills.

Ella jumped up from morning circle and ran for the block corner. She climbed up on the slide and jumped down. The assistant got up to follow Ella and bring her back to the circle. Ella happily returned but only sat for a moment, and then she was off again. Ella rarely sat through snack. She would take a nibble of food, walk around the table and come back for another nibble. When Ella was allowed to sit in a rocking chair for circle and snack time, her ability to remain seated improved significantly.

Children may seek certain types of movement to screen out uncomfortable sensations from other sensory systems. Slow rocking, linear motions and repetitive, rhythmic movements have a calming effect on the nervous system and can decrease hyper-reactive responses to sensory input.

Children who are under-responsive to vestibular input may not recognize the demands of gravity or adequately register the qualities of movement. These children often need close supervision during play because they may not appreciate the risks that they are taking when climbing and jumping. Recognition and preparation for necessary balance reactions, motor planning and grading of movements does not always occur. Movements may not be well planned or controlled, and insufficient feedback is received to modify movements.

Shawna loved walking on the raised flagstone border of Catherine's garden. At the corner of the garden, Shawna, who usually traveled too quickly, would fall off the edge of the flagstones into the flowers. Catherine would caution Shawna to slow down. Shawna continually walked along the border and fell into the flowers. Catherine wondered why Shawna continually made the same mistake over and over again.

Shawna may not be appropriately registering and orienting to changes in gravitational demands. She may not be aware that her centre of gravity has changed and that if she does not move her body accordingly, she will fall into the flowerbed. Shawna may not adequately register, orient or interpret feedback from her body to help master the demands of her environment. She may have had difficulty forming a motor plan and couldn't correct or adjust her actions.

Vestibular dysfunction can contribute to problems with self-regulation, as it plays a role in the modulation of all sensory systems. Inconsistent responses to sensory input, emotional instability, inappropriate arousal levels and difficulty maintaining and shifting attention may be behavioral features of vestibular dysfunction.

The ability to master the demands of gravity is a key accomplishment in human development. Children need to achieve this milestone to develop a strong sense of security. They need to be comfortable with movement to experience the many joys of childhood that are so important for development.

The Proprioceptive System

The typist who moves her fingers over the keypad while looking at the letter to be typed, the skier who is shifting his body weight over his skis to perform turns while looking at the markers ahead and the cyclist who maneuvers her bicycle through traffic while watching for pedestrians and cars are all employing the proprioceptive system.

The proprioceptive system helps us accomplish the above feats. Proprioception is the unconscious awareness of body position. It tells us about the position of our body parts, their relation to each other and their relation to other people and objects. It communicates how much force muscles must exert and allows us to grade our movements. Receptors for the proprioceptive system are located in muscles, tendons (where the muscles attach to bone), ligaments, joint capsules (the protective lining of each joint) and connective tissue. There are also "mechanoreceptors" in the skin that respond to stretch and traction. The receptors of the proprioceptive system respond to movement and gravity. Fisher et al. (1991) suggest that one really cannot separate the vestibular and proprioceptive systems because many of their functions overlap.

We depend on our proprioceptive system to help us make sense of touch and movement experiences. When you hold a square block in your hand, your skin and the position of your muscles and joints around the block provide information about shape. When you sit in the spinning cup ride at a fair, your vestibular system in combination with the proprioceptive system tells you that your body is sitting still inside a spinning teacup.

An efficient proprioceptive system provides us with the unconscious awareness of our body. This awareness helps to create a body scheme or a body map. We can consult this body map to determine the starting and ending position of our bodies during an activity. This position can be committed to memory and accessed again in the future. A usable body map and memories of movement contribute to the development of motor planning abilities. Remember, motor planning is the ability to create, organize, sequence and execute motor actions.

Certain types of proprioceptive sensations can help the brain to regulate arousal states (Wilbarger, 1991; Williams & Shellenberger, 1994). These proprioceptive sensations are provided through activities that require muscles to stretch and work hard. These activities include play wrestling, playing tug of war, hitting punching bags, pulling heavy wagons and chewing crunchy foods. Proprioceptive sensations rarely overload the nervous system, and some sensations can have both calming and alerting abilities, depending on the individual nervous system (Williams & Shellenberger, 1994). For example, if you have been working at your desk for a long time and are beginning to fall asleep, you may decide to stand up and stretch your body to help you become more alert. Other times you may be working at your desk and are anxious because you are unsure if you're able to make a deadline. Standing up and stretching helps you relax and decrease your anxiety.

Proprioceptive input can help decrease over-responsive reactions to other sensations. Many of us unconsciously use proprioceptive input to screen out uncomfortable sensations. When you are in a dentist's chair and the needle to numb your mouth is piercing your gums, you grasp and squeeze the arms of the chair to block out the pain. When the professor is writing on the chalkboard and she keeps breaking the chalk, making awful squeaking sounds, you tense your shoulders, arms and hands and clench down on your teeth to block out the noise.

Proprioceptive Dysfunction

Some children do not adequately receive or process information from their muscles, joints, tendons, ligaments or connective tissue. This results in insufficient feedback about movement and body position. Vision must be used to compensate for poor body awareness and poor grading of movements. Motor planning abilities can be compromised, and fine and gross motor skills may be delayed. Proprioceptive dysfunction is usually accompanied by problems with the tactile or vestibular systems (Fisher et al., 1991 & Kranowitz, 1998).

> *Liam was always crashing into things. He would crash into his classmates when lining up at the door. When he held the door open for his teacher, he would push too hard on the door and it would crash into the wall. He had difficulty coloring because he would always press too hard and rip the paper.*

Some children cannot position their body correctly to get on a bicycle or step on an escalator. Once engaged in an activity, some children may find it difficult to change their body position in response to the demands of the activity. When playing ball, it may be difficult for some children to move right or left or up high to catch a ball coming from different places. Some children have difficulty playing appropriately with toys because they are unsure of how to adjust their bodies to appropriately move or adjust toy parts. Children with proprioceptive problems often appear clumsy. They may fatigue easily and appear inattentive because they have to work hard and concentrate to determine the position of their bodies.

One indicator of difficulty processing proprioceptive input is the inability to determine the amount of force necessary to hold or move things. Objects are frequently inadvertently broken. Written work can be messy. Writing can be too light and difficult to read or much too heavy and laborious.

Mira had difficulty managing any tool in her hand. Her toothbrush often fell from her hand as she tried to brush her teeth. She couldn't seem to maneuver the hairbrush and often brushed her hair with the back of the brush. She held her pencil too loosely and seemed to have difficulty putting enough pressure on her pencil tip. Her letters appeared faint and poorly formed. Mira used her vision to direct her movements and to control objects in her hands. She could not print while looking at the blackboard or a book.

Children who are under-responsive to proprioceptive input may seek out additional proprioceptive sensations to increase their knowledge of where their bodies are in space. This additional input can increase body awareness and one's sense of security.

Kumiko would lean up against any person or any object that might offer her support. At circle time, she was always leaning on her neighbor, much to the dislike of her classmates. At her desk, Kumiko leaned against the edge with her tummy and was often seen supporting her head with her hand. She was unable to walk down the middle of a hall but would drag her hand or roll along the wall.

There are some children who constantly seek out proprioceptive input because they are not adequately receiving and processing this input or because they are using proprioceptive stimulation to reduce over-responsivity to other sensations. These children often like to rock and bang their backs and heads against the couch or the chair. They may like to jump on beds and couches, squeeze between furniture and hide under heavy blankets. These types of behaviors are frequently reported by parents and teachers of children with ASD.

Tom was over-responsive to touch and sounds, but he liked to be squished and cuddled. He pushed against everything, He loved rough house play and could only sleep when the blankets were pulled tightly around him. When he was frustrated, angry or disorganized, Tom would push his chin into the arm, back or leg of his parents. Tom's parents often gave him back rubs to help him stay calm. He would find tight spaces to climb into and would often bury himself under pillows. Tom's search for pressure seemed to occupy most of his time and energy.

Tom's search for proprioceptive input was his attempt to help provide sensations that his nervous system needed to stay calm and organized. The deep touch pressure may also help to reduce his hyper-reactive responses to touch and sounds.

The ability to respond appropriately to proprioceptive input is critical for motor development. Many children instinctively use proprioceptive input to help regulate their nervous systems. This is a useful strategy that can be easily taught to children and incorporated into daily routines. Part Two of this book will review these as well as other strategies designed to compensate for problems with sensory integration.

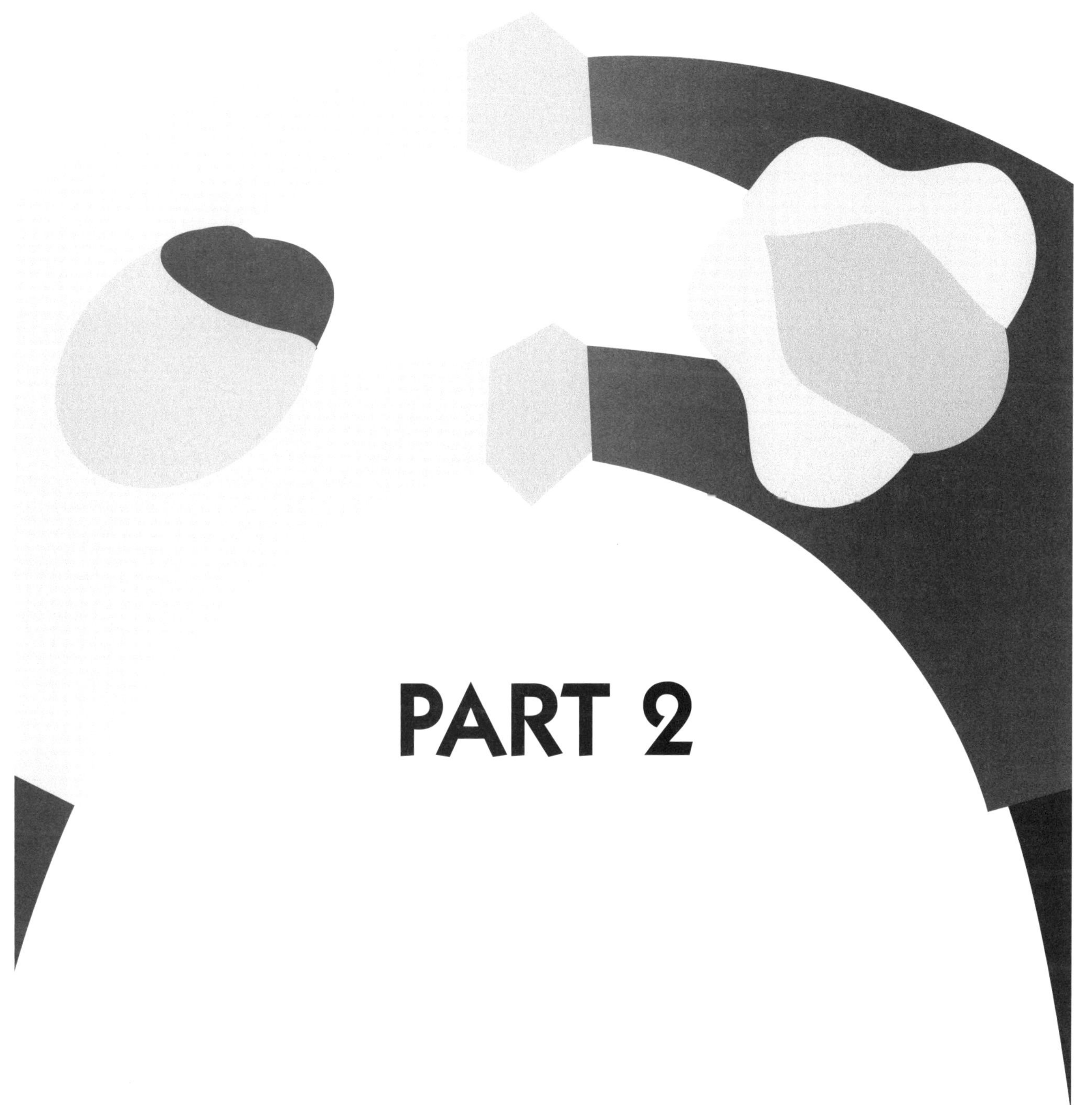

PART 2

CHAPTER 4

IDENTIFYING PROBLEMS WITH SENSORY INTEGRATION

How do I know if my child has difficulty processing sensation?

In order to determine where sensory integration breaks down, we need to look at each sensory system carefully. This is a complex process that can be confusing and requires considerable detective work. Children can be over-responsive in one sensory system and under-responsive in another system. Sometimes a child's behavior seems to suggest that they are seeking out sensation. Sensory seeking behaviors can reflect both an over-responsive or under-responsive nervous system.

Consider a child who moves their fingers in front of their face. An under-responsive child may be seeking out extra visual input that is provided by the fluttering of fingers in front of their eyes. This behavior can also function as an accommodation for a child who is over-responsive. Focusing on the fingers moving in front of the face can help the child screen out, or ignore, overwhelming visual input. Visual fixation on an object can not only provide distraction but can actually reduce the registration of uncomfortable sensory input. You really need to be a detective when you are trying to assess your child's ability to process sensation. Your OT can help!

Sensory integration, the use of sensory information for function, is a process that begins prior to birth and continues throughout our lifetime. Sensory integration is fundamental to our self care, our play and our work. We organize and use sensory information automatically; we never really think about it. This automatic process frees us up to focus our attention on other tasks.

The diversity among children with ASD encourages parents and professionals to observe for uniqueness in each child. Observations need to be collected and analyzed across environments. Possible conclusions are formulated which provide the basis for potential intervention strategies. Observations of behaviors help us identify recurring behaviors and troublesome environments. In order to determine where sensory integration is breaking down, we need to look at each sensory system.

Sensory History and Profiles

Obtaining a sensory history and profile is the most vital way to evaluate sensory integration. Sensory-related behaviors are identified and the settings and situations in which they occur can be carefully considered. Formal assessments may not be useful because they may not provide information about how the child responds in natural situations. Children can be anxious during formal testing, and their responses to sensation may not represent typical reactions. This is particularly true for children with ASD who may be anxious, may not comprehend instructions or may not be motivated to cooperate.

Every day, parents make evaluations of sensory integration without recognizing it and without having the language to describe their observations.

> "Annie has always been a poor sleeper and wakes very easily with the slightest noise. The sign on my front door says, 'please don't ring the bell, baby sleeping.'

> "I can't vacuum or blow dry my hair when David is home because he covers his ears, screams and runs in circles."

> "Adam seems fine in the grocery store until we get to the frozen food section and he hears the buzzing of the refrigerator units."

These accounts from parents have identified that their children have unusual responses to auditory sensation. The recording of these observations forms a sensory history and profile which can be collected through published, standardized questionnaires or informal checklists. An interview to discuss and clarify answers should always follow the completion of a questionnaire or checklist.

Published Questionnaires

Reisman and Hanschu's article, "Sensory Integration Inventory-Revised for Individuals with Developmental Disabilities" (1992), looks at responses to vestibular, tactile and proprioceptive input. The accompanying manual provides excellent information on the significance of the observations reported in the questionnaire.

Morton and Wolford also published an excellent questionnaire titled "Analysis of Sensory Behavior Inventory" (1994). It reviews all of the sensory systems and is divided into observations which may suggest sensory-seeking versus sensory-avoidant behaviors. It includes a method to organize your observations and a worksheet to help summarize your observations, discuss implications and note recommendations.

Dunn (1994) developed the "Sensory Profile," which consists of 125 behavioral statements organized into all the sensory systems and includes observations about activity level and emotional and social behaviors. This is the questionnaire that was used to compare the performance of children with and without ASD, which indicated that 85% of the items differentiated between the sensory processing abilities of children with ASD from those children without ASD (Kientz and Dunn, 1997). The "Short Sensory Profile" comprises 38 items and has been shown to be more accurate in discriminating atypical sensory processing in comparison to the long version (Dunn, 1999).

Another useful tool is the "Durand Motivational Assessment Scale" (1998). This scale looks at types of unusual behavior and helps to analyze what motivates the behavior. Questions about the behavior are presented, and the answers help to determine if the behavior is motivated by a sensory need, the need for attention, the need to avoid or escape or an attempt to communicate a wish for a desired item or action.

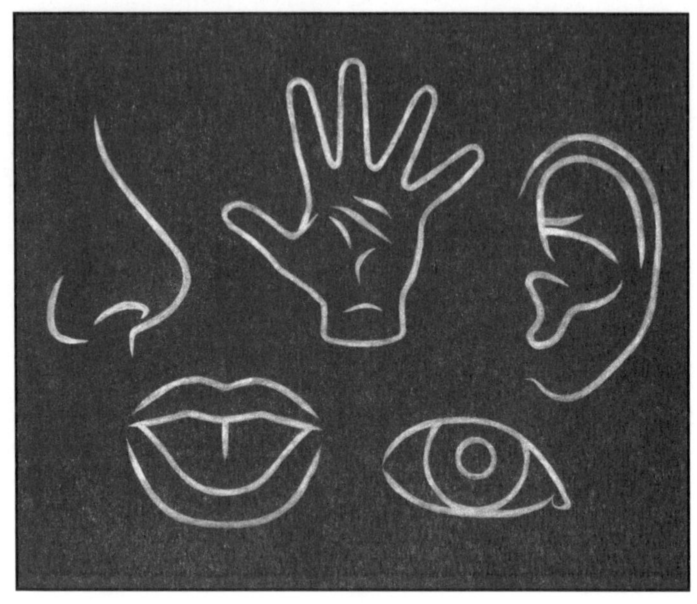

The "Sensory Processing Measure" (SPM) includes a school form and a home form so that sensory processing can be seen across environments and teams could better problem solve and collaborate. (Home form, Parham & Ecker; Main Classroom and School Environments Forms, Kuhaneck, Henry, & Glennon, 2011). It was normed on children ages 5 through 12, from Kindergarten through to Grade 6. The Sensory Processing Measure – Preschool (SPM-P) is for children ages 2 through 5 and again includes both home and childcare setting forms.

A variety of informal questionnaires and screenings is available online that can help identify sensory challenges. The following questionnaires, which we developed, are organized into over-responsive (sensation can be overwhelming and difficult to process) and under-responsive (a lot of sensation is needed for the child to even notice the sensory event) categories. Look for patterns in behaviors that can indicate sensory processing challenges and be mindful of the sensory environments where these behaviors occur. Collecting this information can help you develop strategies to support your child's ability to process sensation.

Building Bridges Sensory Screening

VESTIBULAR

Hyper-responsive

- ❑ appears fearful of playground equipment
- ❑ becomes sick easily in cars, elevators and rides
- ❑ appears fearful of heights/stair climbing
- ❑ avoids balancing activities
- ❑ avoids participation in sports/games

Hypo-responsive

- ❑ seeks fast-moving activities
- ❑ engages in frequent spinning, jumping, bouncing and running
- ❑ constantly moves their head
- ❑ has difficulty staying still

TACTILE

Hyper-responsive

- ❑ avoids touch or contact
- ❑ dislikes and avoids messy play
- ❑ appears to be irritated by clothing or food textures
- ❑ becomes irritated if someone is too close

Hypo-responsive

- ❑ constantly touches objects
- ❑ seems to have difficulty using an object (pencil) unless it is heavy/textured or vibrates
- ❑ constantly mouths objects

PROPRIOCEPTIVE

Hypo-responsive

- ❑ exerts too much or too little pressure when handling objects

Get the free print PDF of this page at www.sensoryworld.com/BBForms

- ☐ has difficulty assuming body positions necessary to perform different tasks
- ☐ seeks more than typical rough-and-tumble play
- ☐ seeks deep pressure by squeezing into tight places
- ☐ needs extra-firm pressure to relax when massaging

VISUAL

Hyper-responsive

- ☐ appears uncomfortable in sunlight or strong light
- ☐ appears sensitive to changes in lighting
- ☐ has difficulty looking at screens
- ☐ has difficulty watching faces
- ☐ moves their fingers in front of their eyes constantly
- ☐ likes to watch falling items

Hypo-responsive

- ☐ notices visual differences
- ☐ focuses on shadows, reflections and spinning objects
- ☐ seeks out new visual sensations

AUDITORY

Hyper-responsive

- ☐ becomes upset with loud or unexpected sounds
- ☐ hums or sings to screen out unwanted sounds
- ☐ dislikes certain sounds (vacuum, hair dryer)

Hypo-responsive

- ☐ seeks out sound
- ☐ turns up the volume on electronic devices/the TV

OLFACTORY (SMELL) / GUSTATORY (TASTE)

Hyper-responsive

- ☐ dislikes strong smells or tastes

Get the free print PDF of this page at www.sensoryworld.com/BBForms

- ❑ has a limited food repertoire
- ❑ gags at the sight/smell of certain foods

Hypo-responsive

- ❑ frequently has his/her hands in his/her pants
- ❑ smears his/her feces
- ❑ eats non-edible foods
- ❑ seeks out new smells/tastes

Identifying Difficulties in Self-Care Skills General Self-Care Checklist

TOUCH

Hyper-responsive

- ❑ has difficulty tolerating the touch of a facecloth/towel
- ❑ rubs spots that were touched
- ❑ seems to accept touch within a predictable routine
- ❑ dislikes the feel of the toothbrush
- ❑ complains that the toothbrush/hairbrush hurts him/her
- ❑ reacts aggressively to touch
- ❑ often strips clothing/takes off shoes and socks
- ❑ has difficulty tolerating temperature changes
- ❑ has difficulty with nail care

Hypo-responsive

- ❑ seeks out touch; loves to feel textures on body
- ❑ feels textures with his/her mouth

PROPRIOCEPTION

Hypo-responsive

- ❑ constantly drops objects
- ❑ applies too much/not enough pressure with objects of self care (squeezes toothpaste so that too much comes out or lacks enough pressure to remove the cap)
- ❑ really enjoys the shower, rough toweling or firm hair brushing
- ❑ seems unable to change body position to accommodate the task (e.g., expresses difficulty getting into the tub)

VESTIBULAR

Hyper-responsive

- ❑ demonstrates resistance to a change in head position (difficulty leaning back to have hair rinsed)
- ❑ prefers to hold head upright

Get the free print PDF of this page at www.sensoryworld.com/BBForms

- ❑ gets disoriented following a change in head position
- ❑ has difficulty weight shifting to balance for a change in position (bending down to dry his/her feet)
- ❑ has difficulty bending over the sink to spit out toothpaste
- ❑ seems fearful of sitting on the toilet, especially when feet are off the ground

VISUAL

Hyper-responsive

- ❑ has difficulty tolerating the reflection of light off the water or shiny sink
- ❑ prefers to keep the light off
- ❑ over focuses on a visual event in the room, like a closing door
- ❑ has difficulty guiding movement in front of a mirror (get distracted by the mirror)

Hypo-responsive

- ❑ has difficulty finding visual items on busy backgrounds
- ❑ seems fascinated with changing visuals (bubbles, dripping water)

AUDITORY

Hyper-responsive

- ❑ gets upset by loud noises (toilets flushing, water running, hairdryer)
- ❑ hums or sings to screen out incoming auditory input
- ❑ gets easily distracted by sound
- ❑ covers ears with hands to screen the louder, more hollow sounds of the bathroom
- ❑ struggles with the sound in the bathroom, so that self care skills have to be completed outside the bathroom

Hypo-responsive

- ❑ enjoys loud sounds and repeat them often (flushing toilet)
- ❑ likes the echo of the bathroom

SMELL/TASTE

Hyper-responsive

- ❑ has poor tolerance of fragrance in soap and shampoo
- ❑ has difficulty tolerating toothpaste

Get the free print PDF of this page at www.sensoryworld.com/BBForms

- ❑ smears feces
- ❑ holds nose/gag during toileting

Hypo-responsive

- ❑ seems not to notice smells
- ❑ smears feces
- ❑ craves strong tastes; eats soap/toothpaste

GENERAL OBSERVATIONS

- ❑ is sedentary; prefers sitting tasks
- ❑ has difficulty staying still
- ❑ has difficulty staying in one place long enough to complete a task
- ❑ fidgets
- ❑ has strong desire for movement, even during a task
- ❑ constantly shifts in position during seated activities

EMOTIONAL/BEHAVIORAL

- ❑ demonstrates poor confidence
- ❑ has difficulty planning the action even though the task is understood
- ❑ exhibits poor self-esteem
- ❑ requires more preparation and support through an activity
- ❑ seems immature
- ❑ can be overly sensitive to criticism
- ❑ acts fearful/anxious
- ❑ has difficulty with transitions
- ❑ requires predictability in effort to compensate for poor planning skills and sensory defensiveness
- ❑ gets easily frustrated
- ❑ has difficulty with rhythms of the body - sleeping, hunger, elimination
- ❑ has difficulty with self-regulation
- ❑ has difficulty interacting with and making friends

Dressing Checklist

TOUCH

Hyper-responsive:

- ❑ dislikes rigid clothing (jeans) and bindings in clothing (waistbands, cuffs)
- ❑ dislikes sleeves on shirts
- ❑ dislikes dressing, opposes changes in clothing (day/night)
- ❑ has difficulty with seasonal changes or changes due to weather
- ❑ has a very narrow collection of clothing items which can be tolerated
- ❑ requires new clothing to be washed several times before it can be worn
- ❑ tolerates undergarments and socks better when worn inside out
- ❑ require socks to be seamless
- ❑ pulls at hats, mitten, scarves
- ❑ constantly adjusts clothing
- ❑ needs all tags cut out
- ❑ experiences extreme stress while shopping for new clothes/shoes
- ❑ finds dressing to be anxiety provoking
- ❑ can strip clothing or take off socks and shoes when anxious
- ❑ feels that cold shoes/clothing feel wet and are not tolerated

Hypo-responsive

- ❑ frequently holds or rubs certain textures
- ❑ enjoys trying on clothing/footwear of different textures

PROPRIOCEPTION

Hypo-responsive

- ❑ frequently drops items from the hand (belt, socks)
- ❑ has difficulty adjusting the pressure in dressing (lets go of the pants when pulling them up or pulls them up hard)
- ❑ is easily fatigued during dressing

Get the free print PDF of this page at www.sensoryworld.com/BBForms

- ❑ has difficulty accurately placing the body's position in relation to the clothing (e.g., correct leg in the corresponding leg hole of the pants)
- ❑ struggles with the finishing touches—ensuring the shirt is tucked in, the zipper is up
- ❑ does not seem to notice when clothing is twisted on the body
- ❑ does not seem to notice when clothing is too small (even shoes)

VESTIBULAR

Hyper-responsive

- ❑ has difficulty maintaining balance during dressing, especially during a change in head position while bending over to put socks on
- ❑ loses orientation when the head is moved (looks down to put shoes on)
- ❑ has difficulty maintaining attention on the task as the need to balance takes up so much energy
- ❑ tends to rush through the activity within the ability to balance
- ❑ has difficulty pacing the activity

Hypo-responsive

- ❑ craves movement during the dressing activity
- ❑ fatigues easily

VISUAL

Hyper-responsive

- ❑ has difficulty finding clothing in closet and drawer; gets overwhelmed by the visual sense
- ❑ doesn't look at clothing when hands are feeling the texture of fabric
- ❑ struggles with balance
- ❑ gets distracted by patterns, may prefer a solid color

Hypo-responsive

- ❑ struggles with matching socks and shoes
- ❑ has difficulty finding a button/zipper on a garment
- ❑ has difficulty matching button to button hole

Get the free print PDF of this page at www.sensoryworld.com/BBForms

- ❑ demonstrates poor guidance of movement with vision
- ❑ becomes distracted with moving the clothing (flicks the arm of the shirt to provide extra visual input by watching it fall)

AUDITORY

Hyper-responsive

- ❑ has difficulty with clothing that makes noise when the body moves
- ❑ gets distracted by the sound of items in pockets (keys/change)
- ❑ is easily distracted by sounds during dressing

Hypo-responsive

- ❑ struggles to hear verbal prompts during the dressing routine

SMELL/TASTE

Hyper-responsive

- ❑ will not wear new clothing because of the smell unless it is washed
- ❑ prefers clothing to be washed and dried with non-perfumed detergents/fabric softeners
- ❑ demonstrates poor tolerance of the glue from decals/iron-ons due to the smell
- ❑ dislikes freshly ironed clothing, as the heat from the iron can bring out the smell

Hypo-responsive

- ❑ repeatedly smells clothing items
- ❑ enjoys smells others may find noxious, like soiled clothing and dirty socks/shoes

Eating Checklist

TOUCH

Hyper-responsive

- ❑ prefers food of consistent texture and temperature
- ❑ dislikes 'surprise' textures in foods (e.g., a noodle in the soup)
- ❑ gags when the texture of food is changed or even perceived to be changed
- ❑ has a very limited diet because of sensitivity to food textures
- ❑ has difficulty tolerating utensils in the mouth; prefers to eat finger foods
- ❑ drinks frequently during eating to wash food out of the mouth
- ❑ uses only fingertips when eating, has difficulty tolerating touch inside the hand
- ❑ is a picky eater
- ❑ has difficulty tolerating temperature changes in food
- ❑ often eats one type of food at a time
- ❑ demonstrates food preferences that become more limited in times of anxiety
- ❑ can't tolerate any food on lips, cheeks or chin

Hypo-responsive

- ❑ seeks out food and non-food objects to explore texture
- ❑ presents a safety concern; decreased processing of touch can lead to choking as the child may not feel the food reaching the back of the throat
- ❑ does not feel food on face
- ❑ demonstrates poor awareness of pain and temperature in the mouth

PROPRIOCEPTION

Hypo-responsive

- ❑ prefers chewy or crunchy foods to increase sensory input (fruit chews or chips)
- ❑ does not chew foods well (safety issue: choking)
- ❑ fatigues easily, especially during meals with a lot of chewing
- ❑ has difficulty maintaining posture to eat

Get the free print PDF of this page at www.sensoryworld.com/BBForms

- ❑ has decreased force in bite (may not be able to bite into an apple or chew meat)
- ❑ props body up using a hand under the chin or leans the head on the arm/body to stabilize posture for eating

VESTIBULAR

Hyper-responsive

- ❑ has difficulty with sitting balance
- ❑ has difficulty maintaining attention to the task when the head position changes to accommodate the fork/spoon
- ❑ has difficulty stabilizing vision to guide eating

Hypo-responsive

- ❑ needs movement; frequently stands up then sits down while eating
- ❑ needs to swing feet during eating
- ❑ constantly shifts position in the chair
- ❑ fatigues easily

VISUAL

Hyper-responsive

- ❑ becomes overwhelmed by the colors and patterns of food, plate and tablecloth
- ❑ has difficulty guiding movement with the eyes as the eyes prefer to look at an unchanging object
- ❑ is distracted by visual input
- ❑ hangs head close to food to block out extra visual input

Hypo-responsive

- ❑ has difficulty finding food/cutlery against a busy background
- ❑ adds items to plate to increase visual interest
- ❑ moves items on plate around to increase visual interest

AUDITORY

Hyper-responsive

- ❑ gets distracted by the noise of the food, utensils, people talking
- ❑ dislikes the sound of other people chewing

- ❑ dislikes the sound of chewing from themselves
- ❑ has difficulty eating when someone else is eating or talking

Hypo-responsive

- ❑ seeks out more sound when chewing/drinking

SMELL/TASTE

Hyper-responsive

- ❑ has difficulty with some tastes/odors
- ❑ gags easily when confronted with certain smells/tastes
- ❑ tolerates a narrow range of foods
- ❑ is very hesitant to try new foods
- ❑ is a poor eater
- ❑ becomes upset with the smell of food as it is cooking
- ❑ has strong preferences for some foods and wants to have them at every meal
- ❑ has difficulty eating out or at school, as the smells of the food of other people may not be tolerated

Hypo-responsive

- ❑ exhibits pica (chewing and eating non-edible items)
- ❑ seems not to smell things; is not motivated to eat because there is no taste
- ❑ seeks out the food of others

School/Work Checklist

TOUCH

Hyper-responsive

- ☐ has difficulty tolerating touch from others; struggles to stand in line, sit in a small circle or work in a confined space with others
- ☐ avoids expression of affection, such as hugs, comfort from teacher/peers
- ☐ dislikes holding writing or cutting utensils in the hand
- ☐ dislikes touch by an unpredictable texture: paint, glue, stickers, tape and/or objects that are wet or dirty
- ☐ has difficulty tolerating close one-on-one instruction and hand-over-hand demonstration
- ☐ tends to use the mouth, not hands, to learn about toys and other objects
- ☐ reacts aggressively to touch by others
- ☐ has outbursts during lining up or circle time
- ☐ has difficulty putting clothes on in a small cubby area
- ☐ dislikes holding the tools of the trade on the job
- ☐ has difficulty traveling in tight places, like the elevator or stairway
- ☐ has difficulty tolerating a uniform
- ☐ prefers to work alone to minimize touch
- ☐ avoids riding public transit during peak times

Hypo-responsive

- ☐ engages in excessive touching of objects and people
- ☐ has difficulty understanding space and the social boundaries of touch
- ☐ doesn't seem to notice changes in temperature
- ☐ doesn't seem to notice when they are hurt

PROPRIOCEPTION

Hypo-responsive

- ☐ has difficulty staying in one place; likes to take frequent movement breaks

Get the free print PDF of this page at www.sensoryworld.com/BBForms

- ❑ stabilizes self against furniture or others (can lean against other children in circle time or hook an arm or leg around a chair to hold themselves up)
- ❑ 'locks' joints to maintain upright posture
- ❑ has a weak grasp
- ❑ has difficulty maneuvering around the classroom, especially when there are physical changes in the environment due to impaired body awareness
- ❑ frequently drops books, pencils, tools, etc.
- ❑ tires easily
- ❑ uses chewing as a strategy to maintain attention and focus
- ❑ uses self stimulatory behavior to maintain attention or relieve stress

VESTIBULAR

Hyper-responsive

- ❑ is distractible, can easily lose visual attention, especially if the head is moved
- ❑ can use a self-stimulatory behavior with the head in order to maintain attention (rocking the head)
- ❑ has difficulty with visual tracking; easily loses place during reading
- ❑ feels fear and avoidance of the playground, gym and stairs
- ❑ dislikes car/bus rides, especially when travelling in reverse, as the eyes can't help process movement
- ❑ dislikes stops/starts and changes in direction of movement
- ❑ panics if stopped on the stairs
- ❑ dislikes changes in body position

Hypo-responsive

- ❑ needs to take frequent movement breaks
- ❑ has poor sitting balance in chairs and on the floor; is constantly in search of movement
- ❑ takes unnecessary risks during movement in the playground and in the gym

VISUAL

Hyper-responsive

- ❑ is overwhelmed by too much visual stimulation on the walls/around the blackboard, can easily get lost

Get the free print PDF of this page at www.sensoryworld.com/BBForms

- ❑ pays attention to detail as a way to screen out overwhelming visual input
- ❑ demonstrates strong visual memory
- ❑ squints to decrease the intensity of the light
- ❑ prefers to wear a hat or sunglasses in class or at work
- ❑ prefers the dark
- ❑ closes blinds or dim lights
- ❑ has difficulty when the natural light changes with seasonal changes
- ❑ hesitates going down stairs, as depth can be difficult to judge

Hypo-responsive

- ❑ has difficulty finding objects against a cluttered background
- ❑ is unable to visually scan across a page without losing the sentence
- ❑ easily loses place when reading
- ❑ is interested in visually stimulating objects and will create visual stims by spinning or dropping objects
- ❑ has trouble staying between the lines when coloring or writing
- ❑ looks intently at people or objects
- ❑ does not have enough visual information to judge stairs properly
- ❑ looks intently at light sources or sharp contrasts

AUDITORY

Hyper-responsive

- ❑ covers ears frequently
- ❑ is very fearful of fire alarms
- ❑ speaks in a loud voice to screen out incoming noise
- ❑ startles at loud noises (PA system, door banging)
- ❑ is distracted by noise
- ❑ has difficulty tolerating background noise; can't focus
- ❑ is very sensitive to noises from other sources (next classroom)
- ❑ prefers activities that enable screening of auditory input (paper tearing, door opening and closing, humming)

Get the free print PDF of this page at www.sensoryworld.com/BBForms

- ❑ is anxious in new situations because of potential sounds

Hypo-responsive

- ❑ does not respond when name is called
- ❑ seeks out activities to increase the variety and volume of sound

SMELL/TASTE

Hyper-responsive

- ❑ dislikes cleaning days because of the smell of cleanser
- ❑ reacts negatively when people wear new smells
- ❑ recognizes people by the way they smell
- ❑ is sensitive to smell due to allergies
- ❑ has difficulty with self-regulation at lunch time when there are many smells
- ❑ is anxious in new situations because of the potential smells

Hypo-responsive

- ❑ feels excessive need to smell items/people
- ❑ likes small spaces, as it is easier to smell others
- ❑ is hyposensitive to taste and may snack on crayons, chalk (safety issue)

Play Checklist

TOUCH

Hyper-responsive

- ❑ prefers predictable touch, as the expectation helps harness attention and improve processing
- ❑ dislikes getting messy
- ❑ avoids arts and crafts, cooking, gardening
- ❑ does not use the whole hand; prefers to use fingertips
- ❑ reacts aggressively to touch by others
- ❑ mouths objects if the hands are overly sensitive to touch
- ❑ has a strong preference for certain textures in toys
- ❑ chooses predictable toys to prevent surprises
- ❑ prefers dry to wet/dirty play
- ❑ uses toys differently than intended; may be used for a sensory purpose, not a play purpose
- ❑ prefers solitary play to play in small groups

Hypo-responsive

- ❑ feels excessive need to touch objects and people
- ❑ has decreased awareness of pain and temperature
- ❑ seeks out play with a lot of tactile input

PROPRIOCEPTION

Hypo-responsive

- ❑ prefers gross motor toys to manipulative because of the full body motion
- ❑ seems to have weak muscles
- ❑ tires easily
- ❑ has a weak grasp
- ❑ is unable to grade movement
- ❑ seems accident prone
- ❑ seems to enjoy falling and crashing

Get the free print PDF of this page at www.sensoryworld.com/BBForms

- ❑ doesn't easily change body position in relation to the toy or the play
- ❑ drops pieces of the toy or uses excessive/not enough force when playing with the toy
- ❑ does not play with the toy appropriately; may use it for a sensory purpose
- ❑ chews on toys to increase attention and/or postural stability
- ❑ 'locks' joints in order to maintain position
- ❑ has poor endurance
- ❑ prefers sedentary activities

VESTIBULAR

Hyper-responsive

- ❑ becomes fearful when the feet leave the ground
- ❑ dislikes being upside down
- ❑ avoids playground activities
- ❑ avoids play activities which call for movement
- ❑ uses eyes to compensate for balance challenges

Hypo-responsive

- ❑ has an excessive need for movement
- ❑ has difficulty adjusting the body to prepare for changes in position
- ❑ creates self movement through rocking
- ❑ constantly shifts in chair
- ❑ takes risks in movement

VISUAL

Hyper-responsive

- ❑ is uncomfortable in bright light; prefers to be in the dark
- ❑ concentrates on detail and is unable to see the 'whole picture'
- ❑ gets lost easily
- ❑ hesitates going up/down stairs
- ❑ prefers smaller spaces
- ❑ prefers less visually stimulating activities

Get the free print PDF of this page at www.sensoryworld.com/BBForms

Hypo-responsive

- ❑ has excessive interest in moving, spinning, patterned movements
- ❑ has difficulty putting puzzles together
- ❑ loses their place when reading
- ❑ has difficulty visually tracking or finding an object against a busy background
- ❑ gets lost easily
- ❑ has trouble matching and sorting

AUDITORY

Hyper-responsive

- ❑ is defensive about sound; covers ears
- ❑ startles easily with loud, unexpected sound
- ❑ constantly makes sound to block out other sounds (humming)
- ❑ stops playing in the presence of unfamiliar sounds
- ❑ is easily distracted by sounds
- ❑ has difficulty participating in social play

Hypo-responsive

- ❑ is fascinated by certain sounds and repeats them often
- ❑ seeks out new sounds/volumes

SMELL/TASTE

Hyper-responsive

- ❑ dislikes new toys that have a strong smell

Hypo-responsive

- ❑ smells or tastes toys prior to play

Get the free print PDF of this page at www.sensoryworld.com/BBForms

Social Skills Checklist

TOUCH

Hyper-responsive

- ❑ isolates self from touch by others
- ❑ dislikes crowds and groups of children for fear of being bumped/touched
- ❑ reacts aggressively when bumped/touched by others
- ❑ has difficulty tolerating hugs, kisses and signs of affection
- ❑ has difficulty playing with others in close proximity
- ❑ can be self-injurious
- ❑ needs predictability in touch to harness attention to process it better

Hypo-responsive

- ❑ seeks out deep pressure and frequently bumps into others
- ❑ exhibits excessive touching of objects and people

PROPRIOCEPTION

Hypo-responsive

- ❑ plays rough in an effort to gain more input
- ❑ seeks out deep pressure, hugs
- ❑ squeezes self into small spaces (to increase the deep pressure input)
- ❑ exerts too much/not enough pressure when giving a handshake
- ❑ performs excessive clapping crashing and other pressure-seeking behaviors
- ❑ can be self-injurious

VESTIBULAR

Hyper-responsive

- ❑ avoids movement
- ❑ body moves as a unit; can't move head independently of body
- ❑ balance challenges can make moving toward or standing beside another difficult

Get the free print PDF of this page at www.sensoryworld.com/BBForms

- ❑ can become dizzy watching other children
- ❑ becomes anxious in an environment full of movement; may stand near the wall
- ❑ does not play movement-based games with others

Hypo-responsive

- ❑ craves movement
- ❑ becomes excited when there is a lot of movement in the activity

VISUAL

Hyper-responsive

- ❑ is more comfortable in the dark
- ❑ looks intensely at objects/people
- ❑ finds eye contact very stressful and therefore avoids it
- ❑ cannot process or tolerate color in different intensities
- ❑ squints
- ❑ prefers to wear a hat/glasses
- ❑ stares off into space
- ❑ looks at a familiar object

Hypo-responsive

- ❑ has difficulty reading facial expression/social cues
- ❑ has difficulty visually scanning to find friends in class or on the playground
- ❑ has difficulty locating and keeping friends in the visual field, especially in a busy environment
- ❑ doesn't use eyes to guide movement

AUDITORY

Hyper-responsive

- ❑ is over sensitive to sounds from others
- ❑ constantly hums and sings to screen out environmental noise
- ❑ dislikes crowds and noisy places
- ❑ covers ears

Get the free print PDF of this page at www.sensoryworld.com/BBForms

Hypo-responsive

- ❑ appears not to hear sounds, even his/her own name
- ❑ seeks out sounds in variety and volume

SMELL/TASTE

Hyper-responsive

- ❑ overreacts to new people, new scents
- ❑ breathes through their sleeve, as it is a familiar smell
- ❑ smells a familiar smell during a transition

Hypo-responsive

- ❑ prefers a small space so that it is easier to smell others
- ❑ sniffs or licks an object or a person to interact or to discover more about him/her/it

CHAPTER 5

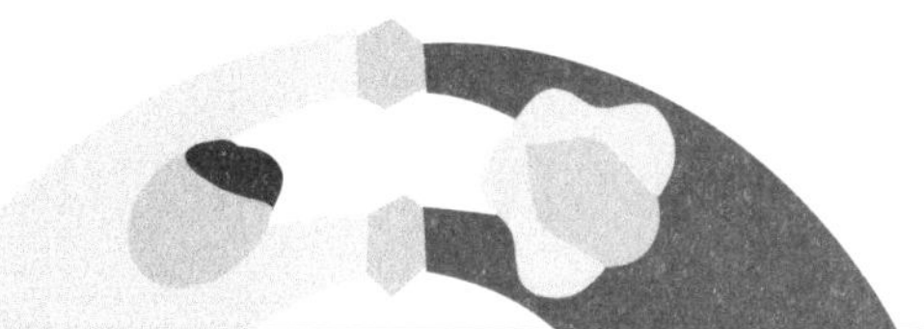

STRATEGIES FOR CHALLENGING BEHAVIORS

The first to step in managing challenging behaviors in children with ASD is to understand the reason behind the observed behavior.

Williamson (1996) identifies many factors affecting behavior in young children with ASD, including the physical environment, the child's current emotional state, the availability of a caregiver, general level of arousal and accumulated negative reactions to sensory buildup. Certain behaviors may reflect a child's response to an inefficient nervous system which may not be able to accurately register, orient or interpret sensory information.

Children with ASD can act as a barometer, reflecting the emotional states of others. Greater understanding can prevent negative responses to the behaviors these children sometimes exhibit. The theory of sensory integration, as presented in chapters two and three, can help you better understand some of these behaviors. Chapter four provides tools that can be used to help determine if a child is experiencing a problem with sensory integration.

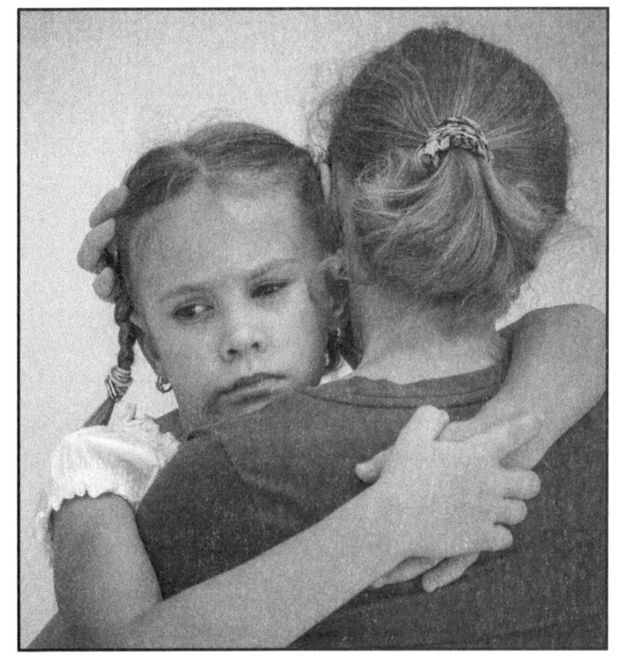

The second step is preventing the occurrence of problem behaviors. Strategies based on sensory integration theory can accommodate sensory needs and help prevent some inappropriate behaviors. These strategies include the implementation of a sensory diet and the use of the Wilbarger Protocol.

The third step to managing challenging behaviors is to develop consistent procedures to employ when the behavior occurs. This chapter will describe some very specific problem behaviors and will offer strategies to implement when the behavior occurs. It will also provide some general calming and alerting ideas. These strategies are most helpful for those children who have been identified as having sensory-related problems. It is not always clear why certain behaviors occur. Sometimes a particular behavior to cope with a sensory need develops into a habit or a learned pattern of response. Sometimes a traditional behavioral approach needs to be used alone or in conjunction with a sensory integration approach. Some behaviors which may appear related to sensory-motor needs may be involuntary tics or reflections of other neurological problems.

Children can be taught to recognize and understand their own sensory needs and be given strategies to increase attention, decrease stress and improve reactions to sensory stimulation. Many of the strategies presented throughout this book can easily be taught to children. At the end of this chapter, we provide a program that has been adapted to teach relaxation techniques to children with ASD. Also in this chapter, you will find:

1. The Wilbarger Therapressure Protocol for Sensory Defensiveness
2. The Sensory Diet
3. General Calming and Alerting Strategies
4. Strategies for Specific Problems
5. A Relaxation Technique for Children

The Wilbarger Therapressure for Sensory Defensiveness

The Wilbarger Therapressure Protocol (Wilbarger, 1991) is a specific, professionally guided treatment regime designed to reduce sensory defensiveness. It involves the provision of deep touch pressure throughout the day. This technique was developed by Patricia Wilbarger, M.Ed., OTR, FAOTA, an occupational therapist who specializes in the assessment and treatment of sensory defensiveness. Patricia Wilbarger is one of the co-founders of Sensory Integration International and is a globally recognized expert in the field. She conducts workshops and has produced videotapes, audiotapes and publications that are available through Professional Development Programs (651-439-8865 or www.pdppro.com). The Wilbarger Therapressure Protocol has origins in sensory integration theory, and it has evolved through clinical use. Ms. Wilbarger offers training courses through which professionals can learn how to administer her technique. In these courses she also shares strategies on how to integrate the protocol into intervention plans and how to train parents, teachers and other caregivers.

There is currently a lack of documented research to substantiate this technique's long-term goal of reducing sensory defensiveness. However, Kimball et al. (2007) report that cortisol levels decreased in children immediately following the administration of the protocol. Many occupational therapists have noted positive long-term results with a variety of populations. Many parents of children with autism have reported that their children have responded positively to this technique, including reduction in sensory defensiveness as well as improved behavior and interaction. Many adults with autism have also reported reduction in sensory defensiveness, decreased anxiety and increased comfort in the environment through the use of this technique. In our own practices, we have observed significant behavioral changes in many of our clients following the introduction of the Wilbarger Protocol.

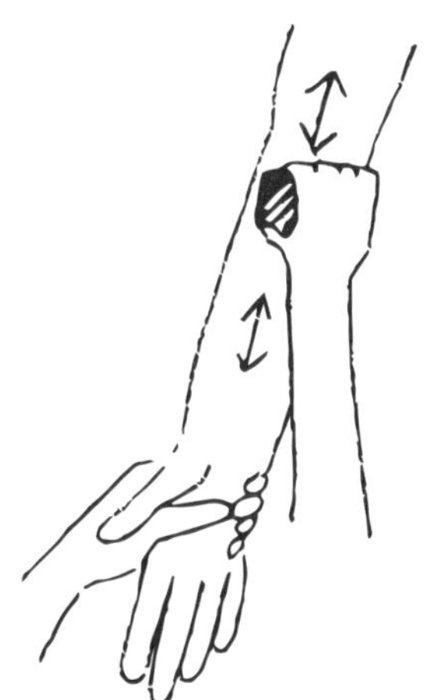

The Wilbarger Protocol represents one of those difficulties in clinical practice in which positive results are observed in treatment regimes that have not yet been fully validated by scientific research. However, because of the strength of anecdotal reporting and our own observations, we feel we would be doing a disservice to our clients if we did not advise them about this technique. When we discuss this option with our clients, we review why it is being recommended and provide them with information on sensory defensiveness. We also inform them about the absence of research in this area, and we make it clear that it is their decision if they want to include the technique into their treatment regimes.

The technique needs to be taught and supervised by an occupational therapist who has been trained to use the technique and who has knowledge of sensory integration theory. This statement cannot be emphasized strongly enough. If the technique is carried out without proper instruction, it could possibly be uncomfortable for the child and may lead to undesired results. The first step of the Wilbarger Protocol involves providing deep pressure to the skin on the arms, back and legs through the use of a special surgical brush. Many people mistakenly call this technique "brushing" because a surgical brush is used. The term "brushing" does not adequately reflect the amount of pressure that is exerted against the skin with the movement of the brush. A more appropriate analogy would be that it is like giving someone a deep massage using a surgical brush. The use of the brush in a slow and methodical manner provides consistent, deep pressure input to a wide area of the skin surface on the body. Ms. Wilbarger recommends a specific surgical brush she has found to be most effective. The face and stomach are never brushed.

Following the massage stage, gentle compressions are provided to the shoulder, elbow, wrist/fingers, hips, knees/ankles and sternum. These compressions provide substantial proprioceptive input. Ms. Wilbarger feels that it is critical that joint compressions follow the use of the surgical brush, and if there is no time to complete both steps, then it should not be administered.

The complete routine should only take about 3 minutes. This technique can be incorporated into a sensory diet schedule. The procedure is initially repeated every 90 minutes and then, after a period of time, the frequency is reduced, and eventually the procedure can be stopped, but gains can be maintained. Some children immediately enjoy this input, and others resist the first few sessions. You may distract the child by singing or offering a mouth or fidget toy. Some children really like the administration of this protocol and will seek out the brush and bring it to their parents, teachers or caregivers. Other children tolerate it with little reaction, and occasionally a child is resistive. If the child continues to resist and negative changes are observed, the use of the technique needs to be reconsidered, and the supervising therapist needs to be contacted. This has rarely occurred in our practices.

Sensory defensiveness is often a major factor that can lead to challenging behaviors. In the following case studies and discussions about specific behaviors, the Wilbarger Protocol is often the first recommendation to be explored. However, it may not be a feasible choice for all families or classrooms. Other deep pressure techniques can be explored, including bean bag tapping, resistant or heavy work (push, pull, carry, lift) and various types of massage.

Case Studies

As you will note in the following case reports (involving children in our practices), sometimes the results of using the Wilbarger Protocol can be very dramatic. At other times, although the changes have not been as dramatic and have occurred over a longer period of time, they have been significant in positively changing the lives of the children and their families.

Pat

Pat is a 4-year-old boy who has a diagnosis of autism. His occupational therapist concluded that he had sensory defensiveness. Pat was particularly reactive to light touch and unexpected or loud noises. He was very uncomfortable in settings with lots of people and activity. In these environments, Pat became very anxious and would run around the perimeter of the room or setting he was in. This could be quite dangerous in parking lots where Pat would attempt to run, and his parents had to hold him securely. It also presented a problem when his parents took him shopping or to family gatherings. The Wilbarger Protocol was recommended as part of an intervention plan which also included a variety of prescribed sensory activities throughout the day. After only one week, Pat's parents noted a significant decrease in his level of anxiety and his running behaviors. After one month, it became much easier to take Pat shopping and to family gatherings. He even became more willing to interact with his peers and unfamiliar adults!

Amy

Amy is a 6-year-old girl who has a diagnosis of autism. Her occupational therapist concluded that she had sensory defensiveness. Amy avoided light touch, was uncomfortable with many clothing textures and resisted many self-care routines including face washing, tooth brushing, hair washing and hair brushing. Brushing Amy's hair was the biggest battle for Amy's parents and babysitter, and Amy would often cry for long periods of time after hair brushing. The Wilbarger Protocol was recommended as part of an intervention plan. The Protocol was started over the weekend, and no other intervention was provided during that time. Amy's babysitter came to work on Monday morning and did not know that the Protocol was being considered or that it had been initiated. She babysat Amy during the day and was responsible for her self-care routines. When Amy's parents came home from work that day, her babysitter reported that Amy did not resist hair brushing and was more comfortable with washing routines. She asked Amy's parents if they had started giving her medication over the weekend!

Reducing Hypersensitivity in the Mouth

Patricia Wilbarger has also developed a specialized program to help reduce hypersensitivity in the mouth. This type of sensitivity, sometimes called oral defensiveness, can result in limited food choices and interfere with tooth brushing and face washing. This technique involves the use of the thumb to apply pressure along the base of the upper teeth (a surgical glove may be used). The pressure should be similar to the amount of pressure used when rubbing an eyelid. Follow the sweeping motions, gentle downward pressure is applied to the lower jaw by placing fingers over the middle of the lower teeth and pressing down.

Sensory Diet

A sensory diet is a planned and scheduled activity program designed to meet a child's specific sensory needs. Wilbarger and Wilbarger (1991) developed the approach to provide the "just right" combination of sensory input to achieve and maintain optimal levels of arousal and performance in the nervous system. The ability to appropriately orient and respond to sensations can be enhanced by a proper sensory diet. A sensory diet also helps reduce protective or sensory defensive responses that can negatively affect social contact and interaction.

There are certain types of sensory activities that are similar to eating a "main course" and are very powerful and satisfying. These activities provide movement, deep touch pressure and heavy work. They are the powerhouses of any sensory diet, as they have the most significant and long-lasting impact on the nervous system (Wilbarger 1995, Hanschu 1997). There are other types of activities that may be beneficial, but their impact is not as great. These sensory snacks or "mood makers" are activities that last a shorter period of time and generally include mouth, auditory, visual or smell experiences.

A sensory diet does not simply indiscriminately add more sensory stimulation into the child's day. Additional stimulation can sometimes intensify negative responses. The most successful sensory diets include activities in which the child is an active participant. Every child has unique sensory needs, and a sensory diet must be customized for individual needs and responses. An occupational therapist needs to be consulted to help evaluate sensory processing abilities and determine what types of sensory activities would be beneficial.

The sensory diet can be a powerful behavioral tool. If the sensory diet is properly designed and implemented, it can help prevent many challenging behaviors, including self-stimulatory and self-abusive behaviors. Engaging children in sensory experiences on a regular schedule can help them focus, be attentive and interact. A child can feel less anxious when he or she feels more comfortable and in control.

One of the main aims of the sensory diet is to prevent sensory and emotional overload by satisfying the nervous system's sensory needs. However, it can also be used as a recovery technique. Knowledge of the child's sensory needs or sensory profile and activities which create calming responses can be of great assistance when the child becomes overwhelmed and out of control. Adults need to be taught to take prompt action if they see the child becoming overwhelmed or are approaching what some parents call a "meltdown". Common indicators that a child's sensory processing system needs help include silliness, giddiness, noise making, aimless running or pacing. These behaviors may intensify into repetitive stereotypic behaviors, including self-injury. Sometimes the child will simply "shut down" – becoming passive, sleepy or self-absorbed.

There are many ways to implement a sensory diet at home and in the classroom, but it takes commitment on the part of the whole team. Depending on the needs of the child, a sensory diet can be comprised of very specific activities carried out at prescribed times. The following form allows you to list specific times to provide activities and methods to compensate for sensory problems during self-care routines.

For children with ASD, the use of visual aids (pictures and words) is helpful to ensure that the children understand their daily routines and can anticipate when they will be engaging in certain activities. Sensory diet activities can easily be incorporated into visual schedules and choice boards. A clear beginning and end to all activities is necessary. A small poster hung in a classroom or at home can display pictures that represent regular daily activities. The picture can be put away in an envelope marked DONE. This type of visual system can help children, as it adds a sense of order and predictability to the class or home environment.

Sensory Diet Accommodations

A Sample Preschool Sensory Diet

This sensory diet was established for Philip, a hyperactive four-year-old boy with little verbal language. He was also sensory defensive to touch and sound. He attended his community day care every day. Recommendations included both highly prescribed suggestions (relaxation techniques at start of day and Wilbarger Protocol every 90 minutes) and a list of activities that Philip should be offered on a regular basis.

Recommendations

Progressive relaxation exercises (see page 113) started Philip's day to assist with transition to the daycare setting. The Wilbarger Protocol was provided every 90 minutes to address the touch and sound sensitivities.

Free play activities were chosen from the following list:

Name: ____________ Date: ____________

Time	Daily Events	Activities/Accomodations	Comments
	Wake-Up		
	Self-Care		
	Breakfast		
	Arrival at School or Childcare		
	Mid-Morning		
	Lunch		
	Mid-Afternoon		
	Arrival Home		
	Dinner		
	Evening Activity		
	Self-Care		
	Bedtime		

Get the free print PDF of this page at www.sensoryworld.com/BBForms

- try having him jump on a mini tramp or an old mattress, using the sit 'n' spin, rocking boat, swinging, jumping on cushions, "diving" into big box or futon, having someone lie on him, making a "hot dog" and jumping into sand or snow
- use hop balls (on soft surfaces) – try making them into "chairs" by turning them
- with the handle down, stabilize the ball beside the wall, in a corner or in an inner tube.
- introduce regular climbing toys, slides, tunnels and big blocks
- use balance beams
- create obstacle courses for planning movement
- engage in running, running errands
- do jumping jacks
- do wall pushups (stand in a door frame and "push out" the sides)
- fill a large pot with water, try lifting/carrying it and dumping it out
- swing across monkey bars, hang from your hands
- ride bikes and other riding toys; provide a destination by allowing "crashes" into a soft big ball or bean bag

Tactile Activities

- provide daily access to dry sensory play materials (rice, sand or beans)
- hide preferred toys in sensory play materials—"squish" hands before and during
- give high fives and push fives throughout the day!!
- draw in sand or salt
- provide therapy tubing or band to pull on, therapy putty, koosh balls, balloons or rubber gloves filled with things like corn, rice and flour
- give hand massage
- participate in wheelbarrow walking over various floor surfaces

Sitting/Circle Time Ideas

- have staff member give deep pressure during circle sitting to his back, hips
- use a weighted lap toy (instructions on how to make a weighted lap toy can be found in chapter nine)
- give the child fidget toys to hold quietly while listening ("stress" ball, vibrating pen)
- encourage him to assume more challenging body positions (high kneel, on tummy, half kneel; this adds calming, proprioceptive input.)
- have him sit in a padded chair or bean bag chair, sit in staff's lap, sit against body pillow, sit in a "move 'n sit" cushion
- give any oral toy (kazoo, harmonica, party blowers, etc.) that requires breath support
- define his "spot"—use laundry basket, carpet square or something similar to
- define his space

Observed Changes as a Result of the Sensory Diet

Philip began to enjoy attending day care, as his anxiety and need for uncontrolled movement decreased. He became calmer and engaged in transitions more easily. At home he stopped complaining when brushing his teeth and would wash his own face and hands. He would seek out his sensory pictures to request a specific activity, such as playing on the big ball. Many of the activities that were included in Philip's sensory diet were activities that were already part of the classroom routine. His classmates began happily joining Philip for many activities. He soon was better able to interact with his peers, as his discomfort with having the children near him decreased.

General Calming, Organizing and Alerting Techniques

The following list provides methods that can help calm, organize or alert the nervous system. The list must be used only as a general guideline, as activities that calm one child may be alerting to another. These strategies can be incorporated into a sensory diet, or they may help deal with a specific situation.

Calming Techniques

Sensory soothing or calming experiences can help any child who is anxious, but are particularly useful for children who are sensory defensive. They help to relax the nervous system and can reduce exaggerated responses to sensory input.

- provide a warm or tepid bath
- give deep pressure massage, backrub using comfort touch
- perform joint compressions
- have him sit in a sleeping bag, bean bag chair, or on large pillows
- provide a blanket wrap (neutral warmth) or swaddling for a younger child
- guide the child to perform stretches (active and passive)
- have the child snuggle in a sleeping bag, bean bag chair, padded floor seat, how 'da hug, or life jacket
- give firm pressure and skin-to-skin contact
- engage in slow rocking or swaying – rocking chair, in adult's lap or arms, or on tummy in a head to heel direction (rhythmic motion)
- perform slow swinging – back and forth – in a blanket
- provide lycra/spandex clothing
- have the child wear a neoprene vest, snug vest life jacket
- provide a weighted vest or collar
- provide a lap snake (instructions for making a lap snake are in chapter nine)
- produce lavender, vanilla, banana or other soothing smells
- encourage sucking

- provide a hideout, fort or quiet corner
- provide fidget toys
- perform progressive muscle relaxation
- provide white noise or quiet music with a steady beat
- give bear hugs (child faces away from you)
- have the child hug a teddy bear, give self hugs
- give finger hugs and tugs
- provide reduced noise and light levels (turn off the TV, radio and lights)

Organizing Techniques

Organizing experiences can help a child who is either over or under active become focused and attentive.

- encourage the child to suck a pacifier, hard candy, or curly straws
- employ vibration—use a vibrating pillow , battery vibrating wiggle pen, toy massager
- engage in proprioceptive activities (see list in chapter eight), especially hanging, pushing, pulling or lifting heavy objects
- engage in chewing, blowing (see oral motor activity list in chapter eight)
- provide opportunities for swimming
- adding rhythm to the activity through chanting, singing or rapping in time with the child's movements

Alerting Techniques

Alerting experiences can help a child who is under-reactive to sensory input, passive or lethargic become more focused and attentive. It is important to determine if the child is in a "shutdown" mode in response to sensory defensiveness. If this is the case, alerting strategies should not be used. Alerting activities need to be closely monitored to prevent over stimulation.

- introduce bright lighting and fresh, cool air
- facilitate fast swinging
- introduce quick, unpredictable movement (bouncing on a ball, lap or mini trampoline)
- have the child drink ice water or a carbonated drink
- engage in cold water play
- run – use tag games, hide and seek, run errands
- have the child sit on a ball chair, water mat or air pillow
- provide cool water mist from a spray bottle on the face
- play loud, fast music and sudden noises
- provide cause and effect toys with sounds and lights
- introduce strong odors (perfume, peppermint, etc.)
- create visually stimulating rooms

Strategies for Specific Problem Behaviors

In the following section we will present some approaches to commonly seen behaviors. The purpose of certain behaviors may be to seek sensory input or avoid sensory input.

Strategies for specific behaviors related to self-care routines (problems with food texture, hair cutting, etc.) are included in chapter seven, "Ideas for Self Care Skills."

Sensory Seeking Behaviors

Many children with ASD crave sensory input and seem to have an insatiable need for certain types of stimulation. The motto for sensory input, "feed the need," is generally good advice. However, there are times when sensory-seeking behaviors may not provide the most organizing, calming or socially acceptable input. It is appropriate to redirect behavior, always striving to provide appropriate input in the most socially acceptable manner.

Biting and Teeth Grinding

Why?

The child may be hyposensitive to this input and probably has no idea that he is actually hurting himself£ Teeth grinding may bc used as a calming strategy. It's also seen in children with poor balance, perhaps in an effort to stabilize themselves.

Try this:

Provide a s ensory diet with appropriate opportunities for strong sensory input to jaw muscles, oral and tactile discrimination experiences. A child may enjoy chewing on beverage tubing to alleviate stress and calm their nervous system. Whatever strategy is used, it will be most effective if used in all settings. The child will then be able to generalize the coping strategy.

Look for the circumstances prior to the biting (the antecedent). If the root of the aggressive behavior is sensory defensiveness to sound, touch or movement, try to identify the sensory sensitivity and eliminate it or position the child to minimize exposure to this noxious sensory input. Warn the child and teach coping strategies. Use the Wilbarger Protocol to reduce sensory defensiveness.

Another oral pressure technique to try: place the flats of the index and middle fingers against the space between the upper lip and nose and press gently but firmly so that the child is receiving deep pressure.

Running, Spinning or Movement Seeking

Why?

Running, spinning, and other movement provides strong vestibular and proprioceptive stimulation.

Try this:

Provide a sensory diet with appropriate opportunities for strong vestibular and proprioceptive input. Preschoolers love to play tag or "come and get me" games; older children can run around the track, do relay races, roller blade or find alternative ways to get that vestibular fix (see chapter eight, "Gross Motor Activities").

Crashing, Bumping and Clinging

Why?

These activities provide soothing proprioceptive, vestibular and deep pressure touch input. If the child has a high pain tolerance, he or she may actually need a very strong stimulus just to register some sensation. Ear infections should also be ruled out as a source of pain, as a child may be unable to localize the source.

Try this:

Address the source of pain (if an ear infection or other medical condition and treat appropriately). Consider introducing the Wilbarger Protocol to reduce sensory defensiveness. If the child engages in head banging, allow chances to wear a weighted hat or bike helmet for calming.

Hitting, Slapping, Pinching, Squeezing, Grabbing and Pulling

Why?

The hand may be extremely sensitive compared to other body parts, and sensory input in the palm may help override the painful response to light touch.

Try this:

Learn alternate means for obtaining some deep pressure/heavy muscle work. For example, a child may push/pull on the seat of his desk chair, press very hard into the desk top, or press hands together. Try a hand massage. Use the Wilbarger Protocol to reduce sensory defensiveness. Ask your OT for help in picking out appropriate Fidget Bag Tools (see chapter nine); these are tools that your child can have with him or her to keep the hands occupied. Experiment with various bracelet wristbands and watchbands which provide pressure. Toys which offer vibration may also be helpful.

Playing with Saliva

Why?

This provides tactile input to the mouth, fingers and spot rubbed. The mouth is the first accurate sensory receptor of the body and is often used by children who are still developing the ability to receive and accurately process tactile input through the hand. Always include hand activities to increase accuracy in receiving and processing tactile input when you provide an oral program designed to increase sensory-seeking behaviors of the mouth (see chapter eight). If the child seems to be using the saliva for visual input, you may need to add alternative eye tools or strong visual play opportunities.

Try this:

Enhance the opportunities throughout the day for oral and tactile experiences through a sensory diet (see chapter eight).

Flapping

Why?

This jarring of the body's joint and muscles provides proprioceptive sensation to the muscle and joints of the wrist, arm and shoulder. This calming sensation may be a sign of sensory overload.

Try this:

Enhance opportunities for proprioceptive experiences throughout the day in the sensory diet.

Use the Wilbarger Therapressure Protocol to reduce sensory defensiveness. Try wall push-ups, jumps with hands held, climbing and wheelbarrow walks (also hand-walking with the child's tummy on a physio ball). Be sure to look for "heavy work" for the hands when choosing toys (see chapter eight).

Preseverative Play

Why?

Often children with poor body awareness and coordination have poor motor planning. Repetitive play builds on existing skills only and does not require sophisticated motor planning. Every time play changes, the child must plan for the change. The child must actively participate in the environment to plan movement and play. This can be stressful and difficult for children, and they may remain stuck' in specific movements. The play may feed a visual need for pattern and order (such as lining up cars).

Try this:

Build the child's gross and fine motor skills (see chapter eight); provide opportunities to play with toys that require patterning (e.g., puzzles, dominoes, lotto, beading, tangrams), as the child may find patterns soothing.

Smelling Behaviors

Why?

Your child likely has a low sensitivity to smell and seeks out very strong smells. Remember that the sense of smell functions from birth and may be an accurate source of information for the child. Children who enjoy smelling cannot respect personal space, as they need to get very close to another person in order to smell them.

Try this:

Provide other smell-oriented experiences as part of the sensory diet (e.g., lotion rubs). Offer a smelling box with small bottles of different scents. If the child has a fascination with cleaning products, encourage a daily chore of cleaning when supervised. Take a cleaning bottle, flush it and fill it with colored water, adding a strong smell that he or she enjoys.

Masturbation

Why?

This provides strong tactile stimulation which the child can tolerate. Many children who may have difficulty processing touch have an easier time processing touch from the genitals, as the feedback is so strong. Feedback is also predictable. Motor action can be learned quickly and repeated with success. A simple motor action can create strong sensory input. Masturbation is a rhythmic activity and rhythmic movements are calming.

Try this:

Enrich access to calming tactile experiences throughout day through a sensory diet. Provide opportunities to process sensory input from another part of the body accurately. Add deep pressure and calming input with weighted clothes or pretend to be mummies by wrapping yourselves up tightly with tensor bandages, rolling therapy balls or bolsters over the child (often with your own weight on them) or having the child crawl deep down into a bin filled with plastic balls. Investigate alternative seating for girls—up off the floor and out of the "w" position, and for boys close to a table where the table top prevents access to the genital area. Use the Wilbarger protocol to reduce sensory defensiveness.

Pica (mouthing or eating non-food substances such as dirt and rocks)

Why?

This eating of non-edibles usually provides strong tactile and proprioceptive input in a child who may not be registering sensation. It also may transmit vibration to the jaw, which can stimulate the vibration-sensitive vestibular system.

Try this:

Provide a rich vestibular and proprioceptive sensory diet. Use the Wilbarger Oral protocol to provide jaw pressure. Find vibrating toys for the child to mouth. Substitute something crunchy for oral stimulation at regular times throughout the day.

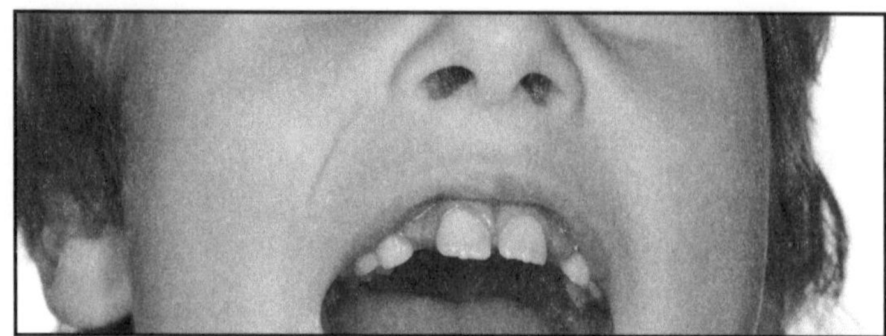

Sensory Avoidant Behaviors

Children who avoid certain sensations are often sensory defensive and are protecting their nervous systems from sensory overload. There are many avoidant responses, but we will discuss only the most commonly seen behaviors that respond very well to a sensory integration approach.

Takes Off Clothing

Why?

This is a clue that the clothes are causing uncomfortable touch input to the skin.

Try this:

Establish a sensory diet to provide opportunities for calming experiences throughout the day. Look for soft clothing, buy used clothes or make sure items are well washed prior to wearing.

Ensure that the child shops and chooses his or her own clothing and learns what characteristics of the clothing he or she can tolerate.

Avoids eye contact

Why?

There are many reasons why children avoid eye contact. Consider these sensory reasons. Peripheral vision may be less stressful than looking directly at something. Processing visual and auditory input may be difficult to do at the same time, so the child looks away in order to process the auditory input more accurately. Peripheral vision can be used as a visual-seeking behavior as the child may seek out lines or shapes, as looking peripherally changes the visual information. Many individuals with ASD are mono channel processors, so looking and listening at the same time is almost impossible.

Try this:

Reduce overall sensory defensiveness by enhancing the opportunities for calming experiences throughout the day in the sensory diet, and use the Wilbarger Protocol. Build trusting relationships with those around the child. Desensitize with various techniques – teach the child to look in the mirror and then at his own image and gradually move to looking at eyes. By building on the child's strengths and interests, (visual patterning fascination with shapes), point out how people's eyes, together with their nose, form a triangle (if one joined them with lines). If he sees that the mouth is an oval and that the face itself is an oval, he will be more comfortable with eye contact. For the child who does not use direct visual contact, teach body positions which indicate listening (for example, when someone is talking, your hands need to be still).

Avoids Car Rides, Swings or any Imposed Movement

Why?

The avoidance of imposed movement suggest this sensation is very frightening to the child.

Try this:

Reduce overall sensory defensiveness by enhancing the opportunities for calming experiences throughout the day with the sensory diet. A very gradual introduction to non -threatening vestibular activities should be a long-term goal. Provide proprioceptive sensations during movement to help decrease fear and anxiety (see chapter eight). Encourage parents to drive out of their driveways forwards, as children can use vision to warn them of movement (backward movement can be frightening). Warn children while riding in the car of upcoming turns and stops. Use a safe, padded car seat which offers lots of pressure. Consult with an OT or physiotherapist who has expertise in treating vestibular issues.

Avoids Stairs or Walking on Different Surfaces

Why?

Some children may experience gravitational insecurity. They are very sensitive to heights and to the demands of gravity. Balance and postural reactions may be immature.

Try this:

As in the previous example, a gradual introduction to non-threatening vestibular activities is ideal.

Avoids Handling Sensory Material

Why?

This is a very common sign of tactile defensiveness, as the hands are particularly rich in touch receptors. Often the temperature and the wetness of the material make a difference in how well it is tolerated.

Try this:

Provide opportunities for calming tactile and other experiences throughout the day with the sensory diet. Use deep pressure touch when demonstrating any tactile play (See chapter eight for tactile activities). Massaging the hands prior to the touch may be helpful.

Limited Use of Hands for Grasping:

Why?

This is another very common sign of tactile defensiveness. Also, as Hanschu and Reisman state (1992), "the hand without a motor plan is a hand without a purpose." If the hand is not grasping, especially when not tactile defensive, this suggests very poor proprioceptive functioning.

Try this:

Build in many proprioceptive experiences. Use hands in function – opening doors, climbing, grasping the ropes on a swing, etc. Explore desensitization with different textures (e.g. kinesthetic sand)

Auditory Sensitivity

Why?

Sensitivity to sounds can differ from sensitivity to speech; hearing problems and ear infections should be ruled out.

Try this:

Reduce overall sensory defensiveness with a sensory diet. Work on helping the child gain control over her own environment (e.g., can she give clues or verbalize when she feels overstimulated? Can she tolerate ear-plugs or use a Walkman?). Reassure the child regarding the source of the sound. Chewing gum or other strong proprioceptive jaw input can compete with external noises and calm the nervous system. Fidget tools also may help for the same reason. Teach relaxation techniques (see chapter five). Consider Auditory Integration Training. Therapeutic Listening, Eaze – CD). Parents, be prepared with an "out-of-order" sign to place on hand dryers in public washrooms to avoid the loud sounds while your child is there.

A Relaxation Technique for Children

Relaxation training can help everyone deal with stress and anxiety. Children with ASD generally operate under high levels of stress. Current investigations by Groden (1998) indicate that new situations, changes at home or school, seasonal changes and strong emotional feelings (even extreme excitement, happiness, worry or anger) can all cause anxiety and stress.

Relaxation techniques have been taught effectively to children with simple line drawings (Doan 1994). To teach children with ASD, these techniques usually need adapting. A traditional relaxation technique that uses auditory, visual and motor imitation may not be successful if the child has poor body awareness and impaired motor planning.

Sensory integration techniques can be used to adapt the traditional progressive relaxation program. Tactile and proprioceptive cues or props can easily be added to the program and can enhance success by increasing sensory feedback. Props such as a squeeze ball can assist children with motor planning problems because they can provide a clear destination for the desired movement (e.g., squeeze the ball with the knees).

Whistles or other blowing toys are often helpful when the child is first learning to take a deep breath on demand. Other children respond to a verbal cue such as "hold your breath," learned during swimming lessons. Children as young as four years old have learned this technique and use it well within the classroom setting at routine times or when prompted. Older children need to learn to monitor their own levels of stress and initiate the relaxation technique when required.

Progressive relaxation is a sequenced task. As sequencing is a common weakness in children with motor planning problems, a book or card format helps students follow directions. Children learn to follow the pictured instructions, then turn the page for the next instruction. In order to be successful in reducing stress, relaxation techniques must be learned then practiced on a regular basis in a variety of settings. This tool has been used across many school, work and home settings and is often a pivotal piece to include in a self-regulation curriculum.

Instructions:

The following four pages contain six pictures to print, cut, and fit into a small photo album (4"X 6"). Customize the program by changing the instructions as needed and deciding on a reward or motivator to include on page six. These have been adapted from Doan (1994). The following is an example of progressive muscle relaxation, and there are other tools available for relaxation, including mindfulness training and yoga.

Many more resources are available that promote self-regulation in the child with ASD (See resources listed in chapter nine).

A. Prepare a picture or write down the reward, especially for initial learning. Most times a sensory toy or small treat to eat or drink is fine. An extra opportunity to run, jump or swing may be enough!
B. Teach your child to follow the directions on the first page by reading out loud and demonstrating, for example, "hold the ball and squeeze tight." Skip to the reward page!
C. Gradually add pages to the sequence until the child can read the whole story and perform the required actions, step by step, with help. Then gradually do away with the prompts – squeeze ball, use your hand, use blowing toys.
D. Identify what anxiety or over-arousal looks like for the child ("Do I lift my shoulders, chew my lip, cry, feel my heart rate go fast, start to make noises?").
E. Teach your child to recognize the emotions they are feeling (e.g., frustration). Teach your child to label the emotion with words or pictures.
F. Help your child connect the relaxation technique(s) that they have used to help their calm feelings. The relaxation techniques found in this book can be made into picture cards to be used within your child's picture communication system.

My Relaxation Book

[Place child's picture here]

Name: ____________________

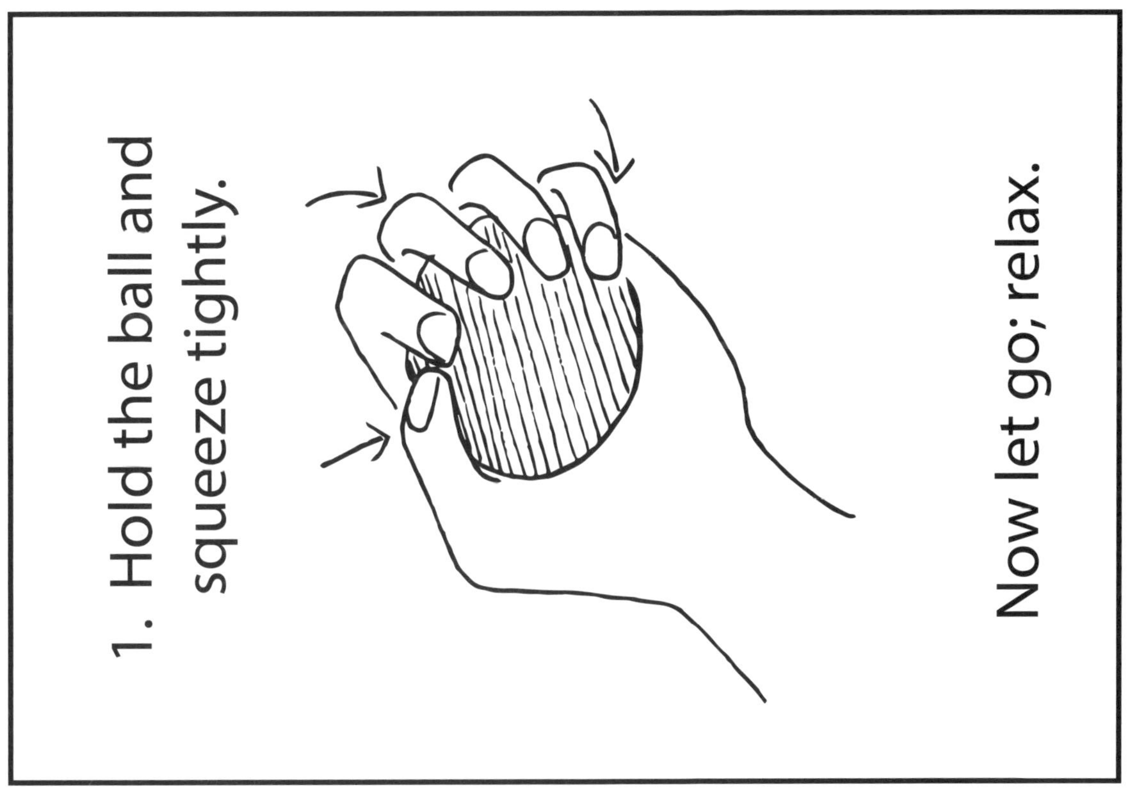

1. Hold the ball and squeeze tightly.

Now let go; relax.

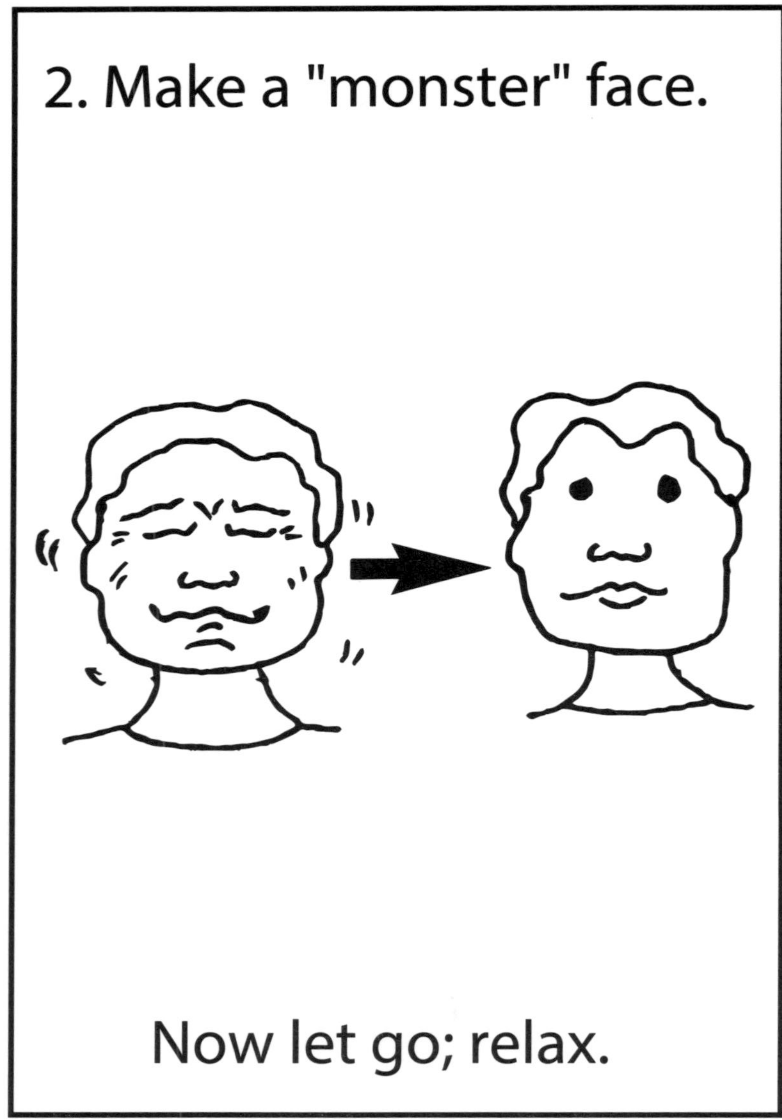

Get the free print PDF of this page at www.sensoryworld.com/BBForms

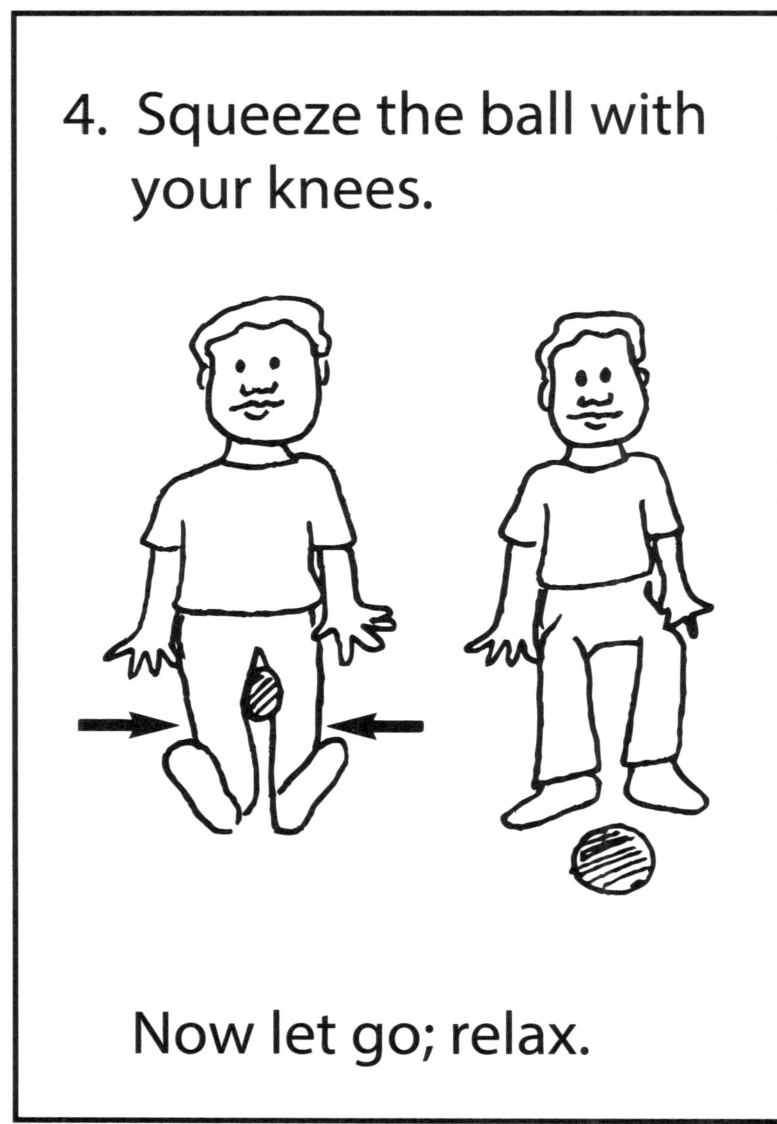
4. Squeeze the ball with your knees.
Now let go; relax.

5. Now hold your breath.
Blow out and relax…

Get the free print PDF of this page at www.sensoryworld.com/BBForms

CHAPTER 6

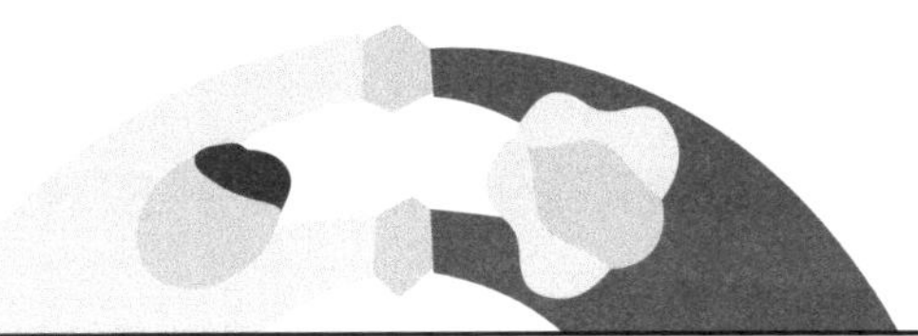

IDEAS FOR SELF-CARE SKILLS

The world can be a very unpredictable place for most children with ASD.

The sensory information these children receive from their body and from the environment while using self-care skills may be processed inefficiently. It is important to support the child with SPD in self-care skills, as these skills are performed daily and can be a source of stress if they are not successful. Performing self-care activities requires handling of towels, brushes, toothbrushes and soap. Your child must motor plan the action and sequence the steps correctly; for example, shampoo must be applied to the hair prior to rinsing. Any other order of this task will not work. Attention must be paid to the task, and your child must monitor the task as he/she is going through it to ensure success.

> Alexia hates when her mother towel dries her hair. She winces in pain as the towel absorbs the water. This is an example of a hypersensitive response to sensory input, interpreting the tactile input as painful and alerting.

Children may also be hypo-responsive to sensory input. They may seek more input in the environment or they may be oblivious to the sensory input.

Ryan does not seem to hear his father calling him to dinner. His father must tap him on the shoulder first to get his attention and then tell him it's time for dinner.

To present an even greater challenge, most children have a fluctuating response to sensory input. Sometimes they are very sensitive to sensory input, and other times they appear to be unaware of sensory input. These children may have difficulty modulating their response to sensory input.

Other factors such as stress, sleep, hunger, thirst or physical ailments can also impair a child's ability to process sensory information. Addressing these underlying physical concerns can better support the child's functioning, including sensory processing.

Children with ASD cannot always accommodate the sensory input of the environment. We can create environments for them that are predictable and that feel safe. The predictable environment and approach can help alleviate anxiety and maximize sensory processing, interaction and learning. Routine and consistency are key to building a learning environment for your child where they feel safe and motivated to take the necessary risks for learning.

This chapter includes a general strategy page and specific strategy pages for each activity of self-care and play. Strategies are divided into sensory strategies and general strategies.

Keep in mind during self-care routines that staying within your child's tolerance allows for the development of a trusting relationship. This relationship can decrease emotional distress. If the environment and those in the environment demonstrate flexibility to support your child's needs, your child can relax, let down their guard and start learning! Good luck with these strategies. We hope you find them helpful.

Sleep

A good night's sleep makes a world of difference to everyone. With a poor sleep pattern, children may not get enough sleep, may have a disrupted sleep or may not get enough deep sleep. They may have difficulty waking in the morning. There is no right or wrong way to perform these strategies. Whatever works for your child is right for your child. Promoting good sleep patterns is a wonderful investment for your child and for you. Remember that pressure touch and neutral warmth are calming to the nervous system.

Sensory Strategies

Proprioception (deep pressure)

- massage and/or joint compression prior to sleep (you can use powder or lotion)
- provide weighted blankets (horse blankets, and blankets with weight sewn into them)
- give your child wrist/ankle weights (have him/her wear them to bed)
- provide body pillows, body socks, sleeping bags
- use swaddling
- have him/her wear tight PJs to bed (under armor or bike shorts/tight top)
- squish child with a physio ball – upper back to feet and back again
- tuck the cover sheet under the mattress to make the bed very tight[S5]
- provide back rubs, bear hugs and massage with a towel in a predictable fashion
- use the body pillows to create a little valley for the child to sleep in or move the mattress slightly away from the wall so that a little valley is created between the wall, side of the mattress and box spring (the body pillows can be arranged under the fitted sheet so that they don't move)

- let the child sleep in a hammock or air walker swing (The company that sells this product is Dynamotion[S6])
- use compression bands on upper arms, thighs and ankles

Vestibular

- place mattress on the floor if child is afraid of heights
- prop up the child on pillows if it is too difficult to change the orientation of the head

Tactile

- provide PJs whose texture is tolerable to the child/child
- provide soft sheets/blankets – flannel or high-count cotton (some children have difficulty regulating their sweat and need an absorbent material like cotton)
- give the child a very soft pillow case
- check for seams/ensure that elastics are covered with soft material
- toss sheets in the dryer prior to putting them on the bed; some children are sensitive to temperature and prefer warm sheets
- provide a soft toy to cuddle
- experiment with different types of pajamas; tight, stretchy, loose, silky, flannel or cotton PJs
- avoid pajamas that have lace or built-in feet, as they may be irritating to the child with tactile defensiveness

Vision

- provide neutral colors on the walls
- use black-out curtains to block light
- provide a night light with diffused light (won't cast shadows)
- provide a tent over the bed to block out light

Auditory

- use a white noise machine to block out competing night sounds
- employ an air purifier for white noise
- play a tape of mom or dad's singing voice
- play the child's favorite music that is slow and rhythmic
- close the windows
- read books in a quiet voice

Smell

- provide a pillow with mom or dad's scent
- provide familiar smells in the room (windows may need to be closed)

Other Strategies

- maintain a predictable routine prior to bed (e.g., bath, teeth, story, bed)
- keep consistent items close to the child as they fall asleep, since they will look for them if they awake during the night
- keep the room organized and clear of clutter
- avoid over-stimulating activities prior to bed (rough and tumble, loud music, eating)
- use the washroom before bed
- maintain a visual schedule
- tell social stories about bedtime

Falling asleep and waking up are two big transitions that we do daily. Just as it can take a long time to fall asleep, it can take a long time to wake up. Gradual introduction of sensation can be gentle to the nervous system as it goes through the transition of waking up. Here is a suggestion of a morning wakeup routine that gradually adds sensation to give the nervous system time to adjust. It has worked for many children in our practice to make mornings more pleasant.

Wake up time – 7:30 AM

7:00 AM – calming music is put on, very low, and the parent leaves the room

7:10 AM – curtains are opened to allow light to gradually fill the room, and the parent leaves the room

7:20 AM – the parent comes in with a physio ball and rolls the ball over the child slowly with pressure (you can do massage, joint compression, squeezes)

7:30 AM – wake up!

Some children are very hungry or thirsty when they wake up, so having a snack and drink right away can help them maintain a sunny disposition.

Dressing

Dressing involves many skills; sensory processing, visual perception, motor planning, balance, gross motor and fine motor skills. Independence in dressing contributes to a real feeling of mastery which contributes to a healthy self-esteem.

Sensory Strategies

Proprioceptive

- encourage deep pressure activities prior to dressing to decrease tactile sensitivities
- try massage with lotion, body squeezes, joint compression, jumping, holding up the wall and burpees to increase body awareness
- under armor are undergarments that add compression to the body and can be worn under clothing (you can also have the child wear a body suit or bike shorts)

- if your child is fearful when body position is changed, dress them in one position (toddlers can have their diaper changed in a standing position)

Vestibular

- if your child has difficulty with balance, have them sit during dressing
- with vestibular sensitivity, your child may not change the position of the head when putting shirts on; ensure a stable sitting surface
- bending down to put socks on may also be challenging; ensure a stable position to decrease the fear of falling
- lifting one foot up to put it through a pant leg requires a balance shift. If this is difficult, sit on a chair, put both feet through the pant legs, then stand and pull the pants straight up.

Tactile

- be conscious of sensitivities regarding texture; buy clothing that you know your child will like (it is more valuable for your child to be at school in an uncoordinated outfit feeling calm than to have your child at school looking beautiful and feeling upset)
- go shopping with your child and point out the commonalities in the preferred clothing/footwear
- build a wardrobe of comfortable clothing for your child
- encourage deep pressure activities prior to dressing to decrease the tactile sensitivities
- wear undergarments inside out to prevent scratching from seams and tags
- allow children to wear clothing that has been "worked in," like hand me downs
- wash new clothing in the washing machine a few times, then introduce it to the child to try
- increase hat tolerance through massage of the scalp and putting the hat on in front of the mirror
- if your child likes to take their clothes off, try the Wilbarger Protocol for sensory defensiveness and massage
- if your child has sensitive feet, wear socks inside out, wash shoes to make them soft prior to wearing them and try laced shoes as they can be more effectively tightened

- cut labels out of clothing or buy clothing with the labels printed on the garment
- ensure that the garment fits well and that does not cut into the skin when your child assumes another position
- be sensitive to the length of sleeve and pant leg your child prefers
- choose softer fabrics like fleece instead of a tougher fabric like denim
- dry clothing in the dryer to soften them and decrease stiffness
- have your child wear briefs instead of boxers; they fit more snugly
- in the winter, cold clothing and boots can feel wet; warm them up in the dryer or use a hair dryer

Vision

- if your child has difficulty guiding movement with the eyes, encourage another sensory system, like touch, to compensate
- minimize visual overload to help distraction; wear clothing of one color
- be aware of patterns in fabrics and the distractibility patterns they may cause
- children can be extremely motivated to wear clothing that has their favorite characters on them
- dress in front of a mirror to add visual cues to assist with motor planning

Auditory

- be aware of the noise made by buttons, zippers, buckles and overall straps during wear
- be aware of the noise of the fabrics (nylon fabrics can make noise as it slides over itself)
- be aware of competing sounds in the environment

Smell

- wash/dry clothing in unscented detergent and fabric softener for the child who is sensitive to smell
- if your child finds comfort in your smell, store his/her clothing with yours

Other

- dress in front of a mirror to add visual cues to assist with motor planning

- break down the dressing task and have your child do the last activity, then the second last and third last, etc.
- use music/songs/rhythm to facilitate motor planning
- start an action and have your child complete the action (e.g., pulling up a zipper) if your child is having difficulty initiating the action
- use augmentative communication strategies to encourage understanding of the task and of the consequences of removing clothing
- use picture symbols and picture strips to help your child with sequence dressing
- perform video self modeling to teach dressing skills
- if your child likes to put their hands inside their pants, try providing overalls and fidget toys to keep their hands busy
- if your child has difficulty telling the right shoe from the left, put a tiny dot on the inside edge of the shoe that matches a tiny dot on the same place on the other shoe
- keep drawers and closets organized to enable a child to choose their own clothing
- keep clothes hung/organized together so it's easy to pick something that matches
- prepare for transitions in seasons; discuss them, prepare for them and use social/video stories to explain the change
- provide shoes with velcro closures and add velcro to button backs and hoops to zippers for children with fine motor difficulties
- a shoe maker can help adapt any shoe if it is difficult to find shoes with velcro as your child grows older
- organize clothing the night before and lay the clothing out on the bed
- encourage your child to put away the clothing so that they know where it belongs
- if balance is difficult, have your child sit to put on socks and shoes
- color code clothing to help your child identify right and left
- put labels in your child's clothing to help identify items if they become lost

- sing the steps while dressing
- try dressing dolls and teddy bears and practice fasteners on them
- try backward chaining, which involves having your child complete the last step of the activity, then the last two steps, etc.
- model making mistakes and recovering from them. Making mistakes as an adult gives children permission to make mistakes and recover.

Grooming

We spend a large portion of our day brushing our hair and our teeth and washing our bodies. Our presentation to others is more inviting if we are clean and well groomed. Difficulty processing touch, poor balance and body awareness and difficulty motor planning can have a negative effect on our grooming.

Whenever possible, let your child do the task independently; it contributes to self–esteem, and it's easier for the nervous system to process self-imposed touch in comparison to touch by another person. If one person is successful in assisting your child with grooming, pay attention to how they do it; what kind of touch do they use, do they speak while grooming, how close do they stand, etc.? Others can imitate that style, and grooming can be more successful.

Adults on the spectrum may need to be taught the level of hygiene that is appropriate in their work setting. Expectations for an adult working in a hospital may be different than the expectations of someone working in a vintage shop. It is important to be candid, respectful and straightforward, as the adult with ASD may not be able to pick up on the nonverbal messages from co-workers concerning their hygiene.

General Strategies for Self-Care Skills

- use communication supports (social stories, video stories, pictures and picture symbols)
- use countdowns or count the number of brushes (for example, when brushing the hair, 5 times on the left, 5 times at the back and 5 times on the right side)

- use visual aids to increase your child's understanding of the task (picture symbols, schedules, sequence strips)
- build in consistency and predictability to decrease stress
- have an organized environment; put things back in place so your child will be more independent in finding them

- label drawers and clothing to promote independence in putting things away
- use calming strategies which are specific to your child to help prepare for the grooming task
- remember that pressure touch has a more organizing effect than light touch
- minimize overwhelming sensory input, wherever possible
- use routines to build predictability
- use motivators so that your child can keep their focus on something they like
- use rhythm and music
- to support motor planning, break down skills into smaller components and teach skills one component at a time

Face, Hand and Body Washing

Sensory Strategies:

Proprioception

- use a heavy face cloth and use pressure strokes on the body
- when shampooing the hair, use pressure touch
- allow your child to wear bike shorts or a bathing suit that adds pressure in the tub
- provide pressure touch from the jets in a whirlpool or jacuzzi

- use pressure and downward strokes with the towel if your child is sensitive to touch
- wrap your child tightly in a soft, warm towel and give them pressure hugs to dry off

Vestibular

- if your child is fearful in balance-related activities, the shower may be a better choice than the bath, as there are fewer changes in body position
- children who are uncomfortable changing the position of the head may not lie down to rinse their hair in the bathtub; try a hand-held shower nozzle or cover their eyes with a face cloth and use a jug full of water to rinse the hair (there is a hat made up of only a brim that is designed to keep the soap and water out of children's eyes when rinsing)
- try a bathtub rail for children who may be frightened getting into and out of the tub (available at most drug stores)

Tactile

- be aware of water temperature and note which is your child's favorite
- have your child test water temperature before they go in
- choose towels and face clothes that are soft
- if your child does not tolerate the touch of water moving over his/her body like in the bathtub, provide a shower, as the water moves in a consistent direction
- provide deeper pressure touch for your child in the shower with the massage attachment on the shower head
- liquid soap may be preferable to the slippery bar of soap
- consider a circular plastic ring children can wear over their ears and around their head to keep the unpredictable water and soap from running down the face and neck
- perform vigorous toweling that is full of squeezes and pressure
- use a small towel to dry, as it's easier to manipulate
- buy soaps with tiny grains in them; these may be preferred by your child

Visual

- be aware of the reflective nature of the shiny metals and water in the bathroom
- some children are fascinated with water coming out of the tub; teach them to use this interest functionally; pouring tea into tea cups, for example
- provide bubbles during bath time
- dry in front of a mirror to help with planning
- dim lights and minimize sound if your child is easily distracted

Auditory

- minimize sounds for the child who is sensitive to sound
- use a white noise machine to overwhelm unexpected sound
- play his/her favorite music

Smell

- use non-perfumed soap and hair products with the child with a sensitivity to smell

Taste

- be careful that your child doesn't eat the soap; keep their mouths busy with a chew tube or eating snacks

Other Strategies:

- inform your child when you plan to touch them with the facecloth or toothbrush
- use cognitive preparation strategies; for example, "we will wash your right arm and then your left arm"
- use visual aids to assist with the comprehension of the task
- provide lots of water play in a sink or bowl with fun toys (squirt gun, boat, diver, squeeze bottle, bubbles, bubble bath, bath foam soap, soap crayons, roll-on soap)
- draw on your child with soap crayons, and as they rub off the soap, they are cleaning themselves
- build up handles of utensils with pipe insulation to decrease dropping
- use music and motivators

Toilet Training

Toilet training can be a real challenge to children with ASD who have sensory integration difficulties. Successful toileting requires receiving and interpreting the sensory information that signals a full bladder or the need to have a bowel movement. The sensory system that provides this information is called the interoception system. The child must then form the motor plan to get to the bathroom and then must conquer the sensory challenges of the bathroom.

Toilet training is one of the tasks of childhood that can reflect stress, and a child can exercise a great deal of control over toileting. Try not to enter a battle of wills on the issue. The process tends to run much more smoothly without stress and expectations. If you experience setbacks with your child, know that this is absolutely normal. Take the pressure off and go back at it after some time has passed. The bowel and bladder are smooth muscles, and the sensory signals they send up to the brain to indicate a full bladder or bowel are like soft whispers in comparison to the messages received by striated muscle (in the arm or the leg).

Sensory Strategies:

Proprioceptive

- if your child wears diapers, draw attention to information from all senses: touch, smell and the added weight of a wet diaper (cloth diapers give more sensory feedback than disposable diapers)
- provide a weighted vest, hat, lap snake or compression vest to encourage sitting for a longer period of time

Vestibular

- if your child has difficulty with changes in head position, encourage them to sit on the toilet instead of standing at it
- ensure that the feet are supported when sitting on the toilet
- cover the hole of the toilet with white tissue paper if looking down into a depth is disturbing for your child

- if your child cannot tolerate sitting on the toilet, try to make it as safe as possible:
  - make the hole smaller with an infant toilet seat or try a padded seat
  - put a stool under your child's feet
  - try to wear a weighted vest, hat, lap snake or compression vest to encourage sitting for a longer period of time
  - a tub rail may be helpful for your child to hang on to
  - use distractions like books, songs, music, and pictures on the walls

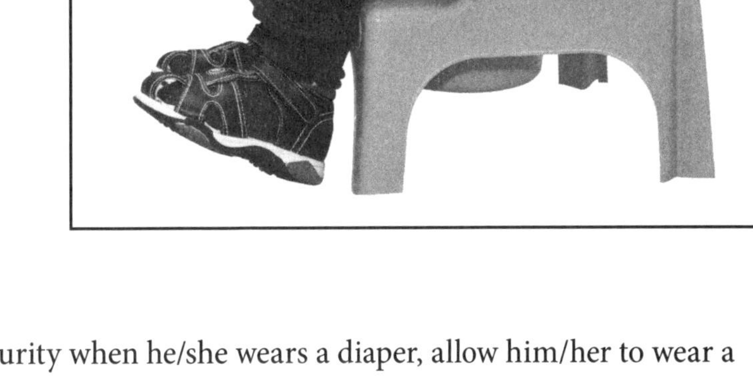

  - if your child loves the feeling of security when he/she wears a diaper, allow him/her to wear a diaper while using the toilet

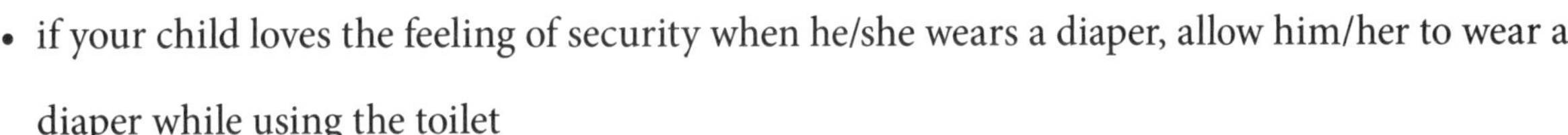

Tactile

- if your child doesn't seem to be aware that he/she is urinating, let him/her go naked; he/she will understand when he/she urinates and connect the sensation with the consequence
- if your child is sensitive to toilet paper, try diaper wipes or a wet face cloth; it can feel softer and is more effective at removal

Visual

- if the visual input is too stimulating, turn off the lights or dim them
- the reflections of light bouncing off the water in the toilet bowl may be distracting; try covering the bowl with white tissue paper

Auditory

- if the noise is too intense, try noise-cancelling headsets, place sound-absorbing towels in the bathroom, or try earplugs, music or running water
- the flush of the toilet may be overwhelming and may need to happen after the child leaves the washroom
- the fear of the flushing toilet may prevent a child with sound sensitivity from using a public toilet. Use the family toilet if available or carry "out of order" signs in your bag and place them on the other toilets and on the hand dryer. Remove them as you leave the washroom.

Smell

- if your child cannot tolerate the smell of bowel movements, have them smell coffee (placed in a small container) while they are going to the washroom
- provide a small container of any strong smell to keep the nose busy while using a public toilet
- if you child smears feces, try your child on a bathroom routine with a caregiver. Smearing often suggests a hyper-sensitivity to smell, and smearing may be a way to block out other smells.

Other Strategies:

- use visual aids, social stories or video modeling to increase your child's understanding of the task
- try to make this task as pleasant as possible
- never force; respect the child's tolerance
- keep a success journal to review during challenging times
- praise the child for their efforts and courage

Hair Brushing

Sensory Strategies:

Proprioception

- push down on the top of the head prior to brushing

- wear a weighted vest/compression vest/weights during this task
- firmly contract the head with the face of the brush prior to brushing
- use consistent, predictable pressure in the same direction
- try a battery-powered vibrating hairbrush (provides consistent sensation and may be better tolerated than a traditional hairbrush)

Vestibular

- if head position changes are challenging, have your child sit during this activity
- use a mirror to help the child predict the sensation he/she will feel
- use a weighted vest or a compression vest during the task

Tactile

- if your child is sensitive to touch, use a brush with a large head
- when brushing, use firm strokes
- brush in front of the mirror so that your child can predict when the brush is coming
- have your child brush his/her own hair
- use massage to the scalp prior to hair brushing
- remember that the air from the blow dryer may be either comforting or problematic

Visual

- use a mirror to predict sensation
- be aware of light bouncing off reflective surfaces
- use a dimmer switch on the lights

Smell

- be aware of scented hair products; use unscented products if your child is sensitive to smells

Other Strategies:

- use a conditioner to detangle as much as possible

- with tangles, start at the bottom of the hair, holding just above the tangle and then work up to the root
- cut hair short

Teeth Brushing

Sensory Strategies

Proprioception

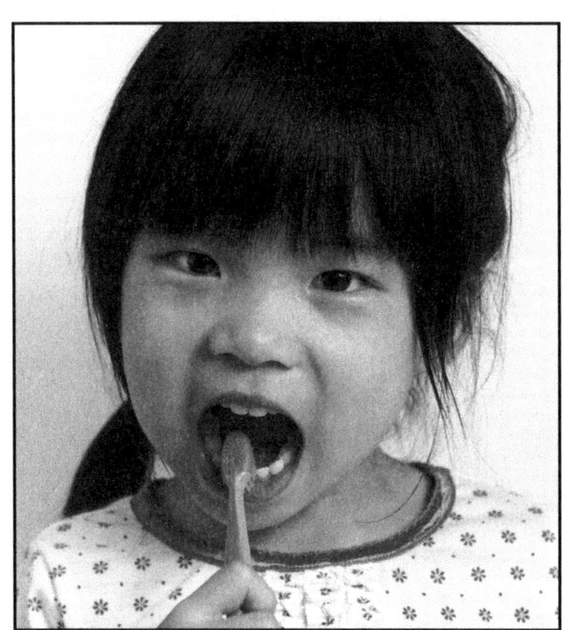

- to decrease sensitivity, apply pressure to the teeth and gums
- prepare for teeth brushing by applying pressure to the outside of the lips and along the jaw
- try a vibrating toothbrush
- use pressure touch with firm strokes
- try joint compression to the neck, shoulders and body to prepare for teeth brushing

Vestibular

- promote balance by standing behind your child to secure the body
- encourage your child to lean against the sink with his/her body if you are not available
- if changes in head position are difficult, have the toothbrush and rinse water ready for the child or teach them how to prepare for the task
- use a mirror

Tactile

- if your child is very sensitive, consider using a face cloth to wipe the teeth
- if your child is sensitive to touch inside the mouth, try the Wilbarger Protocol for sensory defensiveness (oral program)

- try a Nuk brush initially, then move to bristles
- purchase an electric toothbrush, which provides consistent sensation and may be better tolerated than a traditional toothbrush
- warm water may be better tolerated than cold

Vision

- use a mirror to predict sensation
- be aware of light bouncing off reflective surfaces
- use a dimmer switch on the lights

Auditory

- the sound of the vibration or the toothbrush may be a lot to process; distract with music or countdowns
- the reflected sounds may be challenging to process; try noise-canceling headsets or a white noise machine

Smell/Taste

- use a very mild-flavored toothpaste
- rinse the mouth with warm water frequently if your child has difficulty tolerating the toothpaste
- remember that some children who are hypo responsive to taste may love the extra-strong flavor of toothpaste

General Strategies

- provide visual supports like picture symbols, social stories and video self modeling, which can help your child understand and plan for the task
- put on a visual timer and encourage your child to brush for that amount of time (some toothbrushes play music, and the child can brush until the song ends)
- encourage frequent water drinking, which is helpful to remove extra food
- provide a footstool to help your child reach the faucets

- search for toothpaste in a pump can facilitate independence in children with fine motor difficulties
- a plastic cup for rinsing the mouth can be a safer choice for children with developing fine motor skills

Hair Cutting

Sensory Strategies:

Proprioception

- place downward pressure on the head through the neck and shoulders
- use a weighted blanket as a cape or have your child wear a weighted vest or compression vest
- use downward, firm strokes with the comb

Vestibular

- ensure that your child is seated with his/her feet supported
- have the child watch what is happening in a mirror
- if the child has difficulty changing the position of their head, inform the hair stylist so that he/she doesn't force the head shift

Tactile

- use a good cape to block the bits of hair from falling under the clothing
- use the Wilbarger Protocol prior to a haircut
- use a blow dryer to blow away the bits of cut hair
- make touch predictable; count down the number of times you comb through the hair and the number of snips used

- avoid the clipper if it is difficult to tolerate
- use a mirror and verbal warnings to predict touch
- cover the body with a cape to prevent the water spray from touching the skin

Visual

- use a mirror to enable your child to know where their hair is being cut
- if the salon is too bright, ask to turn off some lights

Auditory

- try providing ear buds to listen to music in order to block out the noise of the clippers (they make a vibration sound and may not be well tolerated)
- be mindful of the noise of the salon; you may need to go early in the morning or when the salon is closed if a quiet place is needed

Smell

- be mindful of all the smells of hair products and try to use unscented products with the child who is hyper sensitive to smell
- if the salon is full of smells, create a small smelling kit and have your child smell little containers of coffee, mint and citrus or eat his/her favorite foods

Other Strategies

- look for a flexible and sensitive hair stylist; it will be worth the effort
- be mindful of competing sensory input
- schedule your appointment when the salon is less busy or maybe when it is closed
- use social/video stories to show the entire event
- use visual aids to increase understanding of the task
- use distractions if necessary like a DVD player or an iPad
- use motivators and rewards

- invite the hair stylist to come to your home where it is a more familiar environment
- wash your child's hair prior to going to the salon, to cut down on the time spent there
- go to the salon a couple of times to visit and have your child watch haircuts take place
- follow up with an enjoyable activity or treat
- reward your child's courage

Eating

No skill creates more anxiety in a parent than eating or lack of eating. Children who have difficulty with this skill may have a heightened sensitivity to touch, smell or taste. Children who are hyposensitive to sensory input may have little awareness of their mouth and how to move their tongue and jaw. They may have a poorly organized suck, swallow and breath synchrony. Some children have such a need for movement that they may not sit still long enough to eat a meal. Their meal times may consist of a mouthful with every lap around the house.

Other children may be at the other extreme; they use their mouths to discover their world. Edible and non-edible items are mouthed, chewed and sometimes swallowed. Developmentally, the mouth is the first area of the body that can interpret sensory feedback accurately. As the hands develop in their ability to accurately interpret sensory input, they take over as the primary investigators of the environment.

There are many wonderful courses that OTs and parents can take to increase their knowledge of feeding challenges and strategies to deal with these challenges. Eating is a huge social activity for families, and being able to eat with flexibility (place, type of food) can enable many more social opportunities for you and your child.

Sensory Strategies:

Proprioception

- to prepare for chewing, apply pressure through the teeth, gums, cheeks and lips with a vibrating toothbrush

- prepare for eating with massage with a Nuk gum massage toothbrush
- prepare the posture for eating with movement (sitting on bouncing ball, parent's lap, rockerboard, etc.)
- provide a weighted vest, compression vest, wrist or ankle weights during eating; these can help the child feel more secure and have a better knowledge of the body's position in space
- perform table push-ups, chair push-ups, pushing the hands together and pulling them apart can all contribute to the knowledge of the body's position in space
- if your child is a messy eater, provide pressure touch around the lips and mouth prior to eating and encourage oral motor activity prior to eating (whistling, bubbles) to promote better sensory feedback and build muscle tone for better mouth closure
- if your child has difficulty using utensils, try weighted handles, which give more sensory feedback and therefore make movements more accurate
- try a weighted cup or a cup with a lid and a straw if your child spills drinks often
- use a long curly straw in your child's drink, which encourages a long suck and can be very organizing
- if your child is slumping in the chair, try some pressure through the shoulders to create the muscle tone to facilitate an upright posture

Vestibular

- use movement breaks for the active child
- try a gel seat, Movin' Sit cushion (ASD products), hokki seat, or Mambo seat to promote a small amount of movement during sitting

- tie a theraband around the legs of the chair so that your child can kick against it
- have a rockerboard under your child's feet while sitting
- have your child participate in lots of movement prior to a seated task like eating

Tactile

- be aware of texture, mix of textures and temperature of food; some children prefer certain textures and temperatures and do not tolerate foods touching
- try a plate that has divided sections for food
- some children who are sensitive in the mouth benefit from rinsing out their mouths with water between mouthfuls of food
- if your child is sensitive in the mouth, try the Wilbarger Protocol for a sensory defensiveness oral program or implement an oral desensitization program
- if your child is tactile defensive, arrange seating at the end of the table to minimize touch by others
- a small cafe table can be set up at school or daycare to minimize extra touch
- prepare the mouth to eat with an ice cube or another frosty treat

Vision

- use a small makeup mirror at the table to facilitate accuracy in placing the food in the mouth and clean up after each bite (the visual system can compensate for decreased feedback through the tactile system)
- be aware of how the food looks on the plate; do different foods touch each other?
- have a comforting picture/stuffed animal at the table to look at as a calming strategy
- remember that some children can't tolerate watching other people eat; they may have to eat on their own initially or eat with the family who are with the child but not eating

Auditory

- keep in mind that some children cannot tolerate the sound of themselves eating or the sound of other people eating; try noise-cancelling headsets or eating at different times but enjoying each other's company by doing other activities together

- be aware of competing sounds; use a white noise machine
- remember that the cling-clang of the cutlery may be an issue; try plastic cutlery, cloth tablecloths and cloth napkins, since they are quieter
- listen to music as a distractor to the sounds of eating

Smell/Taste

- be aware of the processing of smells and encourage foods that fall within your child's smell tolerance
- smelling strong smells regularly through a meal, like coffee, can keep the smell receptors too busy to pick up other scents
- try using ice pops or ice cubes/juice cubes to desensitize the mouth

Other Strategies:

- encourage lots of oral motor play with whistles, harmonicas, kazoos, etc., to build oral motor skills and coordination
- encourage your child to take a sip of water in between each mouthful of food to rinse out the mouth
- work within your child's tolerance
- investigate food allergies as well as reasons for fatigue and appetite differences
- try different sitting positions to facilitate an upright posture and focus
- begin with your child's favorite foods and then increase choices
- model with family members and encourage them to model for their children
- encourage children to request the food that they want (or seconds) independently to teach them they have control and can make their own decisions
- try Dycem or a similar non-slip material under your child's plate, to keep it in place
- pre-cut food to encourage independence
- modify utensils to compensate for fine motor and bilateral difficulties
- modify seating to compensate for developing balance
- encourage your child to help prepare the food; shop, select, wash, cut, cook, set the table, mix, serve

to increase positive experiences and interactions around food and to have fun (remember, you can't be anxious and have fun at the same time!)

Play

Play is often referred to as the occupation of childhood. Play offers your child the opportunity to develop gross motor, fine motor, visual motor, cognitive, language, imagination, attention and social skills. Children with ASD often have difficulty with play and therefore they may be at a disadvantage for learning the necessary skills of childhood.

Play activities are among the first social experiences for a child. It begins as solitary and becomes parallel, where children are playing in the same room but not playing together, and progresses to cooperative, where children are actually playing together, sharing fun, imagination and skills. Children with ASD may have difficulty with play because of sensory integration difficulties, problems manipulating toys, poor posture and stamina and difficulties with language, social skills and motor planning (creating and sequencing the steps of play in the right order).

Sensory Strategies

Proprioception

- have the child wear a weighted vest or compression vest during play to provide the proprioception to know where the body is in relation to play
- encourage children who constantly mouth items to use their mouths to gather information about the toy, or they may be self calming—try the Wilbarger Protocol for sensory defensiveness, (oral program) and a sensory program in the palms of the hands so that the child can switch from the mouth to the hands
- use massage in the palms of the hands; also try weighted wrist cuffs to increase feedback
- if your child seems to be unaware of playground boundaries, try using proprioceptive input (deep pressure touch, push, pull, lift and carry) prior to and regularly during play

- encourage your child to slow down and learn about body position and balance by creating an obstacle course on the playground equipment
- if your child is always breaking toys and the tip of the pencil, teach the difference between light and heavy touch and practice playing with specific toys while working on the underlying areas of development (e.g., drums)

Vestibular

- children who are sensitive to balance activities may not participate in playground games or games during which their feet are off the ground – try massage, joint compression and "heavy work" activities prior to going on the equipment
- respect your child's fear, especially during movement and heights; this fear is very real
- if your child is uncomfortable in any position, inform his/her caregiver and teacher to avoid these positions and the stressful situations they can cause
- if your child is afraid of swings, address the underlying skills of balance
- if your child chews on toys, provide a "chewie" (gum, chewy candy, pacifier, etc.)
- increase oral motor input to stabilize posture so that your child feels secure to play
- ensure that your child's feet are touching the ground during play
- experiment with different positions, such as lying on the tummy on the floor, sitting, standing; which is most comfortable for your child?
- if your child needs movement to stay organized, try playing on a swing or a moving surface

Tactile

- children with sensitivity to touch may not participate in messy play; try inhibitory techniques, pressure touch, massage and the Wilbarger Protocol for sensory defensiveness
- encourage your child to participate in messy play using a tool or while wearing gloves; messy activities like finger painting, for example, can be contained in ziplock bags
- consider the temperature and texture of the play material

- grade activities from neat to messy
- use a favorite character or game and integrate a tactile component into it; use motivation to get over the hurdle to avoidance

Visual

- encourage the child to gather information through vision and use memory to create the information needed
- watch your child's eyes; if visual tracking is difficult, place toys within the central visual field and ensure that they feel secure in their posture and balance
- be aware of light intensity; your child may need to wear sunglasses or a hat to block out glare from overhead lights

Auditory

- minimize background noise, as it may be hard for your child to discriminate between sounds
- encourage play with sounds within your child's tolerance

Smell/Taste

- be aware of smell; wash toys with scent-free soap

Other Strategies

- if your child has a comfort toy, one that is taken everywhere, wash it frequently and keep it as long as possible (if your child really likes a blanket or toy, try to buy 2 or 3 for backup)
- if your child is using mouthing to self calm, try oral motor activities like chewing, whistles and bubble blowing, which all provide calming input
- remember that some children use touch excessively and may act in a socially inappropriate manner in their use of touch; try teaching limits through the use of social stories
- use routines which can be calming, as they are so predictable
- if your child seems to be unaware of playground boundaries, try using a homemade stop sign

- if your child is impulsive in play, break down the task into small steps
- teach each step in the style your child learns best – auditory, visual through demonstration, with guidance the child through the movement (please see motor planning section for more strategies)
- cause and effect toys are excellent for children with motor planning difficulties, as the motor response is consistent and repeatable
- provide predictable toys that give children a feeling of control and anticipation
- always look at function; what toy will enable your child to use the behavior functionally?
- give the child the experience of the game turning out different ways. You may even video it unfolding in different ways. An unpredictable ending can be difficult for the child with planning challenges and/or language challenges to accept, and they may want to play the game in the same way.
- attach language to each step
- try turn taking during play and teach your child to pause and check in with his/her friends (board games are excellent for this)

- give lots of opportunities for gross motor play and alternate between gross and fine motor play to address balance, attention, regulation and play
- make play motivating and fun; fun is contagious!
- teach specific play skills and then provide opportunities where they can be generalized
- encourage willingness to share and communicate affection and appreciation for the efforts of others. Reward these skills, as they are essential to building and maintaining relationships
- modify toys for fine motor difficulty
- teach your child strategies to stay regulated during play, like language scripts: "I need a minute" or "I can do this another way." When children have options, they can stay organized and continue to play.

CHAPTER 7

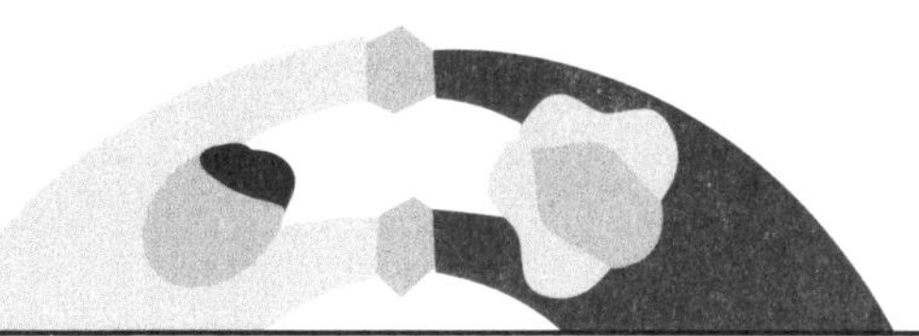

ADAPTING HOME, SCHOOL AND CHILDCARE SETTINGS

All children function better in a predictable environment.

This can be as simple as having a tidy room and storage for their own things. Providing routine and structure can compensate for your child's difficulty with language, sequencing, attention shift and memory. Developing habits or consistent ways of doing things is very helpful and can reduce stress for most children with ASD. It also allows for the provision of more consistent and reliable sensory information. As the child grasps the new learning, this learning can be generalized across settings and between caregivers. Introduce small changes to the task, as the child can tolerate, to contribute to better problem solving abilities and the ability to generalize the skill. Generalization promotes flexibility in the skill which makes the skill functional and useable.

Susie knows she always eats in the kitchen. She knows that her shoes, jacket and backpack are always at the side door and she knows she sleeps in her own bed. This consistency in her environment reduces Susie's behavioral outbursts.

If we have a consistent place for our car keys, we would know where to find them each time we had to use the car. Many of us spend stressful moments looking for the car keys while destroying any chance of punctuality.

BUILDING BRIDGES THROUGH SENSORY INTEGRATION

We need to consider consistency in the environment, schedule and approach with children with Autism/ASD. If we study the child's individual style, we can strive for consistency across environments—at home, at grandma's, in the classroom and in the childcare setting.

Children spend most of their time at home. It is the first environment they know. Their favorite people live there, so home can be a place of relaxation and a place of learning. Many families use the home as the first school setting for children. Activities that offer your child the opportunity to integrate sensory information can be incorporated right in your home. Take into account your space, the needs of other family members and the needs of your child prior to purchasing equipment. A consistent play area and an organized home will offer your child the chance to regulate activity level and increase their comfort and relaxation. Organization can give a child with ASD a sense of control as they are able to predict their day.

Transition times, the times between activities or between environments, are often stressful for children with ASD. There is a whole new set of expectations that demand attention, processing and motor planning. Change is almost always difficult, and a sensory plan with a visual schedule can minimize the anxiety in a transition. For example, when it is time to have dinner, your child can be given the direction to come to the kitchen and be given a juice box. Sucking the juice up through the straw can provide a very organizing sensation and can help make the transition to the kitchen smooth.

Prepare sensory activities for a child when entering a new space to facilitate the transition. For example, if your child loves sand play and has difficulty entering his daycare space, a sand play table can be set up right inside the door. The sensory activity is motivating and provides calming sensory input. The transition to the daycare can be facilitated through the use of the sand table. The schedule can be set up so there is an opportunity for children to perform a familiar "safe activity" right away, like singing a favorite song or carrying the chair to the table. Other children can also participate in the sensory plan. Sensory strategies are listed to give the reader ideas to compensate for sensory integrative dysfunction and make use of the sensory systems the child can process best. We have also included some general strategies to provide ideas which do not have a sensory base, but we've found them helpful in our work with children with ASD.

Environmental Accommodations - Home

Sensory Strategies for the Home

Many children will benefit from having the environment set up to provide calming input such as music, pressure touch with lotion, slow rhythmic swinging in single directions of movement, slow rocking and sitting on a therapy ball or an oral activity like drinking with a straw from their own water bottle. Children may participate in the Wilbarger Protocol for sensory defensiveness and may have an organized sensory diet that has been set up by an occupational therapist.

Please refer to chapter six for strategies specific to self-care skills.

Sensory Strategies

Proprioception

- in your home, offer hide-out places, like beanbag chairs, small tents, pillow corners
- provide a sleeping bag or a body sock for your child to curl up in
- use body pillows, weighted blankets, heavy quilts, compression vests or weighted vests to offer calming input
- have 'heavy jobs' available for your child (e.g., carrying in groceries, carrying laundry, dragging the clothesline in, watering flowers with a heavy watering can, pushing the grocery cart, stacking cans in the food cupboard, vacuuming the carpet, shoveling, gardening, washing the car, scrubbing the walls)
- provide lots of opportunities for active play; for example, trampoline, swimming, biking, rollerblading, climbing, skiing

Vestibular

- if your child responds well to movement, have a quiet place in your home to hang a hammock swing or porch swing (chin up bars in doorways can be very effective)
- provide lots of opportunities for active play; trampoline, swimming, biking, rollerblading, climbing, skiing

Tactile

- consider a water bed, which is soft and warm, and can be comforting and relaxing
- use touch to get your child's attention if calling their name does not work (if touch is well tolerated)

Visual

- decrease visual stimuli to decrease distraction
- have the right type and amount of light for your child (natural spectrum light is readily available, softer lights (lamps and incandescent lighting), instead of the overhead glare of pot lights or fluorescent lights
- use soft lights reflected against a wall to decrease visual glare
- dimmer switches on the lights
- if you use a computer in your home, see if your child responds better to a laptop or a desktop screen
- when using a computer, angle the screen so that your child doesn't get a reflected glare
- be aware of light that comes in from windows (street lamps, light from passing cars, lights from neighbors' windows, sunlight, moonlight). If light is distracting for your child, consider blackout curtains.

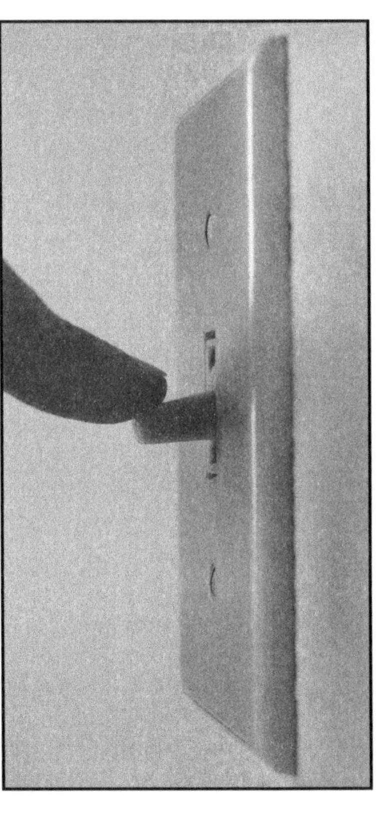

- be conscious of your child's response to color
- paint your child's room a soft pastel color and do not cover the walls with visual distraction
- if your child needs lots of visual stimulation, consider painting the walls a bright color and adding mobiles
- give visual cues when giving directions to supplement auditory processing
- minimize visual clutter; put extra toys and clothes in boxes and label them

Auditory

- use soft objects, rugs and pillows to absorb noise
- provide noise-cancelling headsets
- white noise machine (especially helpful at night)
- provide children with sensitive hearing a bedroom in a quiet corner of the house
- be aware of background noise from the radio, television and telephone
- decrease auditory stimuli to decrease distraction

Smell/Taste

- smells: do they need to be added or eliminated from the home? (Be mindful of cleaning scents; they can be very strong)
- the smell of a parent on a pillow can help the child feel secure and sleep better

Other Strategies for the home

- try to schedule calming activities in between more demanding activities to maintain the nervous system in a calm state (see sensory diet section)
- pay attention to the type of person to which your child responds well (voice,
- volume, proximity, style, verbal and facial expression)
- provide equipment to build obstacle courses (boxes, tunnels, hoola hoops, step stools, balance beams, bean bags, bubbles, etc.) to assist with the development of motor planning
- consider a therapy dog for your child
- prepare auditory and visual materials ahead of time to assist in transitions. Timers, docks with alarms, watches (with a timer) and concrete transitional objects may be helpful during transitions.

Children may benefit from a transitional object to be successful with the transition, as it helps with their understanding. For example, handing Andi her jacket facilitates her ability to get ready for recess. She understands the task and transitions well. Without this understanding, children can resist the change even though a favorite activity is next.

- have a specific place for objects so that your child so that you can find them easily and encourage your child to return items where they belong
- use visual aids to assist in the understanding of tasks
- use a schedule to let your child know what will be happening that morning
- break chores down into small steps to facilitate learning; give your child enough time to process the directions
- set up reward systems for chores – earn allowance, earn books or video games and trips to the ice cream shop
- use a timer to help your child complete tasks and to alert your child to the beginning and end of an activity
- minimize the use of chemical substances in your home – keep it natural, as some children can react negatively to artificial substances
- use technology as a reward sparingly and employ programs that enable use as a family (Wii, Kinect)

When planning activities for your child with ASD, keep the whole family in mind and try to plan activities that would be enjoyable to all. You will maximize fun family time!

- establish routines and be consistent in following them; this helps your child predict upcoming events and feel calm
- prepare for school (clothing, lunch, homework) the evening before to minimize stress the next morning
- share duties whenever possible; every team member likes to feel needed and important
- enjoy each other's company!

Equipment for Home and School

In our clinical experience, we have seen the most success with programs or homes that offer access to lots of movement, pressure touch and consistency. The following is a list of suggested items. An occupational therapist can help guide your choices of equipment.

Supplies and instructions for make-your-own activities are included in chapter nine.

Outdoor

- trampoline
- mini trampoline inside
- large therapy or hop 45 balls
- swings; inner tube type, platform swing, hammock, sling swing, disc swing
- bean bag chairs
- small child-sized table and chair
- sandbox/sensory bins
- tent, ball pit, large box line with cushions, home-made 'fort' to provide a safe place to retreat
- soft surfaces to crash and bump, such as big pillows and old mattresses
- weighted objects to play with and throw (bean bags, beach balls filled with water for the backyard)
- boxes to climb into/out of/under and through
- small fidget toys for the hand or mouth
- general messy play/tactile adventures
- edible fine motor/oral motor activities (lacing licorice beads)
- scooterboards
- rockerboards

- stepping stools
- gel seats
- roller blades, skates, trampoline shoes, pogo sticks, stilts
- kitchen utensils for cooking and baking
- opportunities for open-ended art; an easel and crayons/paint, etc.
- musical instruments and music to enjoy
- noise-cancelling headsets
- smell library—different foods/spices in zip lock bags to smell (mint, orange peel, coffee, basil, garlic, etc.)

This list is by no means complete. Use your imagination and the imagination of your child to add to this list. Dollar stores, second-hand stores and garage sales are great sources for toys and equipment. Always be aware of safety concerns and provide adequate supervision. An occupational therapist can customize a program for your child's needs. Updates to the program can also be provided on a regular basis to support new learning.

Watch for the wear and tear on your equipment, and have fun!

Environmental Accommodations—School and Childcare Settings

Communication Between the Home and School

Children with ASD often thrive on consistency and routine. Skills will be learned more quickly and generalized more easily if they can be practiced both at school and at home. This consistent approach is dependent upon good communication. Many schools and child care centers have a communication book already set up connecting home and school. Parents are very dependent upon this book for feedback regarding their child's day, especially if their child's communication skills are developing. The communication sheet can serve as a vehicle to share strategies between home and school to streamline support for your child. Conflicts and challenges can be caught early and addressed through teamwork. The communication sheets provide a written record of your child's year, and this record can help emphasize patterns in behaviors week to week or year to year. For example, Joseph struggled to manage his behaviors in March. He was restless and had difficulty attending in class. His mom reviewed the communication notes from the previous year and found that he had demonstrated the same behavior at the same time of the year. His sensitive auditory system could not screen out the winds of March. Joseph increased the time he wore his noise canceling headsets and was able to better manage his behavior.

Communication sheets can be sent between home and school electronically. A template can be filled in and sent between home and school. A parent can send in information about the child's night and morning before the child arrives at school, and the teacher can send back information about the child's day before the child gets home. This information enables both the parent and teacher to plan for the time ahead.

Creativity and information sharing are important tools in modifying the school and childcare setting for the child with ASD. We must often step outside our traditional roles of teacher, child care worker or therapist to accommodate the needs of children with ASD. Use abilities, interests and even perseverative behaviors to accommodate the areas of difficulty. Remember, we must modify the environment, our approach and activities, as the children may not be able to accommodate their behaviors to the school environment. There is no road map for children with ASD who also have sensory processing challenges. This can be exciting and challenging.

Each child with ASD presents with a unique set of abilities and difficulties; consider the individual child, not the label, when creating your program. Incorporation of strategies and modification of the environment can go a long way in promoting independence and function in the child with ASD.

There are many strategies to apply in this section. If you try a strategy and find that it is not helpful, do not give up. Problem solve with your colleagues and teammates; perhaps you need to try the strategy in a different way or at a different time of the day, or maybe you need to try a new strategy. Children seem to know when you are trying to understand them, and they will be patient as you learn the ropes. Fixations are often viewed as problems, but they can be a great asset to your program. Fixations can act as motivators which can increase a sense of calm and increase the ability to focus attention. Scheduling fixations into the routine of the day or using fixations to teach concepts can be very helpful. The decisions to incorporate areas of special interest have been well documented. Ensure that all members of your team are in agreement with how the fixations are used.

Ian loved trains. He would line them up over and over again and watch the wheels turn. His teacher painted letters on each train car and taught Ian how to spell small words by arranging the train cars in order. Ian was thrilled as he got to participate in his favorite activity, and his teacher was thrilled that Ian learned how to spell so easily.

Children with ASD may have difficulty processing information from more than one sensory channel at a time. Eye contact may be especially difficult for children with ASD. "Listen to me," rather than "look at me" may be a more helpful request. Consider an assessment by a behavioral optometrist to determine how your child sees. They may be overly sensitive to visual input in the central field of vision and can use the peripheral field to look at you. The use of the peripheral visual field means that the child looks at you from the side of his or her eye.

Which sensory system enables your child to learn most accurately? Is she a visual learner? An auditory learner? Does she have to DO the task to learn it? A functional approach that uses sensory strategies can be more concrete and easier to learn. Abstract skills may not be easily understood by children with ASD, as these skills require language skills. For example, practice writing letters on the schedule board where they will be used, rather than practicing them in a printing book.

A voice recorder cannot record sound and play sound at the same time. Some children have the same difficulty; it takes them time to process the sensory information received during the school day and switch to the output channel where they can express their knowledge. Good communication between the home and school can accommodate this delay in switching channels. Use a communication book daily and supplement with video or sound clips. Some children with ASD require decompression time following a transition. The school and child care settings offer lots of wonderful sensory input. Even desired sensory input needs to be processed and can take time.

School and Child Care Sensory Strategies

Multi-Sensory

- build sensory activities into the entire day so that the student's nervous system can be maintained in a calm state (sensory diet)
- allow for self-soothing behaviors
- incorporate self-soothing behaviors into function (e.g., read while rocking in the rocking chair)
- if your child is overwhelmed by sensory input, try to offer input through one sensory channel at a time
- time is often needed to switch from taking in information and expressing new learning
- determine how sensory input is used in the activity; is it a sensory input to support the child's regulation, is the sensory input needed to develop a skill, or is it both?
- use the most accurately processed sensations to teach new activities
- consider using a physical prompt to start a movement for child with motor planning challenges
- remember that the position of the student in the class is important; sit near the window for natural light, near the door for movement breaks, near the wall so that the no one can come up to the student from behind
- use a vibrating pen, play dough, theraputty to "warm up" the arm to prepare for written work
- make an "office" out of a large box which can be a quiet place to do work

Proprioception

- investigate the use of weighted vests, hats, wrist cuffs or compression garments during the school day
- use oral motor strategies to build organization and introduce a sense of calm (beverage tubing, harmonicas, bubble toys, etc.)

- have the children practice deep pressure activities (activities where you push, pull, lift or carry) in their daily physical activity and in their duties
- try a lap snake
- if the child often slips out of their seat, try using a non-slip rubber surface on the chair and under the book being worked on

Vestibular

- build movement breaks into the child's schedule
- have a rocking chair available, as this can be very calming
- use alternative seating like a hokki stool, move 'n' sit cushion, or a ball chair to support the deskwork for a child who needs to move
- work on a stand-up easel or a table top easel to offer a position that works better for the child who has difficulty moving their head position

- try a rockerboard under the feet (beneath the desk)
- if the child is uncomfortable when his or her feet are not connected with the earth, have chairs low to the ground where the feet can touch or place a little stool under his or her feet

Tactile

- provide a quiet corner with a tent or pillows where the child can go to relax and refocus
- place the child's cubby at the end of the row of cubbies if touch information is challenging to process

- position the child at the end of the line or holding the door if touch is challenging to process
- place the child's desk in a quieter area of the classroom, preferably with his or her back against the wall to minimize unexpected touch

Visual

- minimize visual clutter
- define physical space visually; consider the placement of the child's seat, the position of the door, the location of the scissors (Keep things in a consistent place and label that space to increase independence in school tasks)
- use color-coded binders to help keep work in order
- offer a baseball cap or sunglasses to minimize visual glare
- use a desktop rather than a laptop for students with visual sensitivities
- if the child has light sensitivity, he or she may not prefer to sit near the window

Auditory

- match your voice to your child's ability to process sound. Be aware of tones, rhythm and rate of your voice that your child responds best to. You may use a calm, consistent, loving tone when speaking with the child, or you may need a boisterous, fun voice!
- remove sources of loud, unpredictable noises (PA or fire alarm), or warn the child before the PA system/fire alarm goes off
- be aware of competing sounds in the classroom (an FM system may help a child who has difficulty hearing the teacher's voice over the sounds of the classroom)
- music that is played at a low volume or a white noise machine can help drown out extra sound

> Olin was proud that he handled the fire drill at school without becoming upset. He said, "The principal told me that there would be a fire drill at 10:15. I knew it was coming... I was ready!"

Smell/Taste

- be aware of the smells of the daycare or school, especially in centers that make their meals
- be aware of the scents of cleaning products
- provide an object from home with a parent's smell; this can be very comforting to a child

General Strategies

- ensure that the student is in a comfortable place so that learning can happen
- if sitting posture is a problem, offer movement breaks, T-stools, large balls or a gel seat to sit on
- use communication aids/visual strategies to enable the child to understand requests and upcoming events of the day
- make new learning as concrete as possible
- make tasks motivating and understandable to the child
- use a laminated timetable/schedule
- use sequence boards to teach skills
- give ample time to prepare for change, especially when motor planning is challenging
- use humor; it works wonders for everyone
- use timers to signal the start/end of an activity
- learn about successful strategies used at home and use these in school
- use motivators to promote attention and focus
- give the child some control in the daycare/school setting; allow for choices
- keep environment, routine and verbal directions as consistent as possible
- facilitate communication between the home and the school; contact should occur daily in a recordable form
- keep a success journal for review on difficult days
- encourage the child to sit with the legs crossed in front, not behind; it keeps the hips is good alignment and prevents others from tripping over the feet

- use visual cues on the floor to help guide the child to a specific activity or place (like colored masking tape)
- give duties to the children to help them feel important and a part of the teaching team

Sitting and Staying in the Circle

Sensory Strategies

Proprioception

- try a bean bag chair or soft chair that will give support through a large portion of the body's surface
- fidget toys, vibrating toys or favorite toys may be helpful; offer special toys which are only used during this time (stuffed animals with vibrators inside can be very helpful)
- offer a weighted vest, weights, compression vest or lap snake to help your child stay in the circle

Vestibular

- movement that provides proprioceptive, kinesthetic and vestibular input prior to and during sitting may assist with attention (Movin' sit, t-stool, howda hug chair, large ball)
- be aware of head position changes in the child with gravitational insecurity; he or she may need to sit on a chair to avoid the up/down of sitting on the floor and may need to sit opposite the teacher
- asking children to bring things up to the teacher is a great way to integrate movement
- daily physical activity in the circle is healthy and fun!

Tactile

- be aware of tactile feedback of classmates; be prepared to make more space around the child with tactile defensiveness to prevent unexpected touch
- child who is hypo-responsive may respond to tickles on the back and back of the neck to maintain attention

- providing a textured stuffed animal or favorite blanket during circle time may help increase attention

Visual

- use a carpet square to designate the child's place
- be aware of competing visual input
- cut down the glare of overhead lights with a baseball cap
- for the child who is constantly seeking out visual input, integrate this input into circle time. For example, the child who likes superheroes may be able to pay better attention to the teacher who wears a superhero mask when giving directions

Auditory

- be aware of competing sounds and unexpected sounds in children with sensitive hearing
- use music, including singing the instructions, to help engage your child
- provide noise-canceling headsets for the child who cannot filter unwanted sounds and becomes overwhelmed

Smell/Taste

- be aware of the smells of others and the effect that has on your child
- remember that your child may seek out new smells and may have difficulty keeping the appropriate distance between them and the child they are interacting with

Other Strategies

- work within success; if your child can stay in circle well for 20 seconds, use this as your baseline and increase time from this point; try to make it positive
- try a short walk around the circle and then try sitting again
- try music to draw attention and focus
- have the child sit beside the teacher; engagement in handing over items for discussion or engaging

in other duties may help maintain attention and contribute to a student's self-esteem and feeling of worth

- assign duties through which everyone can feel like an important part of the team

Physical Education/Exercise Time

Sensory Strategies

Proprioception

- engage in heavy proprioceptive dance; it can be very organizing and enjoyable
- have the child wear compression vests, weighted vests and/or weights to provide more information about his or her body's position in space
- participate in heavy work activities in regular intervals during PE (rolling and picking up a medicine ball, for example)
- participate in duties which involve pushing, pulling, lifting and carrying (for example, carrying/dragging the bag of balls, pushing open the gym doors, climbing up the rope ladder)

Vestibular

- have a designated area for movement that is safe and open for the child who needs space so that he or she can move and return to the PE activity
- if the child is fearful of heights, try wearing weighted vests, cuffs, hats, or compression vests to provide a feeling of security. Always let the child be in control of their

own movement if they are fearful of heights. This is a real fear and needs to be respected.
- activities which involve changes in position, especially head position, can be difficult for the child with gravitational insecurity

Tactile

- offer the child the opportunity to move away from the other children if he or she has difficulty processing unexpected touch
- be mindful of the change rooms; they can be overwhelming for children with tactile defensiveness (children may need to change a few minutes prior to the class)
- remember that contact sports may also be challenging for children with tactile defensiveness

Visual

- offer a hat when under the glaring lights in the gym
- remember that visual overstimulation may result from teams playing/running/throwing

Auditory

- be cautious of the auditory feedback of large rooms, (like the school gym), as the child may not be able to tolerate the sounds (try the noise-canceling headsets here)

Smell/Taste

- try offering tiny smelling vials of coffee/citrus/cinnamon when entering smelly change rooms

Other Strategies

- use motivating music to attract the child
- encourage activities that invite creative movement so that the child, no matter how they move, will be correct
- encourage animal walks, stop and go and obstacle courses
- when learning a specific movement, break the task down and teach in "bite-sized" pieces for the child who has motor planning challenges

- repetition of movements and music can increase memory of movements
- teach a smaller component of a larger sport (e.g., teach the child how to be a goalie in soccer rather than master the whole game)
- implement a general stamina building program (swimming, stair climbing, walking), which can build endurance in the child with low muscle tone
- attach language to movement to facilitate motor planning and memory
- use familiar movements and modify them slowly, allowing the child time to problem solve
- follow the child's lead; leave an activity open from time to time to observe his or her organization of the task

Manipulatives

Sensory Strategies

Proprioception

- the child may mouth puzzle pieces or other small parts of activities; try offering an appropriate chew toy or a piece of tubing to chew on while playing with the manipulative toy
- offer a compression vest or weighted vest to facilitate posture
- provide weight to increase awareness of the hands and more success in using the hands-in tasks

Vestibular

- a moving chair (Movin' sit cushion, hokki seat, mambo seat, ball chair) can provide vestibular input to facilitate muscle tone and attention

Tactile

- try teaching with a strong sensory base; for example, try putting a shape sorter in the sand table; use the sensory input to maintain attention to the task while learning the task
- keep the mouth busy with snacks or chew tubes while playing with manipulatives if the child seeks out tactile input through their mouth

Visual

- make dropping activities functional by dropping objects into a bucket
- have an interesting visual activity easily available for child who seek out extra visual sensation (like an electric aquarium)

Auditory

- the child may tap on pieces to increase auditory feedback or because he/she doesn't know how to play with the toy. To decrease tapping, teach how to play with the toy or try using only one hand. You may also offer tapping breaks on things that make different sounds.

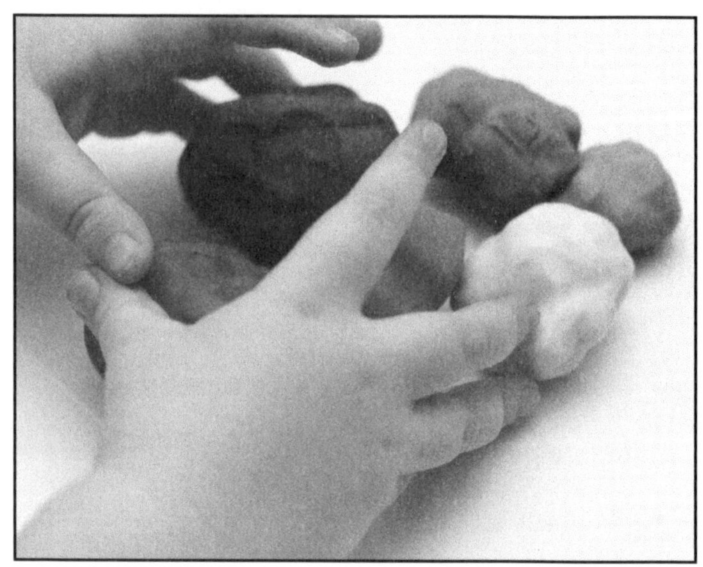

Smell/Taste

- be aware of the smells of objects; wash new toys to remove strange smells
- add smells that are motivating to activities that are challenging (for example, add cinnamon to play dough activities to increase motivation to create)

Other Strategies

- try hand-over-hand teaching with lots of positive reinforcement only if well tolerated by the child
- video modeling can also help a child review and learn a task prior to trying it out
- pictures/sequence strips can be provided to support learning a new skill
- try singing while you are doing the activity ("Here We Go 'round the Mulberry Bush" can be adapted to just about anything!)

Sensory Activities

These activities are often favorites! The child may want to climb right into the sensory bin, mouth the material, pour it out onto the floor or throw it to get the attention of the teacher or other children. Try to determine the underlying reason behind the behavior your child is exhibiting so that the strategy can accurately address it.

Sensory Strategies

Proprioception

- use massage/pressure touch prior to the activity to give the rest of the body sensory input and decrease the desire to lie in the sensory bin
- provide the child with a chewy or similar oral activity to keep the mouth busy while the hands are learning
- provide massage to the hands prior to sensory play to get them ready to receive the input and decrease the use of the mouth
- provide a compression vest or weighted vest to increase your child's awareness of their body and their position in space

Vestibular

- allowing the child to sit on a moving chair or resting the feet on a rockerboard can provide vestibular input to increase muscle tone and attention to the sensory task

Tactile

- if your child has sensitivity to tactile input, offer gloves
- messy sensory activities can be contained in ziplock bags
- tools like spoons and spatulas can be used to mix materials if your child can't touch it

Vision

- provide a pouring activity in the sensory bin – a revolving wheel, strainers, spoons, bowls and an incline – especially if the child likes to watch items falling down
- if the child likes to pour the material onto the floor, place a piece of plastic or a large bowl on the floor to catch it, providing a place to aim the material
- wear a baseball hat to cut down on glare from overhead lights

Auditory

- use noise-canceling headsets to block out noise from the sensory activity

Smell/Taste

- add smells to the sensory activity to enhance attention

Other Strategies

- structure the play with a game and take turns to provide the child with attention and a feeling of being part of play
- if the child wants to get his or her whole body into the activity, use a visual strategy to explain that this is not the way to play or offer the sensory activity in a small container. Placing feet in a sensory bin while playing with the hands may be organizing for a child.
- praise play that is appropriate to the activity and praise often, even if you're praising their breathing
- the sensory table needs a teacher to model play and model and guide interaction with other children
- use video modeling/social stories as a very effective way to learn how to play with a task
- keep the child involved in the activity; sing, take turns pouring
- Many kitchen tasks are sensory tasks (washing dishes, cutting and washing vegetables, stirring juice).

Washroom Time

Sensory Strategies

Proprioception

- children may need to void in a diaper because of the sensory feedback it provides; try having the child wear the diaper to void while sitting on the toilet
- have the child wear a weighted vest, compression vest or a lap snake on the lap while on the toilet to ground your child

Vestibular

- the toilet may be a challenge due to gravitational insecurity; try using a potty or a potty seat with a smaller hole, have the feet firmly planted on a footstool, offer the child your hands to hold, read a book or sing a favorite song
- lying back on a change table may be difficult due to discomfort with the change in position; try holding the child's head during lying down or try changing the child standing up

Tactile

- if the temperature of the toilet seat is uncomfortable, try a cushioned seat or use a towel over the seat with a hole cut out of it
- use wet wipes, as they are more efficient than toilet paper (be aware of temperature)
- some children need to strip off all the clothes as the clothing is touching them differently; give them extra time to get dressed/undressed
- for children with tactile defensiveness, roll up their sleeves prior to hand washing, as the shirt may be too difficult to wear if the sleeves are wet

Vision

- cover the toilet hole with white tissue paper to decrease the visually perceived depth of the hole in the toilet)
- dim the lights to prevent reflected light off the shiny surfaces

Auditory

- there is often a hollow sound in the bathroom; try adding music
- noise-canceling headsets can block out noise

Smell/Taste

- offer a preferred smell as a strategy to combat other smells in the washroom

Other Strategies

- while waiting for a turn to use the washroom or wash hands, try to have another activity set up for the child to do (books, sensory play, songs or fidget toys)
- respect the child's tolerance and never force; this activity can be very anxiety provoking for the child
- positively reward efforts and attempts

Working within the child's tolerance allows for the development of trust between the teacher and the child. It also avoids the increase in emotional distress that can be difficult for children. If the environment and the teacher respect the child and demonstrate flexibility, the child can relax, let down their guard and begin to learn. The child can either put energy into being stressed or into learning. It is our challenge to create the comfortable environment for learning and respecting the sensory processing abilities of children helps us to create this environment.

Snack Time

Snack time can be an anxiety-provoking time for children, especially those with tactile defensiveness. It is important to be aware of sensory challenges to build success in snack time. Social skills and eating often go hand in hand, and snack time provides many social opportunities. There are many wonderful courses available for parents and OTs/SLPs that are specific to feeding.

Sensory Strategies

Proprioception

- have the child wear a weighted or compression vest or a wrist weight to combat poor body awareness
- increase awareness of the hands and mouth with a vibrating toothbrush prior to eating
- use thicker textures of food for children with poor mouth closure and difficulty coordinating tongue movements
- build up handles of utensils with pipe insulation
- offer a weighted cup to help with accuracy

Vestibular

- provide movement breaks if necessary
- if the child is fearful having their feet off of the floor, place them at a small table and chair, or place a foot-stool under their feet at a larger table

Tactile

- if the child is uncomfortable with touch, sit at the table end, as touch is minimized without neighbors
- cold, metal utensils may not be comfortable for the child with tactile defensiveness; try plastic, wood or plasticine over the spoon handle
- children with tactile defensiveness may not be able to tolerate more than one texture in their food; food may need to be pureed to ensure consistency with texture
- introduce foods in similar texture groups

- if the child finds sitting with all the other children overwhelming, set up a small cafe table and encourage the child to invite one other child to eat with him or her to have a snack

Vision

- foods that touch may not be tolerated well, so try plates with dividers that keep food from touching
- try using a mirror to increase visual feedback regarding the face

Auditory

- the sound of chewing food may not be well tolerated; try a white noise machine or music
- offer noise-canceling headsets if sound is overwhelming

Smell/Taste

- respect temperature preferences (the warmer the food, the more flavor it has)
- remember that preferred smells can override the smell of some snacks
- enable the child to have a snack away from the group to decrease the smell

Other Strategies

- if the child slumps or rolls out of the chair, try some downward pressure touch through the shoulders and head
- try posture pillows to support posture
- utensil use can be taught; initially, give the child food items that can be easily speared by a fork, then teach hand over hand
- use a non-slip material under the child's plate and cup to prevent movement
- teach the child to use the napkin to wipe the face after eating
- use a cup with a lid to decrease mess while the child is learning this skill
- if food is a motivator, take advantage of this excellent learning opportunity, as attention and focus will be enhanced
- give a small amount of food at a time to encourage the child to ask for more in order to practice speech

- encourage independent cleanup where the child brings the bowl and cup to the kitchen to be cleaned
- ensure correct table and chair heights; build up the height with a booster seat if necessary
- if anxiety is high, the child may not eat well. Ensure a calm, comfortable environment during mealtime

Music

Sensory Strategies

Proprioception

- offer a weighted vest or compression vest to help your child with body awareness
- allow the child to hold a balloon and feel the vibration while music is playing as a good alternative if he or she is not permitted to touch the instruments

Vestibular

- incorporate movement and dance into music
- ensure a stable sitting surface if your child is gravitationally insecure

Tactile

- be aware of the child with tactile defensiveness and their position to others in the music class
- musical instruments also introduce tactile sensation; have a towel nearby for wind instruments

Vision

- the lines of the music and notes can jump about; try color coding the notes

Auditory

- offer headphones to children with sensitive hearing
- be aware of sound preferences

- be aware of fluctuating volume
- warn the child before an unexpected or loud sound
- whenever possible, engage your child in a helping role; let him or her turn the music on and off

Smell/Taste

- allow the child to smell a preferred smell to facilitate tolerance of the smells in the music room

Other Strategies

- offer consistency in songs to encourage memory and the ability to sing along
- offer fidget toys to increase attention and focus or provide a musical instrument to play
- investigate listening programs (Tomatis method, Therapeutic Listening, Integrated Listening Systems)
- consider an assessment of auditory processing abilities
- use music often, if motivating
- use visual strategies/video self modeling to assist with learning and understanding
- have a list of activities to increase the child's ability to predict what comes next
- take advantage of the motivating nature of music to work on:
    - turn taking – use a song like Old MacDonald
- eye contact/eye gaze – withhold the next verse until the child connects verbally or with eye contact
    - interaction
    - incorporation of movement; rhythm
    - sequencing of activities – due to the predictability of the song

Fine Motor Work

Sensory Strategies

Proprioception

- use weight on writing utensils for the child who is developing body awareness

- if the child is sensitive to feedback through the hand, massage the hand prior to fine motor work
- if the child is developing body awareness, wear a wrist weight
- wear a weighted vest or compression vest to increase attention and information regarding the position of the body
- put weight on the shoulder to increase awareness and support posture
- use a vibrating pen to increase awareness of the hand and arm

Vestibular

- try a gel seat, hokki seat, mambo seat, ball seat or a t-stool for the child who needs movement to increase attention
- use a tabletop easel if changes in head position are challenging
- ensure that your child's feet are firmly on the floor

Tactile

- offer tactile sensory play to the child who is developing fine motor skills
- if the child cannot accept touch through the hands, try wearing gloves during sensory play
- use a glue stick rather than sticky, tacky glue for the child who dislikes textures
- a vibrating pen can decrease tactile sensitivity

Visual

- wear a hat to block out overhead light
- promote the use of different color plastic overlays to increase visual attention
- use a tabletop easel to decrease glare
- use color-coded lines to help with writing

Auditory

- the scratchy sound of pencils on paper can be irritating; offer noise-canceling headsets, white noise or music to help

Smell/Taste

- use smencils, smelly markers and crayons to increase interest in writing

Other Strategies

- build up the handles of writing utensils with pencil grips and pipe insulation to make them easier to grip
- give a physical prompt to get started
- use visual strategies for sequencing tasks
- decrease the amount of written work by considering quality vs. quantity of written work
- use another method for expression of knowledge; tape recorder, oral expression, video, multiple choice sheets
- provide more time for assignments and encourage self-checking
- use a computer program for written expression
- give math problems which are already written out and have the child write the answer only
- use graph paper in math to assist in keeping the numbers in the correct place
- have the child circle or underline the correct answer rather than writing it out
- break large projects down into small pieces
- have the child write on a vertical surface rather than a horizontal surface (e.g., tape the paper to the blackboard or use an easel)
- have a stamp with the child's name to decrease the need to write out the name many times
- glue correct answers on a prepared sheet rather than writing them out
- watch for perseverative behaviors, as they can indicate stress
- be aware that cognitive functioning may not be on the same level as the writing skill. It can be very frustrating when the child demonstrates uneven development, both for the child and for the person supporting the learning. Be creative!
- when the child is having difficulty, try to determine if the concept is the challenge or the fine motor work is the challenge

- ensure proper table and chair heights where the feet are resting on the floor and the elbows can be comfortably held at a 90-degree angle

Social

Sensory Strategies

Proprioception

- if the child needs pressure touch, teach appropriate ways to get it (doing wall push-offs rather than hugging their friend all the time)
- your child can be taught how to respect the personal space of others

Vestibular

- if the child is developing balance skills, position them where there is something "safe" to grab onto if balance is threatened rather than grabbing a friend
- introduce active games or sensory play to encourage interaction
- if there is too much movement in a social interaction, encourage a job where your child can be in one place, preferably sitting

Tactile

- if proximity to others is hard to handle, encourage the child to be at the front or the back of the line in order to minimize touch by others
- be aware of negative reactions to touch, as the student may respond to random, light touch with aggression
- teach other students to alert the child that they are approaching, especially when they are approaching from behind (this is especially true for students who can become fearful of new sensory input)

- if the child has tactile defensiveness, encourage interaction games which offer distance (e.g., rolling a ball back and forth)

Visual

- teach the child to gather information through vision as well as touch
- if eye contact is challenging for your child, teach them how to "check in" using eye gaze

Auditory

- the child may not seem to hear other children; teach other students to use visual cues to initiate interaction
- minimize sound if the child is sensitive; talk in whispers, speak one at a time
- if your child often misunderstands friends or has trouble organizing what was heard, consider an assessment of central auditory processing

Smell/Taste

- preferred smells can help your child be in proximity of others who may have a different smell
- social events that do not include eating are preferred in those children with a sensitive sense of smell

Other Strategies

- teach self-regulatory strategies to enable the child to keep calm and organized
- teach others in your child's life what your child needs to be successful in social interaction
- do not demand eye contact, and teach others in the school setting that eye contact can be very stressful to the child
- promote listening by cueing "Listen to me," not "Look at me"
- use social stories or video stories to explain rules and social situations
- use augmentative communication strategies if necessary and teach fellow students how to use this system so that they can interact with your child
- build opportunities for social interactions by structuring them; have the student hand out the books, hold the door, collect the trip money, etc.

- promote independence in self-care and teach your child how important taking care of yourself makes it nicer for your friends to be around you
- provide choices to promote independence and interaction
- provide students modeling for strategies to display and receive emotion or an interaction (like a handshake)
- if the child has difficulty finding a friend due to poor visual scanning, teach how to call out their friend's name
- encourage interaction through activities and play rather than by verbal interaction
- practice turn taking; make it fun!
- practice cleaning up after oneself
- encourage child to be responsible for a job in order to be a contributing member of the family and class
- practice role playing, plays, skits and puppet plays to build interaction within the safety of a script
- teach the child how to play board games to provide a structured setting for social interaction
- keep a success journal of friends and fun times
- involve the whole team in your journey
- encourage employment where social interaction is structured (e.g., waiter: "Can I take your order? Would you like french fries as well?")

Preparation for the School Years Ahead

The greater the independence in self-care and the ability to organize work and get along with others, the more choices for education will be available for your child. Early attention to these areas will pay off in the future. Independence in these areas also contributes to a sense of mastery and control over the immediate environment which, in turn, leads to greater self-esteem and confidence. A feeling of mastery also contributes to better organized behavior, as movements have more purpose, and frustration is minimized.

- encourage independence in self-care to determine the amount of support the child needs in the school setting and the type of setting the child can go to
- encourage independence in self-care, since it also makes home life easier for parents' establishment of a predictable routine to help the child with motor planning difficulties prepare for activities
- determine which sensory channels are best perceived by the child and try to teach via these channels
- use interests and adapt these interests to learn new skills
- use movement and pressure touch to prepare for an activity
- practice turn taking and waiting skills to prepare for lining up and for communication
- teach how to sit and participate in an activity
- help the child understand which activities offer calming and how to identify rising anxiety
- help the child connect their rising anxiety with calming strategies (There are several wonderful programs that teach regulation: The Incredible 5 Point Scale, The Alert Program and The Zones of Regulation, to name a few)
- teach the child how to tell others in the environment that the calming strategy is needed
- encourage willingness to share and communicate affection and appreciation (this is best taught through modeling respect and affection and shaping responses)

Problem-Solving Worksheet for Students with Sensory Processing Disorder

Students with sensory processing disorder often have behavior that can disrupt a classroom and interfere with a student's learning. With the following list of questions, a school team can problem solve around the behaviors that a child with ASD may exhibit. Remember that each student is unique and that behaviors can be motivated by different factors. This is detective work; answers may not be obvious. Careful observations and investigation can really pay off. Encourage the student's participation in order to observe motor planning, sensory processing and the ability to persevere in a task. Strategies to modify behaviors can enhance your student's learning and participation in the classroom setting.

Child's Name: ______________________________

Date: ______________________________

Occupational Therapist: ______________________________

1. What underlies the behavior?

- Try to understand the reason behind the behavior you are observing.
- Let the student know that you are attempting to understand and that you know he/she is trying hard be respectful.
- Have members of your school team fill out questionnaires to broaden your information base.
- Observe the student and observe responses to different sensory stimuli at different times of the day (take into account fatigue, transitions, etc.)

When do atypical behaviors occur? ______________________________

____

____

What helps the student stop atypical behaviors? ______________________________

____

2. What motivates this student?

Are there sensory motivators that this student is using to self calm? ______________________________

____

Are there toys/activities/topics/music that motivates this student? ______________________________

____

3. Can the behavior be altered so that it is:

Acceptable in the classroom setting? ______________________________

____

The student's need is being met? ____

____

4. Can the schedule and/or environment be changed to accommodate the student's needs?

Can activities involving greater organization and concentration be at the beginning of the day rather than at the end?____

____

Can there be quiet times so that the teacher is available for more individual attention?__________

____

Can offensive sensory stimulus be minimized and sensory stimulus that is organizing be increased?

____

Can calming sensory stimulus be scheduled into the child's day to increase calmness (sensory diet)?

5. Does structure and routine facilitate the student's ability to predict upcoming events?

Can communication aids become part of the student's organization to increase understanding of the day's events and give a sense of control?____

6. Can the perception of sensory stimuli be changed?

Can wearing weighted vests, ear plugs or Irlen lenses be introduced? ____________________

____

Can verbal or visual strategies be incorporated? How? _______________________________

____

7. How can communication between members of the school team, home and community agencies be facilitated to ensure consistent strategies and understanding across environments?

Get the free print PDF of this page at www.sensoryworld.com/BBForms

____

____

____

8. Other Strategies:

____

____

____

____

____

Communication Between the Home and School

Children with ASD often thrive on consistency and routine. Skills will be learned quickly and generalized easily if they can be practiced both at home and at school. This consistency in approach is dependent upon good communication. Many schools and childcare centers have a communications book already set up between home and school. This communication can also happen electronically. Parents are very dependent upon this book for feedback regarding their child's day, especially if their child's communications skills are developing. The communications sheet should outline important points which should be shared between home and school for the benefit of the child.

Activity:

This section asks you to name the activity in which the child participated.

Goals of the Activity:

What is the purpose behind doing this activity? Some suggestions include socialization, learning independence in the tasks of daily life, cognitive skills, fine motor skills, gross motor skills, language, communications, music, and taking turns.

Child's Performance:

How did the child do with this activity? (Be specific so that performance can be measured later on in the school year, against the present time,) How independent was the child? Did they enjoy the activity? How long did they stay with the activity?

Strategies:

Was the activity modified? How? Was the environment modified? How? Were any visual strategies employed? Which ones were used and how were they used? Were any auditory strategies used? Which ones and how were they used? Were any strategies used to compensate for motor planning difficulties? Which ones and how were they used?

Communication Between Home and School

Activity	Goals of the Activity	Child's Performance	Strategies	Home/School Ideas

Get the free print PDF of this page at www.sensoryworld.com/BBForms

Home/School Ideas:

Ideas for Home—Which activities could be practiced at home to strengthen this child's understanding and independence in this task?

Ideas for School—Which activities could be reviewed at school to support new learning done at home?

Keeping Calm in the Classroom

We need to provide an environment for learning which puts the child with sensory processing difficulties in a calm, ready state. If the child presents as anxious, there are several interventions that have been researched to be successful (Groden, 1994). There are many other strategies which by trial and error have been observed to significantly lower anxiety (learning is not taking place if anxious behaviors are occurring). Anxiety presents in many forms and may look like gaze aversion, hand flapping, biting, increased tactile defensiveness (negative reaction to touch) or other irregular motor behaviors. One of the following strategies are often needed: calming techniques and/or removing oneself from the sensory overloading situation.

Fidget Baskets

Look for small, quiet toys that will not disturb the other children. The following are most commonly used:

- silly putty (see chapter nine for a recipe by which to make your own)
- stress balls (many suppliers have wonderful stress type balls, or eggs l; discount stores often have soft squishy balls or toy animals)
- fidget flour balloon (see chapter nine for a recipe to make your own)
- see chapter nine for a more complete list of ideas

Things to Wear (to provide calming deep pressure touch)

- weighted vest (see chapter nine for instructions to make your own)

- compression vest. Hug or squeeze vest
- weighted lap desk or lap snake (see chapter nine for instructions to make your own)
- visor or baseball hat/sunglasses

Equipment in the Classroom

- padded chairs, hokki chairs, mambo chairs, ball chairs, Movin' sit cushions
- noise-cancelling headsets
- theraband leg wraps on chair legs (child can kick for deep proprioceptive input)
- alternative floor-time seating (water pillows, bean bag chairs, laundry baskets, balls stabilized in inner tubes tires, rocking chair, rocker board)
- water bottles or other mouth toy opportunity

Program/Schedule Changes

- additional opportunities to move around
- more doing than listening
- arrangements to leave the room in a non-punitive way (e.g., teacher has prearranged with the office to accept an envelope delivered by the child at any time). The tasks allow the child to feel helpful, provide calming movement and allow for a break from the possible sensory overload of the busy classroom
- relaxation strategies

CHAPTER 8

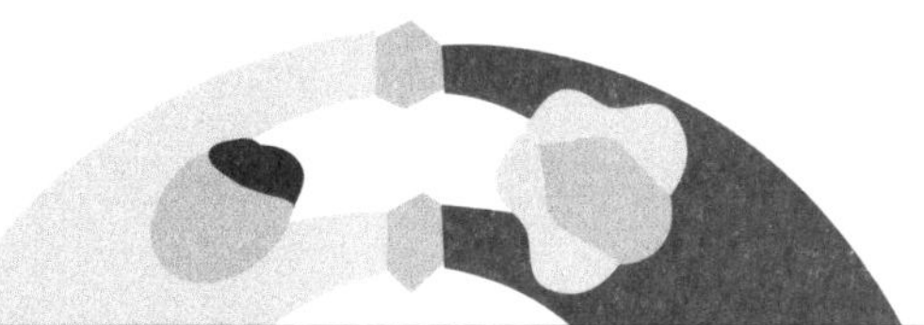

ACTIVITY SUGGESTIONS

This chapter contains a number of multi-sensory activities to provide tactile, vestibular and proprioceptive sensations during play.

All of these activities have been used very successfully with children who have ASD. Some recommendations are traditional games all children like to play. Others have been specifically developed for children with ASD, taking into consideration possible problems with comprehension, sensory integration, motor planning, motivation and attention.

We strive to provide easy, low-cost ideas and try to ensure practicality for parents, teachers and daycare providers. With the availability of resources on the Internet, there are many new ideas posted every day on social media sites including blogs, Facebook and Pinterest. We encourage you to share your creativity by posting your successful activities. Try searching images and the term DIY (Do it yourself) as one way of finding inspiration.

Activities are best provided in environments that offer structure and routine. Activities are organized into the following sections:

- Activities for Sensory Diets
- Tactile Activities:
  - General Activities
  - Learning to Feel with Fingers
  - Recipes for Tactile Play
  - Vestibular Activities

    - Proprioceptive Activities
- Oral Motor (mouth) Activities:
    - Learning to Drink from a Straw
    - Learning to Blow
    - Learning to Chew
    - Keeping Mouths Busy
    - Learning to Keep Your Chin Dry
- Fine Motor Activities :
    - General Activities
    - Heavy Work for the Hands
    - Edible Fine Motor Fun
    - Edible Dough
    - Homemade Silly Putty

- Gross Motor Activities:
    - Swimming Games
    - Backyard and Mini Trampoline Games
- Visual Cues for Gross Motor Activities
    - Roughhousing /Two-Person Physical Games
    - Animal Walks
    - Big Ball Exercises
    - Scooter board Activities
    - Yoga Activities

Please consider possible allergies when using any food items or sensory materials.

Activities for Sensory Diets—General Tactile Activities

Tactile activities can be an important part of a sensory diet or a fine motor skill-building program. Hand and finger awareness, fine motor planning and attention can also be developed with the use of tactile activities.

Activities to Try:

- Arts and Crafts – finger knitting, crochet, rainbow looms, scrapbooking,
- Gardening
- Body Brushing – varied brushes, drawing with soap crayons on body, or chalk, and erasing with various textures
- Massage/back rubs – varied lotions, powders
- Tactile Adventure Bins – cornmeal, oatmeal, water, sand, lentils, popping corn kernels, theme-based bins
- Treasure hunt – hide small objects in play dough or tactile bin to find with fingers
- Play dough – see recipes for edible and homemade play dough
- Painting – outdoors with water, paint roller in bathtub, soap crayons
- Bath time – bubbles bath, soap crayons, back scrub brushes, Do It Yourself (DIY) bathtub body paint
- Foam soap or shaving cream – draw, blow
- Edible Painting – pudding, yogurt or applesauce on a tray; put a paper on top to make a "print"
- Feelie Bag, box or book – collect small items and different textures to match and sort
- Kitchen time – cooking, mixing, tasting, smelling, washing up
- Pet care – grooming, petting
- Forts/hide-outs – pillows, scarves, blankets and a flashlight
- Dress Up – keep a box with gloves, shoes, hats, scarves
- Make Up – face and body paints, tattoos or stickers
- Blindfold games – pin the tail on the donkey, blind man's bluff (caution: this may be scary for some children)

- Tactile Stepping Stones – small carpets, bath mats, rubber mats
- Tactile texture plates
- Bubble wrap
- Sticky Play – tape, MACtac (or other one sided sticky paper)

Learning to Feel with Fingers

The sense of touch is necessary for the manipulation of objects by the hands and fingers. Three-year-old children can usually identify familiar objects by feel and do not need vision to point to indicate which of their fingers has been touched or where they have been hurt. The ability to perform precise finger movements, necessary for a task like fastening buttons, is dependent upon feedback about where the button is on the finger tips. Therefore, most children who have poor touch discrimination will have difficulty with many fine motor tasks.

Some children with sensory integration dysfunction constantly touch and manipulate objects. They may put objects into their mouths without an awareness of their actions (Fisher et al., 1991). These children may be seeking additional tactile input because they are under-responsive to touch sensations.

Light touch activities should be avoided for children with tactile defensiveness. Some children enjoy light touch, and others may find it disorganizing and overwhelming, even if they are not tactile defensive. Activities should be stopped at the child's request if the child is resisting or not actively participating.

A general principle to keep in mind when providing tactile activities is to pair potentially uncomfortable activities with firm pressure, or proprioceptive input, to help modulate the tactile input.

Activities to Try:

- Tactile Adventure Bins:

  Fill large plastic bins or even wading pools with materials of varied textures. If the child still puts things to their mouth, use water, oatmeal, cornmeal, Jell-O or pudding. Older children will enjoy pouring and sifting through sand, rice, flax seed, lentils, or beans.

- High fives and "Push Fives" (a term coined by Meryle Lehn OT, who produced SticKids):

  Push Fives are an alternative to high fives that provides deep pressure touch. Encourage a child to push with steady effort but not to topple you. High fives may escalate arousal levels, and Push Fives can help calm and focus a child. Use these often to celebrate effort or as a greeting, for example, saying goodbye.

- Building Hand Towers:

  Have child hold one hand out, cover with your hand, place the child's other hand on top, cover with your other hand, then show the child how to pull out the bottom hand quickly. Repeat!

- "One Potato, Two Potato":

  Have children make fists and try the old classic pounding game.

- Texture Books:

  Most children with ASD are very interested in books, so combine this interest with a sensory discrimination task. Making a tactile book is easy. Collect samples of contrasting textures. A favorite for young children is an Old McDonald book. On each page, cut an animal shape out of a different fabric and be sure to alternate the feel (e.g., rough then smooth, hard then soft, etc.) on subsequent pages. Use sturdy cardboard and glue down the fabric edges with either colored glue or glue gun glue. Hole punch the pages and place in a 3-ring binder or simply use large rings to hold the pages together. Sample pages may include:

pig = burlap	cow = spots of felt
chick = feathers	duck = terry cloth and silk (pool of water)
horse = suede leather	goose = feathers
cat = sandpaper	grass, sun, etc. = velvet, netting, plastic canvas

  Older children will enjoy a texture book with labels to read (e.g., sandpaper can be labeled as rough)

- Guessing Games:

  The adult rubs the child's finger using different textures and has the child guess which finger or which texture was used.

- Songs:

  Consult any preschool resource book or YouTube for songs and activities. During the song, present different tactile toys such as vibrating bugs, loofah sponges, different bath brushes, feather dusters, etc.

- Finger Tugs & Hugs:

  Adults can provide deep tactile input by grasping each of the child's fingers firmly and tugging and pulling along the surfaces of each finger. Singing "One Little, Two Little, Three Little Fingers" or "Where is Thumbkin?" works well. Older children can learn to do this on themselves.

- Sticky Fingers:

  Use upside down MACtac or double-sided carpet tape fastened on a surface. Children love to place their hands (and feet!) on this.

- Sticker Fun:

  Young children may enjoy peeling off stickers or masking tape after you have placed it on their skin in a spot they can easily access.

- Finger Nail Squeezes:

  Squeeze with a firm pressure on the base of each nail and hold for 5 seconds. Older children can do this independently.

- Tactile Bag:

  Put bits of fabric and small toys into a cloth bag. Some children love the surprise factor of reaching into a bag and choosing items. Other children who are more tactile defensive may need to see what they are touching.

Recipes for Tactile Play

When introducing these activities, the child may have strong reactions to certain tactile input. If the child isn't enjoying the feel of the material, it won't be very motivating or meaningful. Sometimes adapting the temperature or amount of wetness will be all it takes to make the input tolerable. You can also provide tools such as plastic gloves, tongs, spoons and shovels if finger avoidance is evident. If none of these adaptations make the activity tolerable to the child, simply encourage them to watch. Try the new material many times. The goal is to increase acceptance of a greater range of materials or to "widen sensory windows" (Wilbarger, 1998). With the wide range of recipes available on the web, you should be able to find a recipe that works for you and your child.

The following activities are not suitable for children who still persist in mouthing everything. Refer to the "Edible Dough" & "Edible Fine Motor" sections for alternate ideas.

Smelly Play Dough

Combine 2 cups flour with 1/4 cup salt, 1 package Kool-Aid, and 2 tsp. cream of tartar. Then add 1 ½ tablespoons oil. Gradually add 1 cup boiling water to the mixture. It will be sticky because it is hot; let it cool, knead and add more flour if needed. Save in the fridge in plastic. It keeps for several weeks in the refrigerator or about a week in the open air.

Gluten-Free Play Dough

Combine ½ cup white rice flour, ½ cup cornstarch, and ½ cup salt with 2 teaspoons cream of tartar. Add 1 teaspoon cooking oil and 1 cup of water and cook over low heat while stirring for a few minutes until it forms a ball. You may add food coloring as desired. As above, the dough will be sticky until it cools, so knead it into a ball. Store it wrapped tightly in plastic in the fridge.

Bubble Mixture

Mix 1/4 cup dish washing liquid with ½ cup water and 1 teaspoon of sugar. Add a few drops of food color if desired. Many parents suggest Dawn Original dish soap as the best dishwashing liquid for bubbles. Start with bubble pipes or straws if your child has trouble rounding the lips and blowing with the regular bubble wand.

Salt Dough

Mix 2 cups flour, 1 cup salt and 1 cup cold water (food coloring optional for color). Knead mixture until it forms a smooth dough. Add more flour or colored water to reach a desired consistency. The mixture dries well in the air. Try a garlic press for great "spaghetti" or monster hair.

Magic Mud or Goop – Mix cornstarch with a little water and food color. Don't worry if it doesn't stay together. Let kids run their cars through the "mud." When dry, it vacuums up.

Drizzle Goo

Mix 1 cup flour with ¼ cup of sugar, ¼ cup of salt and ¾ cup water with food color. Place in a squeeze bottle. This is great for tactile letters for name cards! Let it dry flat overnight.

Super Simple Sparkle Chalk

Mix a thick paste of white sugar and water, dip sidewalk chalk in paste, then use on paper. It dries great for tactile numbers and letters. Kids will need help using it.

Shaving Cream/FoamSoap/Whipping Cream Paint

Easy as pressing the button on the can! Works well on mirrors, windows or in the tub.

Shaving Cream Foam Dough

This is trial and error fun. Mix approximately 3 to 1 ratio of shaving cream to corn starch and be prepared for a mess!

Vestibular Activities

Vestibular stimulation can have a significant impact on the nervous system. Quick head movements tend to be alerting, and slow head movements tend to be calming. The vestibular organs are located in the inner ear and are sensitive to head movement. Vestibular sensation also helps the nervous system stay organized and balanced. All these activities must be supervised carefully! Watch for signs of overload. You may not always see the response immediately, as it can build up over time. Development of the sensory diet should be done slowly and conservatively with the supervision of an experienced occupational therapist.

Negative responses—Watch for these signs:

- excessive yawning, hiccupping or sighing
- irregular breathing
- facial color change, pallor
- sweating
- motor agitation
- increased anxiety
- pupil dilation
- changes in sleep/wake patterns
- significant changes in overall arousal levels; e.g., falling asleep or giddiness

If the child shows any of the above signs of distress, stop immediately and determine the cause of the child's reaction. Engaging the child in deep pressure touch or proprioceptive activities may be effective in reducing the overwhelming responses of too much head movement (Kawar et al., 2005).

Activities to try:

- Bouncing – on large balls, old mattresses
- Swinging – in blankets, hammocks, toddler swings, playgrounds, aerial yoga swings, ropes
- Spinning – on swivel chair, sit 'n' spin, scooter board, tire swing
- Rocking – on a rocking horse, rocking chair
- Climbing – on playground climbers, ladders, designated furniture
- Riding Toys – trikes, bikes, scooters, roller blades, pedal-less bikes
- Walking/Running/Hiking/Swimming

- Upside-down Play – off couch, off lap, on monkey bars, trapeze, hand stand against the wall, cartwheels, somersaults
- Roughhousing/Wrestling – swinging while someone pushes on legs
- Outdoor Play – slides, teeter totter, roller coaster, rolling down hills, skiing, skating, rock climbing, soccer, baseball
- Recess Games – hopscotch, ball catch, soccer, hockey, tag
- Calming Vestibular Motion – slow, rhythmic, linear swinging, or rocking, gentle bouncing, head to heel rocking while lying on tummy

Proprioceptive Activities

Proprioceptive input can have powerful calming and organizing effects on the nervous system. The precautions are minimal, as this type of sensation is rarely overwhelming. These activities are particularly important to include in sensory diets for children who are over-responsive to sensations. They can help to inhibit or prevent uncomfortable reactions to sensations.

Activities to try:

- Stair Climbing/Sliding – bumping down on bottom or "snake" crawling down head first
- Crawling – through tunnels or boxes on all fours
- Crashing into crash mats
- Playing Tug of War – with ropes, scarves, stretchy bands
- Roughhousing – play wrestling
- Pulling/Pushing – weighted wagon, wheelbarrow, or weighted cart
- Catching/Throwing – heavy weight ball, bean bags, weighted animals, sandbags, cushions and pillows
- Kicking – soccer ball, big ball

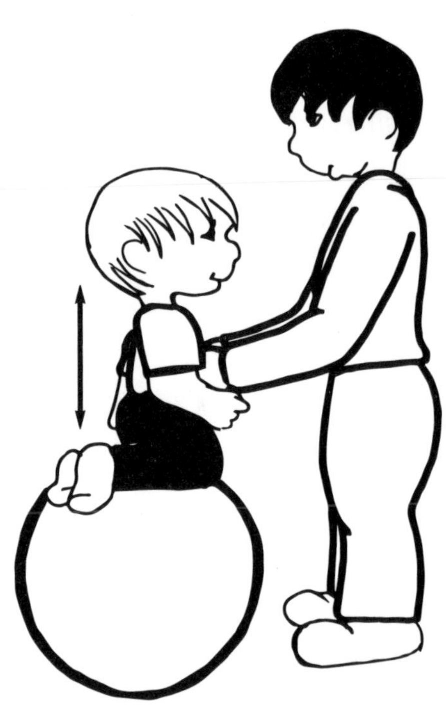

- Carrying heavy items – groceries, boxes, books, pails of water, water babies (fill soda bottles with water)
- Swimming/Extra Bath Time – swim weights can be added
- Big Ball Activities (visual cues follow at the end of the chapter)
- Scooter Board Activities (visual cues follow)
- Animal Walks (visual cues follow)
- Wheelbarrow Walking
- Pulling Apart Resistant Toys/Objects—Lego, pop or snap beads, stretchy toys
- Pounding/Rolling – playdough, clay
- Hitting a punching bag or tetherball
- Squishing between pillows, mats or bean bag chairs
- Body stretches
- Joint compressions
- Any activity that involves pushing, pulling, lifting, carrying, dragging and/or jumping
- Heavy Exercise – pushups, sit-ups, handstands, tug of war
- Batting at balls using a plastic baseball bat
- Swinging while someone stops the child by grabbing the legs
- Hanging from adult hands or from monkeybars, trapeze bar, chin-up/pull-up bar
- Stirring cake batter, pudding
- Pushing against a wall or another person, pushing or pulling on one's own hands
- Vibration (cushions, toys, battery massagers)
- Gross Motor Activities—hiking with backpack, biking uphill, obstacle courses, stretching, toning and strength training
- Massage
- Biting, chewing and crunching resistive foods, or chew tubing
- Belly breathing
- Wearing a weighted vest, compression vest, weighted belt, ankle or wrist weights

Oral Motor Activities

Learning to Drink from a Straw

The ability to drink from a straw is almost essential in our culture. It's convenient and tidy for most families on the go to throw a drinking box in the diaper bag. Sucking is also a calming and organizing activity which requires closing the lips, lip strength and the ability to hold the jaw in a stable position. Sucking also uses cheek muscles, helps breathing and promotes good posture. Most special needs catalogues now include a large section of excellent oral motor products to work on these skills. New products are always appearing, so check with your OT or SLP for the latest products.

Activities to Try:

- If the child is having trouble getting started, try a favorite drinking box drink.
- You can adapt the straw if needed (find a firmer straw with a wider diameter such as a piece of beverage tubing), start by dipping the straw into the liquid, placing your finger over the end of the straw, then putting it in the child's mouth, waiting for or assisting with lip closure then releasing your finger to let the liquid drain into the mouth. Once the child knows the yummy drink is coming from the straw, place it into the drink box and gently squeeze to make a SMALL amount of liquid go up into the straw and be swallowed. Continue gentle squeezes and gradually reduce your level of help.
- You can also adapt many commercially available water bottles. Choose a plastic container with a straw that is squeezable (sports or clear Rubbermaid type). You may need to shorten the straw. Test to determine if it will work by squeezing the bottle, making the liquid go up the straw easily.
- Remember, change is difficult, and many children will resist any new idea. Don't give up!
- Present the straw several times daily for at least two weeks before deciding they just aren't ready yet!

- Increase your child's sucking ability by trying straws of different widths, such as curly straws; use thicker substances such as apple juice mixed with applesauce, smoothies, milkshakes, thinned yogurt or slushies. Try sucking on fruit wedges and popsicles or sipping soup off a spoon.

More Activities

- Harmonicas and whistle-type toys work with air going in and out, so let the child practice alternating these two mouth actions and be the bandmaster!
- Play "vacuum cleaner" – suck a piece of colored lightweight craft foam (about 1" by 1') and move it over into a shallow bowl while sucking. Then suggest they "be the wind" and blow it away.
- You can progress with the child's skills by teaching them to take "big breaths in" (good for relaxation training). Show them how to take and hold a breath by picking up small candies at the end of their straw. Challenge the child to pick them up and move as many as possible within 20 seconds, then EAT! Be sure the candies are not small enough to suck into the straw.

Learning to Blow

Blowing is excellent for facilitating lip closure, respiration, breath support for speech, jaw stability and grading. Blowing helps to develop the muscles of the tongue, cheek, jaw and lips, as well as organizing the sensorimotor system. Ask your child to take bigger and longer breaths.

Activities to Try:

- Blow bubbles in the bathtub with different wands and toys that you can use for bubbles. Many have different mouthpieces which require different mouth positions. Many children who cannot blow bubbles with a regular "bubble wand" do well with a bubble pipe or bubble straw which provides more support to the lips.
- Blow sound makers, party horns, pinwheels.
- Ping-pong ball table hockey (sports-minded kids love this). Dollar stores have many theme-based ping-pong balls or novelty balls to make it more fun; set up barriers on the table such as books to

mark the sidelines and keep balls from flying all over. Make a contest of seeing who can blow the ball off their opponent's end of the table.

- Teach your child to blow bubbles through the straw into the liquid, (... then you have to teach them this is rude!)
- Give the child a harmonica and practice alternating inhale/exhale to make different sounds.
- Give them a whistle (best for outside play).
- Use a feather (from a pillow, bird or craft store); put it in child's hand and blow it off. If it is too difficult; try a feather on a party horn and ball toy. Sometimes a feather is easier than the ball as it is lighter and takes less air to move. Then you can progress to heavier items such as ping-pong balls and cotton balls.
- Have the child blow out candles in various ways (from the front of the mouth or the sides of the mouth). If the child does not have good lip protrusion, they may benefit from you providing stability by holding their chin in your hand. If needed, gently push their lips together into a pucker. Then have the child breathe out forcefully to blow out one candle. Gradually increase the distance and the number of candles.

Learning to Chew

Many children with ASD have poor sensory awareness of their mouths and/or low muscle tone, both of which make chewing food more difficult. They may dislike the feel of certain foods so they don't become good chewers. All mouth activities will be more successful if the child is in a comfortable and secure position. Make sure their feet are supported and the table is at elbow height or just a little lower.

Activities to Try:

- A small battery-powered vibrator/massager (such as Z-Vibe) can be played with for a few minutes before the meal to build up muscle tone in the cheeks and tongue if the child has low tone in these areas.
- Brush the sides of the tongue when you brush the teeth. This can help encourage sideways tongue movement, which is needed for chewing. An electric toothbrush provides another way to brush the tongue.

- Provide a lot of sensory stimulation to the insides of the cheeks with a toothbrush or by pushing outward on the inside of the cheeks with your fingers.
- Chewing is a partnership between the tongue and the cheeks. Often poor chewing coordination is caused by cheeks that are inactive.
- A "chew stick" is a popsicle stick with the end wrapped in gauze and dipped in orange juice, grape juice, etc. (something the child likes). The child chews the gauze at the end of the stick to get the flavor.
- A "chew treasure" is a bundle of something yummy tied in a small gauze square with a sturdy string attached. Moisten the gauze, place the "treasure" on the child's molars and ask them to chew it up to taste the "treasure" Favorites are juicy foods (oranges, apples, sticky caramels, string cheese, etc.). This helps the child keep the food on the molars where it should stay for chewing, and prevents the food from dropping back to the centre of the tongue or to the back of the mouth. With both the chew stick and the chew treasure you may need to place it in their mouth and move the jaw passively for them until they begin to make the motion on their own (Morris and Klein 1987).

Talk Tools (Rosenfeld-Johnson) makes kits for blowing, chewing, and drooling remediation. Note that the research does not support using nonspeech oral motor exercises to develop speech (Bowen, 2014).

Keeping Mouths Busy

Why do these activities?

Williams and Shellenberger (1994) in their book *Alert Program for Self Regulation* suggest that oral motor input is necessary for the organization of the nervous system. Furthermore, Oetter, Richter and Frick (1993) in their book *MORE: Integrating the Mouth with Sensory and Postural Functions* stress the importance of oral motor stimulation in regulating attention and mood. Both of these publications are excellent resources.

Activities to Try

- see previous pages for activities to promote blowing, sucking and chewing
- brush with a toothbrush, NUK brush, toothette, or washcloth
- lick ice cream, popsicles, lollipops, stickers or stamps
- seek out sweet tastes, which are generally calming (sugarless candy, licorice)
- seek out sour things, which are more alerting (sour candy/popsicles, lemonade)
- remember that spicy and bitter foods are most alerting (taco sauce, cinnamon hearts)
- offer frozen things, since cold is alerting (frozen grapes, ice chips, popsicles)
- vibration can be an alerting and organizing input; use electric toothbrushes, vibrating teething toys or small battery massagers

Learning to Keep Your Chin Dry

A wet chin or drool is a frequent concern for children with ASD. Excessive drooling may be a bother to the child and is socially awkward. Children with ASD may drool because of sensory processing problems. If a child is a persistent mouth breather and has a chronic open-mouth posture, they have incomplete lip closure. This decreases the ability to produce the negative pressure required to adequately suck liquid onto the tongue. Often children with respiratory, upper airway, allergies, or sinus problems have open mouth positions, so these problems should be addressed.

Other sensory related causes include:

- Decreased sensitivity in the mouth and subsequent delayed swallow (if the child does not feel the pooling of saliva, they don't get the message to swallow it).
- Decreased tactile sensation of wet versus dry. Many children who drool do not have this sensory dis-

crimination because they are constantly wet around their chin or lips. If we can keep a child's chin and lips dry as much as possible, the child may begin to notice wetness as they now have something to compare it to. They may initiate wiping their wet chin themselves.

Activities to Try:

- If the family members, teachers or support personnel are willing, it is advised to try to keep the child's chin dry for a minimum of two weeks. Always have a dry towel, tennis wristbands or a cotton bandanna available. Use firm patting, not wiping, to soak up the wetness. You may need to check very frequently to begin, then increase the time periods as the child becomes more aware.
- Point out the dry chin, and use the words "wet" and "dry" to comment. Point out the dryness in a mirror.
- Reinforce the concepts of wet versus dry in pretend play with puppets or dolls.
- Another approach is to use verbal or visual cues to increase the child's awareness of the wetness and to follow with a swallow. Tennis wristbands (one on each wrist) can be used to wipe the chin and also act as a visual reminder to think about swallowing. Direct the child with words or pictures when they are wet to wipe with each hand and then swallow: "wipe, wipe, swallow" routine. A pre-arranged wipe signal from the adult or visual cue card may also work.
- If the child's swallow sequence doesn't seem to be effective, practice by squirting small amounts of liquid into the side of their mouth. Tell them you are the mommy elephant feeding her baby or some other silly story, depending on the child's age. Use a drinking box, a squirt toy or syringe for the elephant's trunk. Squirt, swallow, squirt, swallow. Let the child have a turn squirting.
- If the problem persists, refer to a speech language pathologist, ENT or dentist.

Fine Motor Activities

Many children with ASD have significant fine motor delays. These delays may be related to impaired sensory integration. If tactile defensiveness is present, children also will avoid the very activities they need to practice with their fingers, thus contributing to delays. We have provided a list of our favorite fine motor activities.

Tools for general activities:

- spray bottles and squirt guns to develop the skill side (thumb side) of the hand
- tongs for pre-scissors skills
- squeeze toys for water and air play
- eye droppers
- spinning tops
- windup toys
- two-handed building toys - Duplo, Lego, tinker toys, beads, sewing cards
- baking, stirring, rolling, pounding and pouring
- peg boards
- hammer and nails
- bubble paper popping
- playing cards - dealing, counting
- coins in a piggy bank
- puzzles, blocks
- dress-up dolls and action figures
- open and close containers for snack time
- bingo daubers, finger paint, paint with water, chalkboard
- clothespin games
- elastic bands
- arts and crafts
- tablets have many apps that target fine motor pinching skills; one OT favorite is Dexteria and Dexteria Jr.

Heavy Work for the Hands

For kids who need or prefer creating chaos, try giving lots of these types of motor tasks before trying constructive, putting-together type tasks. This type of play offers resistance, which also provides tactile and proprioceptive input for the hands and fingers.

- Pulling/pinching/snipping/poking – try play dough/plasticene/homemade slime (hide and find a small object which was hidden)
- Breaking down egg cartons, cardboard boxes
- Crushing – try a can crusher, see how fast you can go
- Popping bubble wrap
- Ripping up old magazines, newspapers, old sheets
- Catapulting soft objects such as mini marshmallows into a target
- Snapping popsicle sticks and pushing them into a trash bin
- Pounding/poking golf tees into styrofoam or a container of plasticene
- Crushing cookies – put his/her favorite cookies into a strong baggie and pound/crush/break by hand or tool to put on top of ice cream, or in a smoothie
- Picking "Sticker Picker" – laminate a file folder or other card stock, then add stickers, large and small all over, then have him/her pick stickers off
- Punching paper with a hole punch
- Shredding paper
- Throwing/pounding ice cubes
- Squishing water beads
- Shooting Q-tip arrows with a mini-bow at a target.
- Pulling apart toys; e.g., pop beads, bristle blocks, Legos, magnetic toys or any interlocking building toy

Edible Fine Motor Fun

Often children with ASD resist traditional arts and crafts but may be highly motivated by treats. Many children will still be using their mouths as a sensory doorway (Morris and Klein 1987), especially if they are very tactile defensive. This mouthing behavior is a challenge, but if the activity promotes tasting and licking, it will be enjoyed by all. The following activities must be supervised carefully. The ideas generally progress from easiest to more difficult. Have fun, and happy eating!

Creative (visual-motor):

- Powder Power:

  Lightly sprinkle flour, icing sugar, cocoa, jelly, or Kool-Aid powder on a cookie sheet or counter top. Show the child how to draw roads or train tracks through it.

- Pudding Painting:

  Have the child help you make an instant pudding mix or buy pudding. Use paper plates to finger paint on, or if you use paper, it takes a while to dry. If you can stand it, have the child lick his/her fingers for a great oral-motor experience!

- Fruit Juice Painting Cubes:

  Freeze juice with strong colors (e.g., purple, orange, pink) into ice cubes. Take cubes out to draw with on white paper and pop the rest into cold drinks!

- Magic Milk Paint:

  Open a can of sweetened condensed milk and place in muffin tins. Add a few drops of food color and paint with Q-tips. It dries very shiny.

Two Handed Tasks (bilateral coordination, finger dexterity)

- Food Necklaces:

  Start threading with circle-shaped cereal (e.g., Fruit Loops) onto a stable string such as a straw or

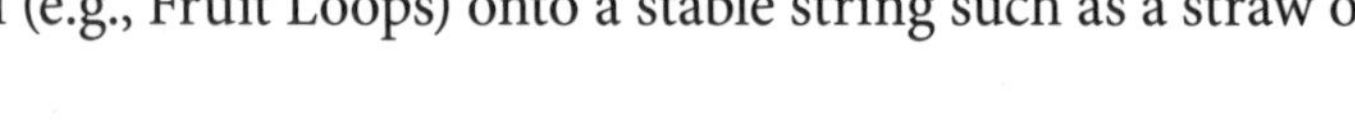

pipe cleaners, etc. "Thread one, eat one" works as motivation! Progress to stringing on a licorice string, then on to stiff plastic string, and eventually onto string. (Twizzler licorice can be cut up into bead-sized pieces for an alternative to cereal).

- Opening Skills:

  Collect small, see-through plastic jars and containers. Carry small cereal or raisin treats with you, but always ask the child to open the jar to get inside! Pop off lids are easiest; turning comes later and is usually done with the dominant hand; the other hand is the "helper" or holding hand. Try hand-over-hand help if needed to start and gradually remove your help.

- Learning to Spread:

  Use plastic picnic cutlery, wooden tongue depressors or popsicle sticks as spreading utensils. Short-handled children's knives are also good. Large rice crackers or flour tortillas do not break as easily as crackers or bread.

- Marshmallow Madness:

  Gather toothpicks and different-sized marshmallows. Create prickly creatures by poking toothpicks into the marshmallows. You can make theme creatures, snowmen, or vehicles.

Edible Dough for Fine Motor Fun

Many children are still using their mouths as their "sensory doorway" when they want to begin play dough activities. These recipes and many more found on the world wide web offer alternatives that are edible! Always begin with clean hands and a few tools to keep the activity interesting (use themed cookie cutters to celebrate holidays). Have fun and happy eating!

Peanut Butter Play Dough

1 cup peanut butter

3 Tbsp. brown sugar

1 Tbsp. raw oatmeal

1 cup corn syrup

1 ½ cups powdered sugar

1 ½ cups powdered milk

Mix with hands, adding more sugar or dry milk until you can knead it. Add oatmeal or Rice Krispies for texture. You can make this dough without the corn syrup, you just have to adjust the dry ingredients "by feel."

Cinnamon Applesauce Dough

2 cups cinnamon

1 cup applesauce

Add enough flour to get desired consistency. Great for fall themes!

Homemade Silly Putty

Many children love to use silly putty or play dough when learning to pound, roll, squeeze or cut. Play Dough may crumble and is often too babyish for older children. This putty can be made very stiff, which makes it ideal for holding in the other hand to cut. Although it may be harder to snip through with scissors, the stiffness provides increased tactile and kinesthetic feedback. This putty is wonderful to use during imaginative play. It can be used to stick things together on a temporary basis. The resistance of the putty helps develop finger strength. This recipe is a low-cost alternative to silly putty but not recommended for children who still put fingers in their mouths! It's fun to make in a group, but practice making it first to get the feel of it.

Homemade Silly Putty Recipe:

Mix together ½ cup water, ½ cup white glue and food coloring (blue food coloring seems the least edible color, to visually discourage kids from putting it in their mouths).

Mix another ½ cup water & 1 teaspoon Borax in measuring cup.

Combine above, knead until the glue forms a putty-like consistency, add cornstarch gradually and keep kneading until it is a solid mass.

Store in any airtight container; plastic eggs or ziplock bags work well. A great thing about this homemade silly putty is that you can keep adding cornstarch to make it nice and firm with a soft texture. You can easily squeeze it, and it takes more effort to pull it and break it than most soft putties. Also, the more corn starch you add, the less sticky it is. This recipe makes enough for 8-10 children.

Silly Putty Activities

- Keep a large plastic tub of putty and dump it on the table with cookie cutters, scissors, rolling pins, etc. Hide small toys or coins in it for finger strength.
- For fingertip skills, use thumb and pincer fingers of ONE HAND ONLY to roll baby dinosaur eggs or alien eggs (whatever small, round-shape eggs fit the play themes). Puppets or clickers held by the other hand "eat" the eggs.
- Make 'creatures' with toothpicks.

Gross Motor Activities

All children benefit from active movement of the large muscles in the arms, legs and trunk. Exercise of these muscles promotes strength, endurance, posture, balance and coordination. Recent research confirms the role of exercise in promoting brain health (Ratey 2008). Participation in gym class and eventual leisure activities are highly dependent on gross motor skills. Children with ASD may be reluctant to practice these activities, especially if the underlying sensory motor foundation skills are weak. They benefit most from routine and easily practiced activities. We have included our favorite gross motor activities as follows:

General Gross Motor Activities to Try:

- walks and hikes
- running, skipping and hopping

- dancing, marching to music
- playing ball hockey, soccer or basketball
- jumping – mini-tramp, trampoline (see trampoline activity sheet)
- walking on stilts (cans with skipping rope handles) or "big feet"
- tumbling and wrestling
- hide and seek
- playing on the playground
- bowling
- ice skating
- skiing – downhill or cross county or snowshoeing
- rollerblading
- bike riding or trike riding
- stand up scooters
- skateboarding
- pogo stick
- tether ball
- tee ball
- hop scotch
- hoop games
- racquet sports
- obstacle courses
- beanbag/nerf ball/frisbee catch and throw games
- track and field activities
- big ball games
- swimming
- scooter board tag
- yoga, tai chi

- Wii fit or Xbox Kinect
- interactive panels (often found in multi- sensory rooms)

Swimming Games

Many children with ASD love to swim, perhaps because it is such a total sensory experience. The weight and pressure of the water against the body is relaxing and increases body awareness. Outdoor swimming pools, lakes or seasides may be preferred for children with ASD due to the natural lighting and sound levels. Indoor swimming pools often have harsh artificial lighting and high noise levels generated by echoes off hard surfaces. The ability to swim is essential as a safety factor in our culture. Many therapy goals can be incorporated into swimming, as it is such a motivating activity.

Activities to Try:

Make laminated pictures for all your child's favorite swimming songs and or chants. Pair the song with the visual cue and the motor actions. Pictures can also go inside plastic bags or clear self-adhesive vinyl covering. Allow your child to make choices of favorite songs/games.

The following singing or chanting activities promote language development and provide sensory input:

- Swimming, swimming in the swimming pool (great actions)
- Motor boat, motor boat go so slow, motor boat, motor boat go so fast, motor boat, motor boat step on the gas! (whirl around on flutter board or holding hands through the water)
- This is the way we blow big bubbles, kick our feet, splash our face... (tune – Here We Go Round the Mulberry Bush)
- The Grand Old Duke of York (wonderful up and down)
- Ring around the Rosy
- Jack in the box, sitting so still, won't you come in – yes I will, (jump into water)

- Humpty Dumpty (jump off tube into water)
- Row, Row, Row Your Boat (use air mattress or flutter board)
- Five Green and Speckled Frogs (jumping in)
- Scrub, Scrub, Scrub our Sillies Out (tune – Shake our Sillies Out, use therapy brush)
- Hokey Pokey (may persuade a reluctant child to put a face, foot or hand in)
- If you're happy and you know it blow big bubbles – start with straws and show how to blow, gradually cut the straw shorter. Blow ping pong balls across the water, take a small mirror underwater to encourage eyes open and bubble blowing.
- add swimming weights, fins or other swimming aides to increase the proprioceptive input

Backyard and Mini Trampoline Games

A large backyard trampoline can be a wonderful therapeutic piece of equipment the whole family can enjoy. An indoor mini trampoline is a versatile piece of equipment that involves movement and body awareness and assists in gross motor skill development.

Unfortunately, a trampoline can also be dangerous. It must be set up and supervised carefully. Usually only one person at a time is recommended to be on the trampoline; however, when dealing with children with special needs, this may be unrealistic, and you may require another person to assist the child. A responsible adult can jump safely with a child, providing they don't bounce too high and stay towards the middle of the trampoline bed. A heavy adult and light child is the most dangerous combination, and adults should practice the stop bounce maneuver right away (stop jumping, bend knees and absorb the bounce, balancing with your hands out if needed). This stop should also be a goal to be taught to the child, perhaps with a visual cue stop sign or red circle which represents a red traffic light. This is an early co-regulation skill; the adult helps the child inhibit the motor action of bouncing or running. Later the child will progress to being able to inhibit their actions themselves; this is an important part of self regulation required for playing safely. Children must practice risk taking!

An indoor mini trampoline is generally a safe piece of equipment if basic rules are followed, such as one person on the trampoline at a time, keep away from sharp or hard furniture and provide hand support if needed to begin.

Activities to Try (general progression from easiest to more difficult):

- Sit and hold hands and sing, Bouncing Up and Down on The Big Trampoline (tune: Bouncing Up and Down in My Little Red Wagon by Raffi) or Row, Row, Row Your Boat while rocking back and forth and gently bouncing.
- Knee bouncing – let the child hold your hands in a face-to-face position.
- Standing up – same as above holding hands OR turn child away from you and provide deep pressure by squeezing with your legs while you sing or count and rhythmically bounce. Have another adult watch the child's face for signs of distress. Most children find this position very secure and love it!
- Bumper Cars – once the child is comfortable running around, introduce "crashing" and falling in a safe, controlled manner. Bump with your shoulders or back, arms crossed, no pushing allowed.
- Jump around the Rosy – after you all fall down, be sure to include the child pulling you up as part of the game! Make a big fuss of "HELP, HELP, pull me up!" The pulling builds interaction skills as well as providing good organizing sensory input.
- Humpty Dumpty Sat on the Ball (bring ball to sit on). The trampoline is a safe and fun place to practice falling.
- Race track – use colored circles of construction paper for red/green traffic lights or use a homemade stop sign. Practice jumping/running and stopping on command.
- Jump like various animals (use visual cues at the end of this chapter).
- Seat drops, knee drops, doggy drops (on hands and knees).
- Rolling games – roll across, over each other, and sing "There were ten in the bed and the little one said, 'I'm tired, roll over...'" Monitor this vestibular input carefully as for sensitive children, since it can be over stimulating.
- Tag games – chase and catch.

Visual Cues and Strategies for Gross Motor Activities

Sensory-motor activities or total body activities that demand heavy work are often recommended. They are recognized for the organizing effect they have on the nervous system. However, many of these activities are difficult to teach a child with ASD due to communication barriers and difficulty with motor planning. Hodgdon (1995) has found visual aids to be an effective strategy for children with auditory processing and communication problems. Many picture symbols are now available (such as Boardmaker by Mayer Johnson), but there is a lack of appropriate pictures for sensory-motor activities. We have included simple visual cues to assist children's participation in specific gross motor activities.

Resources for motor challenges in children with ASD has grown dramatically in the past decade. Visual aids are available in many formats, including YouTube, apps for Smartphones and tablets and computer resources. Refer to the resource section in Chapter Nine for further ideas.

These visual aids were developed by one of the authors, Shirley Sutton, and illustrated by Marion Foubert, an experienced childcare provider. We have also added a yoga booklet, (illustrated by Paula Aquilla), that we have found to be useful with our children.

In our experience, pictures are helpful during OT programs, as they aid with children's comprehension, enhance sequential skills and improve attention to tasks. We have also found children to be more cooperative when they have visual preparation for upcoming changes in the activity program. By using picture sequences that are stable over time, the children learn the game and will often make choices of preferred games. Learning and motivation are enhanced by making therapy exercises more interactive. In fact, self-directed activity is considered crucial to motor planning in Ayres sensory integration therapy (Ayres 1975).

Line drawings are used, as they are less distracting than photographs. The drawings were set up to be customized for your child by printing your favorites, cutting them, and placing them into a standard small photo album. Using these visual aids, or making your own, is well worth the effort! Watch for immediate results with many children in the areas of comprehension, transitioning, and compliance. Pictures also help parents and teachers define the beginning and end of an activity. Quill (1995) also notes that concrete picture cues are invaluable aids that help children with ASD deal with last-minute changes of plans or deviations from routine.

Mackenzie (2010) suggests using a hierarchy when teaching movement modulation for behavioral self regulation. The progression begins with the child imitating the adult's actions in close physical proximity. Secondly, the child imitates the actions from pictures. This is more complex, as the actions are frozen in time and require symbolic thinking. Thirdly, actions are paired with simple verbal labels, (be aware of your child's ability to process sound and visual input simultaneously).

Pictures have been developed for FOUR main types of activities.

- Roughhousing/Two-person physical games:

  These activities feature face-to-face interaction and foster your child's attention span and interaction skills. Communication skills as well as sensory and motor skills are encouraged as you have fun together. Use your child's love of movement and deep pressure touch sensation to foster interactive games. Using a familiar song over and over with the same game is a wonderful way to reinforce language skills.
- Animal walks:

  These challenging positions are excellent for floor time at home, circle times at school or transition times when children need to move to another spot. The positions provide heavy muscle work, which builds body awareness and helps with motor planning. These cues are also excellent for interactive games such as Mother May I. Non-verbal or low-verbal children enjoy having these pictures placed on a large die to throw when it is their turn to move.
- Big ball exercises:

  Big ball activities are often very successful for children as they provide movement input and pressure input which can be motivating and organizing. These pictures can turn playing on a big ball into a series of games that work on interaction and communication skills such as turn taking, choice making, requesting help, saying "stop/go," etc. Mackenzie (2010) recommends teaching the child to be aware of their body parts, beginning with the hands and progressing to the whole body. These pictured ball exercises are excellent for focusing attention on a specific body part as well as modulating the force of one's movements. Some ball skills require big motor responses, ("Hit it hard, make your fist like a rock. Now try to hit it lightly, like a feather.")

Therapy balls are widely available now at many stores and therapy suppliers. A peanut-shaped ball may be more suitable for children with significant balance challenges while also offering a novelty factor. Less expensive balls from toy stores are often acceptable. Hop balls with handles will also work for these activities – just turn the handles out of the way.

- Scooter board activities:

  The pictures provide ideas for this common piece of therapy equipment (see equipment in Chapter Nine for information on how to build your own). Scooter board activities are used for movement and body awareness and for foundation motor skills such as back extension, sitting posture, arm and neck strength, and core stability.

- Yoga activities:

  Yoga exercises can be done while standing, sitting and on the floor. It can be difficult for children to transition from one position to another, so we designed a series of postures that are for standing only. We suggest that you incorporate breathing into each posture. Breathing in the postures helps to build core stability, as the breathing happens while the postural muscles are stabilizing the body's position. Feel free to play with the order of postures and the amount of breaths.

  Here is a sample series to try:

  - Breathe in/breathe out - 5-10 times
  - Low tree – right foot up, breathe in and out
  - Tall tree – right foot up, breathe in and out
  - Warrior 1 – right foot forward, breathe in and out
  - Warrior 2 – right foot forward, breathe in and out
  - Triangle – right foot forward, breathe in and out
  - Changes sides, put the opposite foot forward.

Roughhousing/Two-Person Physical Games

Grand Old Duke of York

Objectives

- To provide movement, paired with language, up and down
- To increase body position sense and head movement
- To develop adult's upper body strength

Start with small lifts until child is comfortable.

Yankee Doodle Went to Town ...

Objectives

- To provide touch pressure to child's tummy area
- To provide linear calming movement
- To develop "protective reactions" in arms when you lower them to the ground

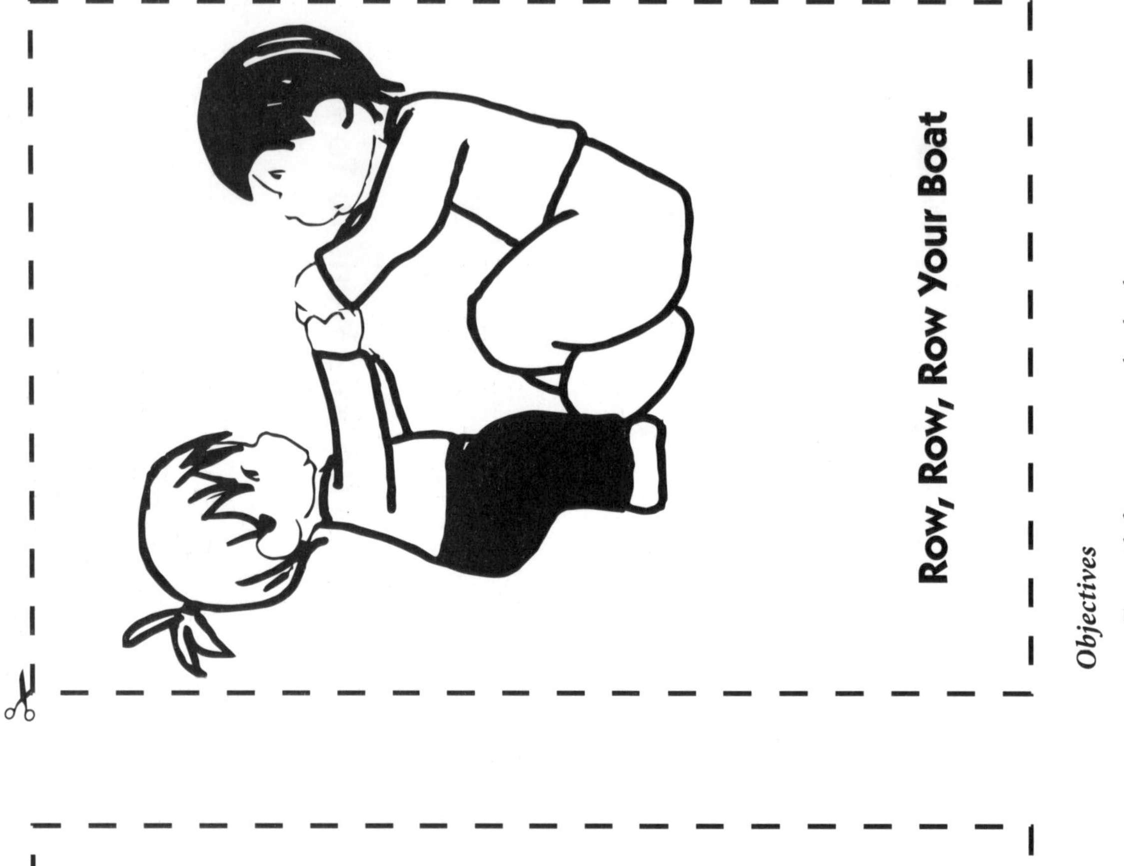

Row, Row, Row Your Boat

Objectives

- To provide firm pressure touch to hands
- To increase body awareness through push-pull activity
- To develop upper body strength
- To promote standing balance

Up and Over

Objectives

- To provide strong head movement in the upside-down position
- To develop arm and hand strength

Be sure the child has good muscle tone before trying–use another adult to "spot."

Get the free print PDF of this page at www.sensoryworld.com/BBForms

Teddy Bear–Climb the Stairs

Objectives

- To provide deep-pressure touch to hands
- To increase body awareness and standing balance
- To develop standing balance

You may adapt the same chant to a variety of motor movements.

Airplane Ride

Objectives

- To provide deep pressure touch to hands and tummy
- To increase body awareness through up, down, sway
- To develop back and neck extension muscles
- To promote basic balance

Objectives

- To provide deep-pressure input to child's tummy
- To develop "protective reactions" in arms when you "shake them off!"

Chant "Trot, trot trolley horse up and down; look out [child's name], don't fall down!"

Objectives

- To provide deep-touch pressure to body
- To provide calming head movement
- To promote language skills

Chant: "Rock the boat 'til we laugh and shout, rock the boat 'til we all fall out!"

Head Down

Objectives

- To provide head upside-down position (strong vestibular)
- To increase eye tracking

Song idea: "Ring Around the Rosey" (We all fall down)

Push-Pull

Objectives

- To provide calming push-pull input without direct touch (especially good for sensory-defensive children)
- To increase body awareness through push-pull activity
- To develop upper body and handgrip strength

Get the free print PDF of this page at www.sensoryworld.com/BBForms

Animal Walks

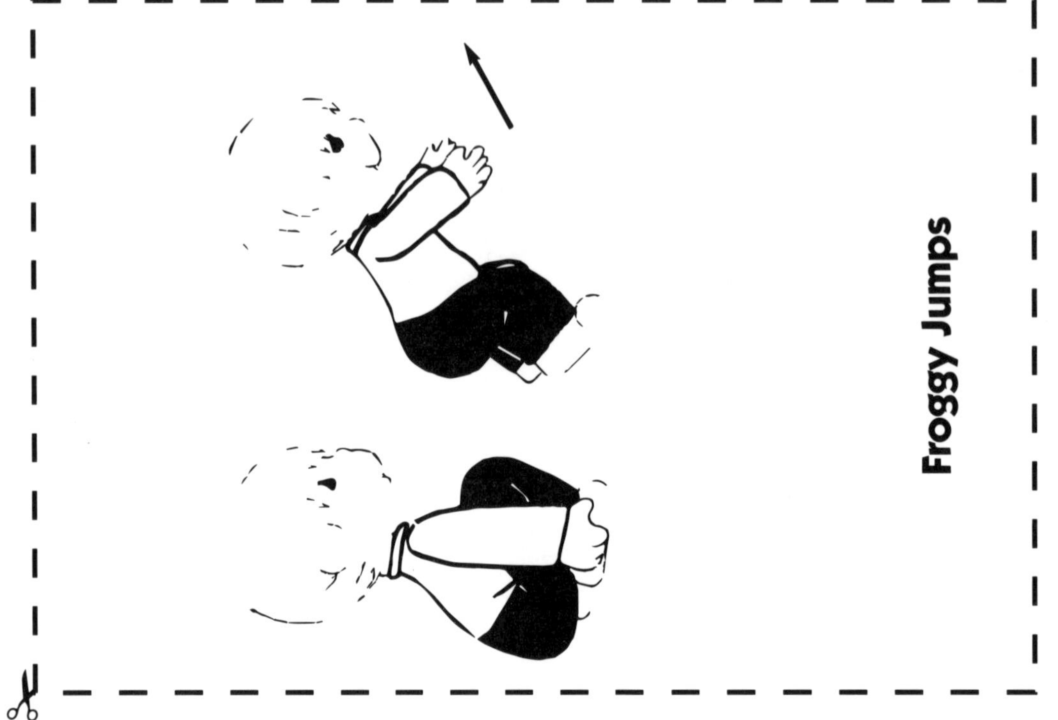

Froggy Jumps

Objectives

- To provide head movement to build body awareness
- To practice two-step, large muscle motor sequence
- To develop muscle endurance

Bunny Hop

Objectives

- To provide touch input to hands from pushing off the floor
- To build strength in legs
- To develop two-sided body coordination
- To promote two-step motor sequence

Get the free print PDF of this page at www.sensoryworld.com/BBForms

Bear Walk

Objectives

- To provide tactile desensitization to hands from weight bearing on the floor
- To increase body awareness

Requires complex coordination of two body sides.

Crab Walk

Objectives

- To provide pressure touch input to shoulders and hands
- To increase body awareness through weight bearing

If too difficult, start by asking the child to move tummy up and down while staying still.

Get the free print PDF of this page at www.sensoryworld.com/BBForms

Objectives

- To provide touch input to back from carrying an object
- To increase body awareness
- To develop upper body strength
- To promote motor control by moving fast versus slow

Objectives

- To provide touch pressure input to hands during weight bearing
- To increase upper back extension strength
- To build arm strength

Get the free print PDF of this page at www.sensoryworld.com/BBForms

Bottom Slide

Objectives

- To provide touch pressure input to hands from floor
- To increase body awareness
- To provide calming input from demanding heavy work from hip, tummy, and arm muscles

Big Ball Exercises

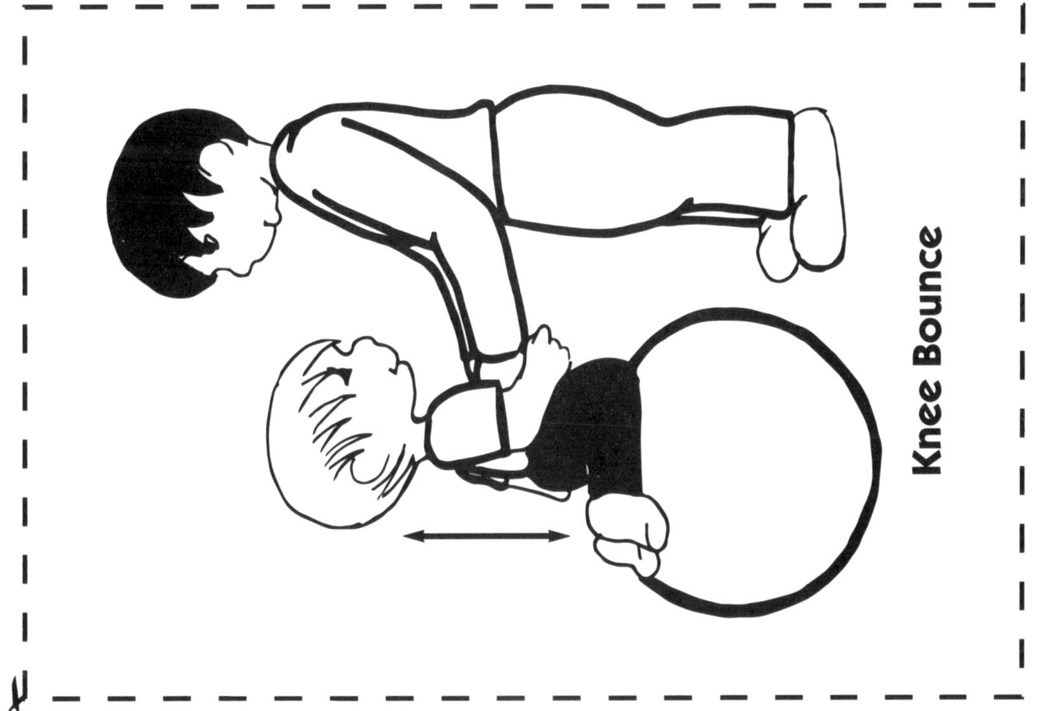

Knee Bounce

Objectives

- To provide calming, rhythmic movement
- To increase awareness through push-pull activity
- To develop upper body strength
- To promote kneeling balance

Get the free print PDF of this page at www.sensoryworld.com/BBForms

Get the free print PDF of this page at www.sensoryworld.com/BBForms

Tummy Throw

Objectives

- To provide touch pressure to body from floor
- To increase back and neck extension strength
- To develop arm strength
- To develop good eye tracking (roll ball)

Hit Big Ball

Objectives

- To provide touch pressure input to hands
- To increase body awareness through hitting activity
- To develop upper body strength
- To promote eye tracking

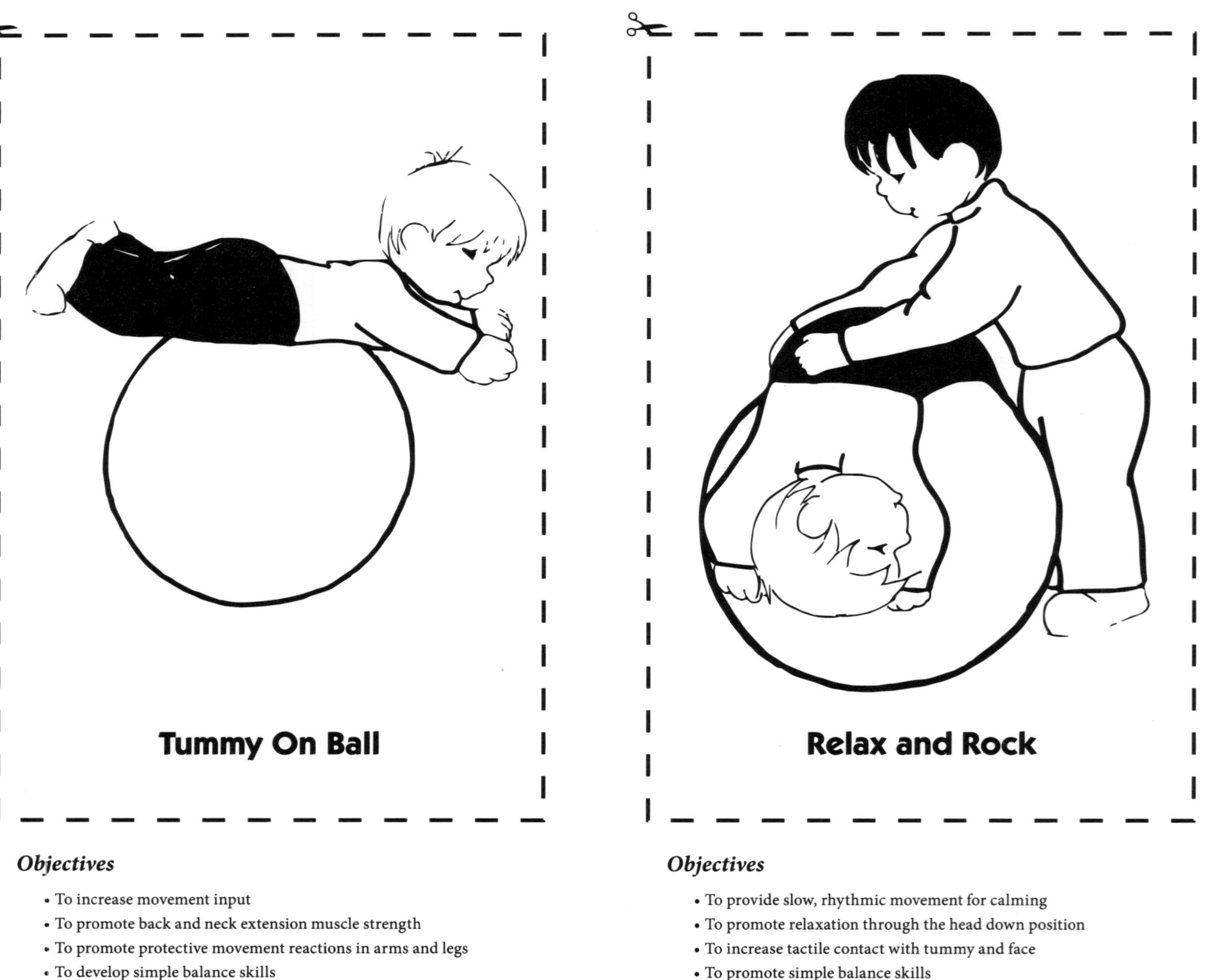

Tummy On Ball

Objectives

- To increase movement input
- To promote back and neck extension muscle strength
- To promote protective movement reactions in arms and legs
- To develop simple balance skills

Relax and Rock

Objectives

- To provide slow, rhythmic movement for calming
- To promote relaxation through the head down position
- To increase tactile contact with tummy and face
- To promote simple balance skills

Get the free print PDF of this page at www.sensoryworld.com/BBForms

Objectives

- To provide up and down head movement
- To increase body awareness through hips and feet
- To promote sitting balance
- To build rhythm and counting skills

Objectives

- To increase awareness of legs and feet
- To develop leg and tummy strength
- To promote two-sided body coordination
- To improve eye-foot coordination and timing

Get the free print PDF of this page at www.sensoryworld.com/BBForms

Push Big Ball

Objectives

- To provide touch pressure to hands
- To provide calming heavy muscle work
- To build strength in wrists and arms

(Note to adult: stand opposite child and provide resistance.)

Scooter Board Activities

Hoop Sit

Objectives

- To provide touch pressure to hands from holding hoop
- To increase body awareness
- To develop upper body strength
- To promote sitting balance
- To increase body awareness through push-pull activity

Get the free print PDF of this page at www.sensoryworld.com/BBForms

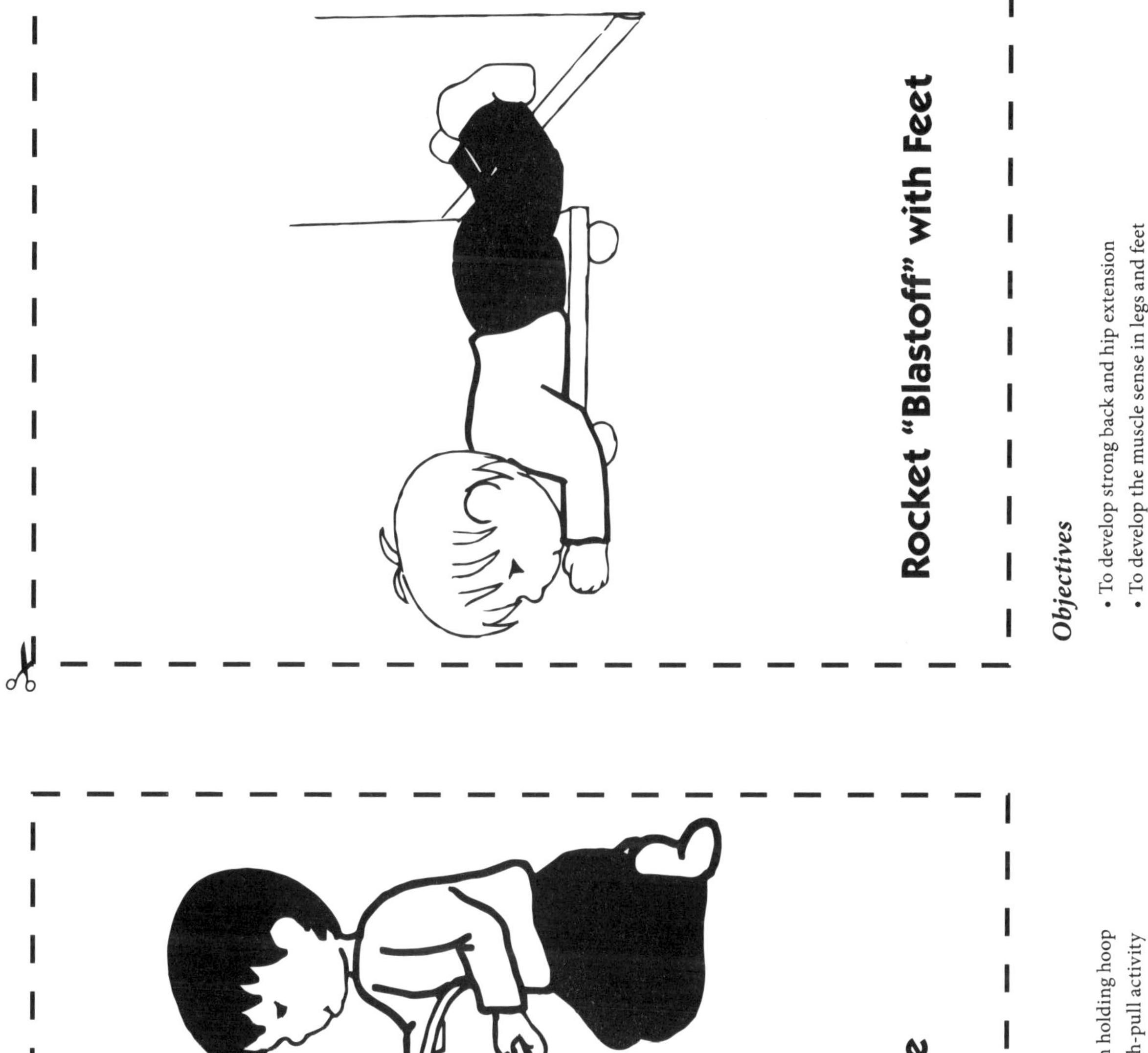

Knee Ride

Objectives

- To provide touch pressure to hands when holding hoop
- To increase body awareness through push-pull activity
- To develop upper body strength
- To promote kneeling balance

Rocket "Blastoff" with Feet

Objectives

- To develop strong back and hip extension
- To develop the muscle sense in legs and feet
- To promote sense of timing (countdown to "blastoff")
- To provide fast movement (acceleration)

Get the free print PDF of this page at www.sensoryworld.com/BBForms

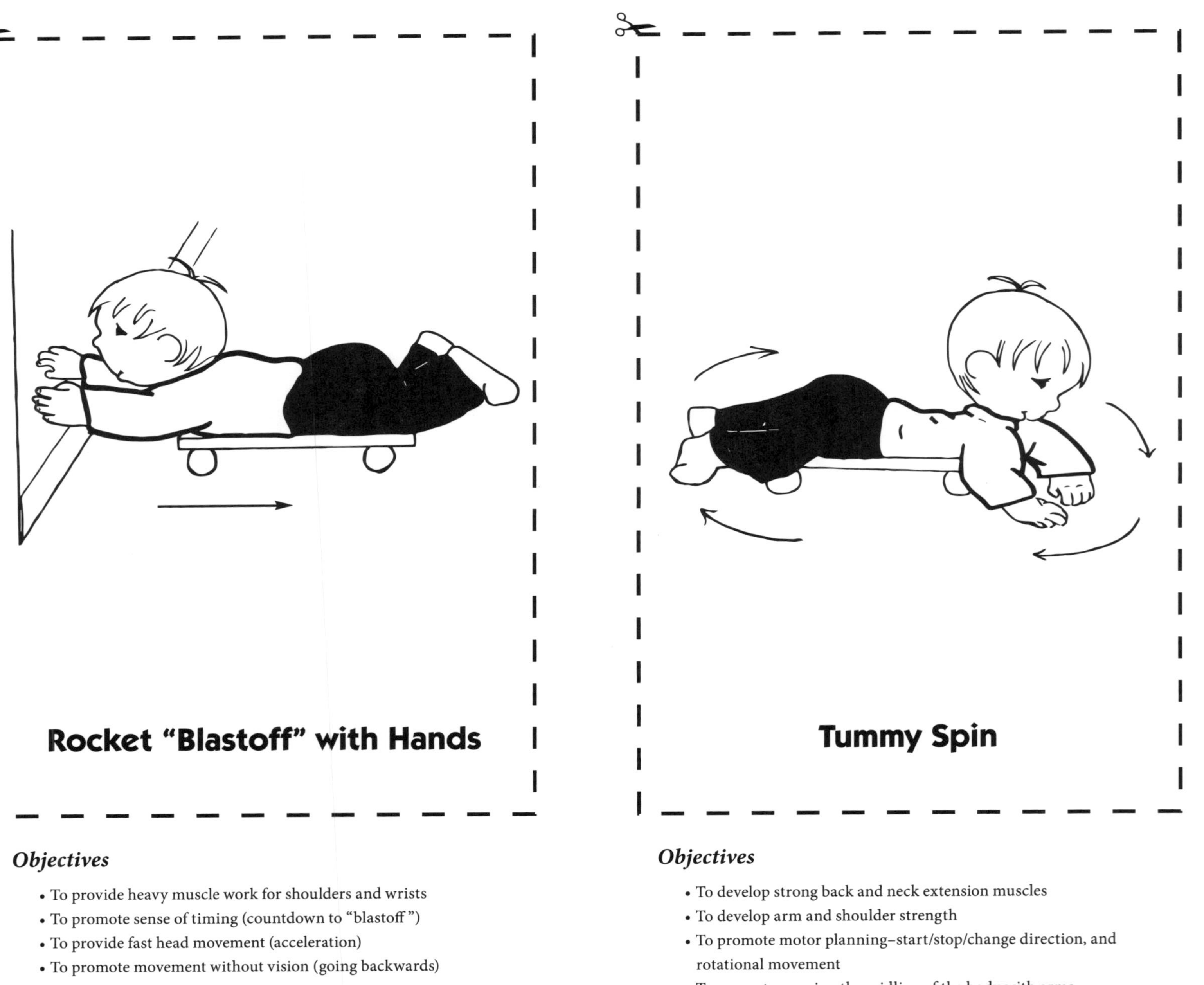

Rocket "Blastoff" with Hands

Objectives

- To provide heavy muscle work for shoulders and wrists
- To promote sense of timing (countdown to "blastoff")
- To provide fast head movement (acceleration)
- To promote movement without vision (going backwards)

Tummy Spin

Objectives

- To develop strong back and neck extension muscles
- To develop arm and shoulder strength
- To promote motor planning–start/stop/change direction, and rotational movement
- To promote crossing the midline of the body with arms

Get the free print PDF of this page at www.sensoryworld.com/BBForms

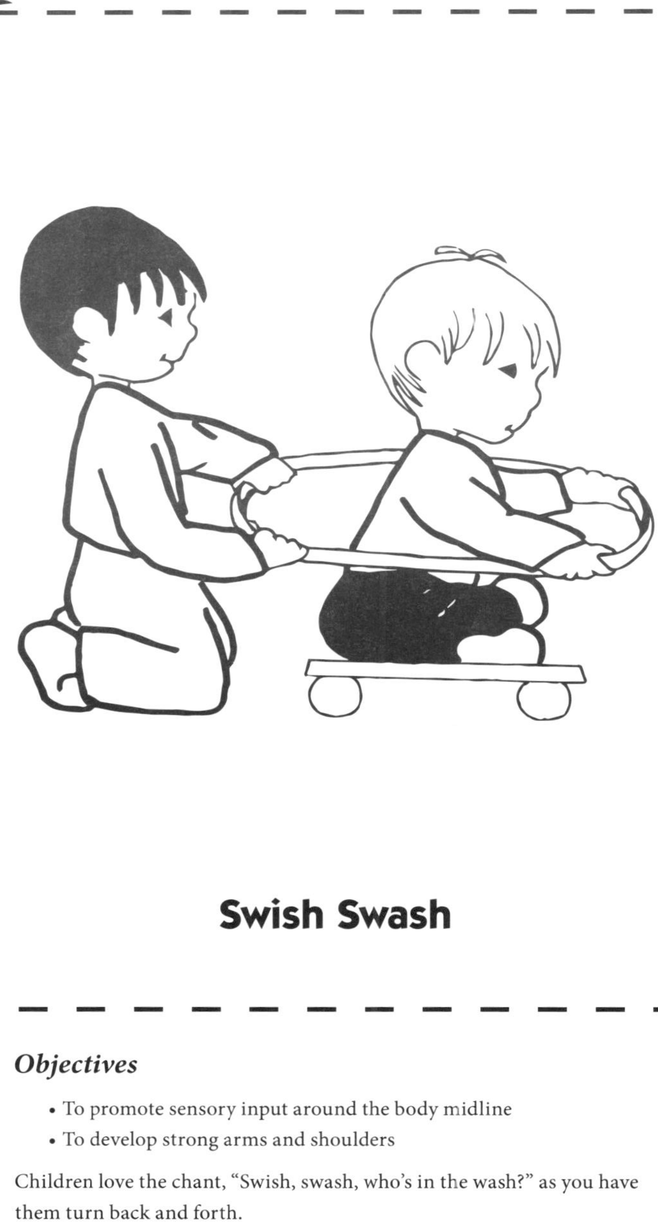

Swish Swash

Objectives

- To promote sensory input around the body midline
- To develop strong arms and shoulders

Children love the chant, "Swish, swash, who's in the wash?" as you have them turn back and forth.

Yoga Activities

Get the free print PDF of this page at www.sensoryworld.com/BBForms

Low tree with hands at heart
Extended right angle

Get the free print PDF of this page at www.sensoryworld.com/BBForms

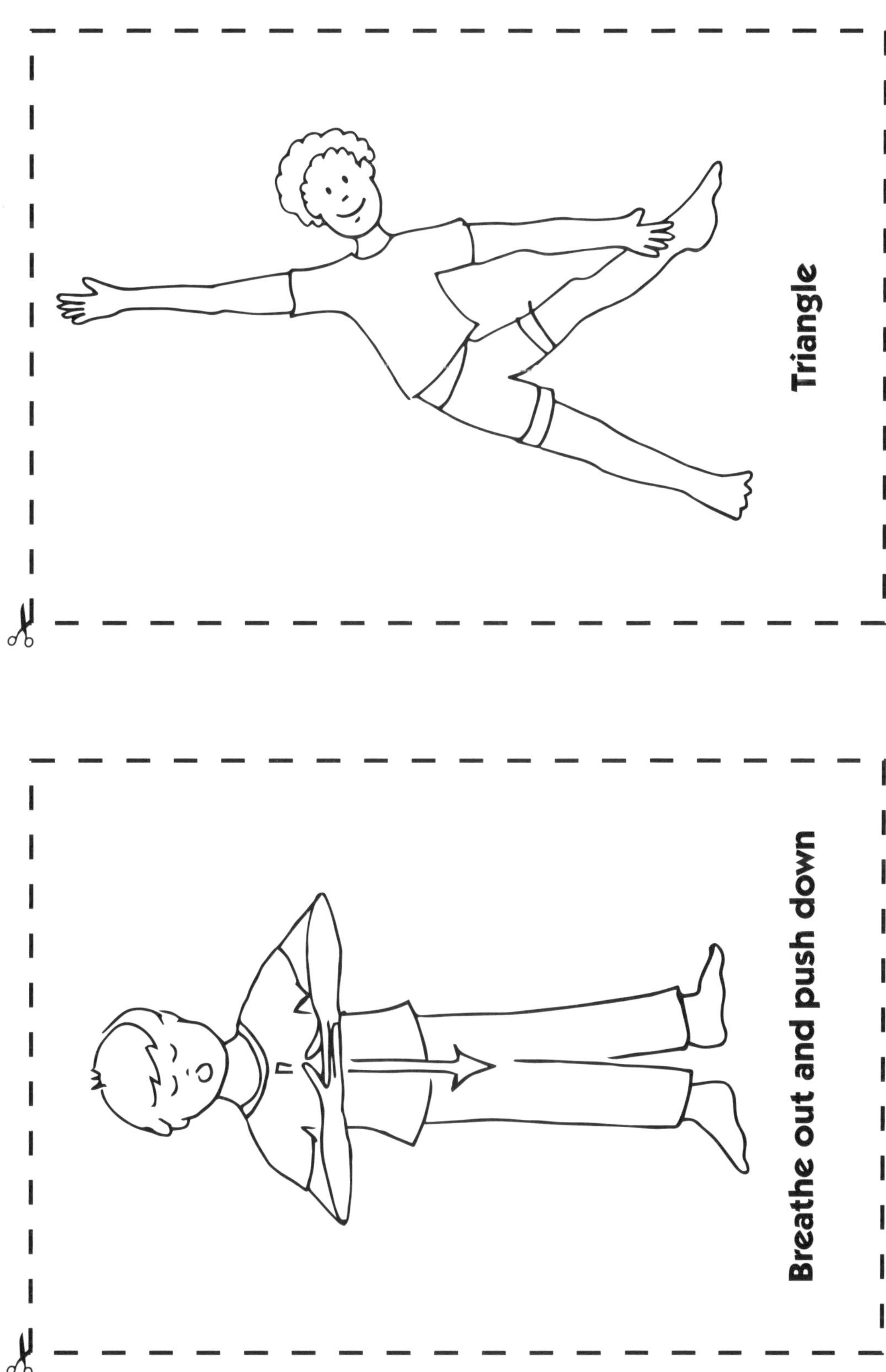

Get the free print PDF of this page at www.sensoryworld.com/BBForms

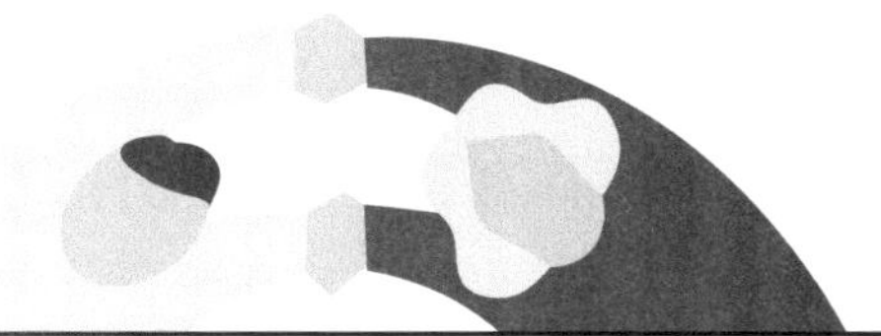

CHAPTER 9

EQUIPMENT AND RESOURCES

This chapter contains a number of instructions for making equipment that we have found helpful in our experience working with children with ASD.

Often parents, schools and child care centers don't know where to find equipment or don't have the resources to purchase the equipment from specialty catalogues. By providing easy and low-cost instructions or purchasing sources, children will have access to the sensorimotor experiences they need. All of these suggestions are very adaptable to your child's size, body weight and personal preferences. A brief explanation of how and why to use the specific equipment is included.

Remember, when introducing any new items or equipment to children with ASD, they may need some time to become comfortable with anything that is unfamiliar. They may initially reject items which are new, as these children typically prefer predictability and may be unsure of their use. You may need to have the piece of equipment within the child's visual field for a period of time without the demand of its use. Social stories, visual aids, video modeling and live role modeling are strategies that may be helpful when introducing new equipment.

Equipment is not used in isolation of other interventions but is used to enhance outcomes or augment educational and behavioral programming.

The resources are organized into the following sections:

Make-it-Yourself Equipment Ideas

- Weighted Products (vest, blanket/punching bag, lap snake)
- Platform Swing
- Scooter Board
- Stretchy Hammock
- Stress Balloon Fidget Tool
- Fidget Bag Tools
- Low-Cost Indoor Sensory Equipment Ideas

Resources:

- Suppliers
- Books
- Web Sites
- Assessments
- DVDs
- Tablet Apps

Make-it-Yourself Equipment Ideas

Weighted Products

Temple Grandin (1986) reports alleviation of symptoms and improved regulation following the use of her "squeeze machine." Donna Williams (1996) feels that padded clothing protects her highly sensitive tactile system from too much sensation. These adults are commenting on the benefits gained from the application of deep pressure touch. Various items that offer deep pressure touch are increasingly used to support self-regulation in children and adults with ASD. The research on the value of these items is mixed, and those that report positive results often have small sample sizes. However, in our clinical experience, children who constantly seek deep pressure touch, are sensory defensive, are easily distracted or have poor body awareness often benefit from the extra weight these items provide. The use of weighted items can be an integral part of a sensory diet. Items should not be used if the child resists their use and if he or she shows discomfort during use.

Weighted Vest

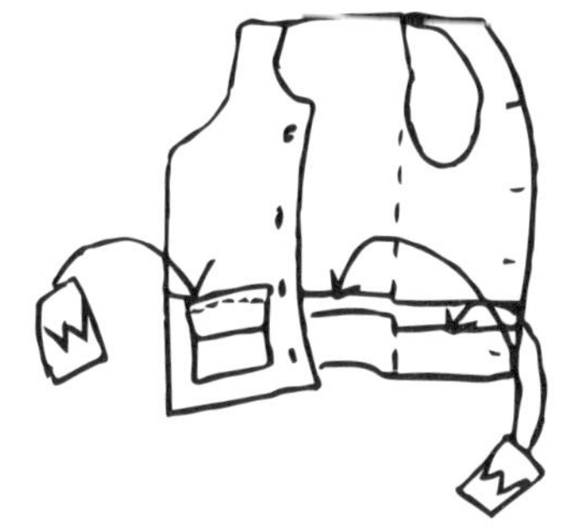

The vest is custom made to fit the child snugly in a comfortable fabric that the child prefers. It is padded and weighted to five percent of the child's body weight for initial application; modifications are made based on therapist clinical reasoning (Olson 2004). Recommendations regarding weight need to be specific for the individual child, as strength, muscle tone and the need for pressure varies.

Protocols regarding wearing time vary, with a 2012 Best Evidence Statement (BESt) concluding that there is insufficient evidence and a lack of consensus regarding wearing times. Initially clinicians recommended 30 minutes of wearing time (VandenBerg 2001) to avoid habituation or adapting to the new sensation, which would decrease effectiveness. This recommendation was altered following a study that demonstrated positive results following a 2-hour period then a 2-hour break (Fertal-Daly 2001). Typically the vest is worn during seat work or when children are in stressful environments. Considerations for wearing time need to include whether the child has difficulty with the tactile input of putting the vest on and off and whether the child dislikes having the vest removed because they begin to rely on the comfort that it provides. There needs to be a flexible approach to determine weight and wearing time. One needs to experiment and take into account both the child and family preferences in conjunction with an OT. Review the Cincinnati Children's Hospital Best Evidence Statement that has guidelines regarding use. www.cincinnatichildrens.org/WorkArea/DownloadAsset.aspx?id=94933

If you want to try this strategy before someone commits to sewing or purchasing a vest, a bag of rice in the child's backpack or fanny pack may provide some insights into this method's effectiveness. Ask your OT if he or she has a vest you may borrow for a few weeks.

Are there risks?

As long as the vest is comfortably fitted, there are no known potential risks to this treatment. If it is very hot, the vest will not be appropriate. If the child shows signs of distress or discomfort, the trial can be ended at any time. Most children begin wearing the vest for shorter periods.

The potential benefits may include:

- decreased stereotypic behaviors
- increased attention to task
- decreased anxiety
- increased impulse control

Precautions:

- avoid use during extreme heat or for children who become easily overheated
- monitor use for children with low muscle tone and poor posture
- ensure proper fit that allows for chest expansion during breathing and no excessive pressure against bony points
- conduct visual scan of body after use to determine if there are any pressure points
- avoid use for children with severe respiratory complications

Are there any alternatives to a weighted vest?

Yes. Although there are currently no studies supporting the use of alternative equipment, there are a variety of items that people use that can have positive results. Compression vests or "snug vests" are increasingly available through therapy supply companies. Although they have not been formally studied, therapists have reported similar positive effects using pressure wraps, lap pads, weighted belts, lap snakes, body socks and weighted blankets.

Instructions for Sewing

If you are lucky, you may find a sturdy new or used vest with buttons or snaps that fits the child. Alternatively, you might sew one from a pattern. Fabrics such as fleece, denim and corduroy seem to work well and can withstand machine washing! When choosing a fabric, also consider summer weather and whether the child will be wearing the vest mainly indoors or outdoors.

Try the vest on the child and consider where you intend the weight to be. Typical placements are below the shoulder blades, on the upper chest and around the hips. You need to create pockets for the weights to sit in. Ensure that the pockets are symmetrical, with equal weight on each side of the body. The weights can be simply ziplock sandwich bags filled with sand or rice, plastic pellets or aquarium gravel. Be aware of the safety risk if the child gets into things and still eats non-edibles.

1. Decide what you are going to use for weights and make the pockets accordingly. Use sturdy fabric or pad the pockets so the child won't feel the weights moving around. The average preschool child weighing forty pounds would typically start with a vest of 4 to 6 pockets, which will weigh four pounds.
2. Sew pockets snugly to fit the weights and distribute the weight evenly. Often you need to put a small piece of Velcro at the top of each pocket to ensure that the weights do not shift. Remove or add weights to adjust the weight; sometimes the child accepts the vest better if the weights are added gradually. When washing the vest, remember to remove the weights first.

Weighted Blanket or Punching Bag

There is controversy over the use of weighted blankets. There was a very unfortunate incident where a weighted blanket was used to inappropriately restrain a student in a classroom that led to his death. Subsequently, there was an investigation that led to the development of specific guidelines regarding the use of weighted blankets. Individual school boards, provinces or states may have their own guidelines that need to be considered.

The following recommendations have been adapted from the Autism Society Canada 2008 guidelines that were developed following this incident.

1. A health professional's advice must be obtained to ensure that the use of the blanket is suitable for the child
2. The weight of the blanket must be in proportion with the client's physique and weight (note: Clinical consensus among OTs suggests a maximum weight of up to 15% of the current body weight)
3. The child's head must never be, or be able to be, covered by the blanket
4. Vital signs should always be observable (breathing, skin color)
5. The child must never be rolled in a blanket (unless a therapist is constantly at his or her side)
6. The child must be able to easily slip out of the blanket if he or she wishes to do so (it is not a tool of confinement)
7. The child must express his or her consent to the blanket, even if consent is not verbal.
8. Many children benefit from the calming input of "heavy work" – using their large muscles against resistance. A weight bag for kicking or punching is often a favorite way to get that calming feeling as well as burn energy. Commercial weight bags are far too hard and heavy for most children to use safely. A low-budget, simply made version is another useful piece of equipment to help your child learn self-regulation.

Some kids like to "vent" safely by punching a bag. You know your child best and know if this is a safe idea. Only put up the bag when they are calm and regulated and use it as a fitness tool.

This style of the weight bag may also be used as a weighted blanket; if it is successful for your child, you might then wish to purchase a commercial version, which is often easier to launder.

How to Make:

Determine the appropriate weight of the bag, considering the child's size, weight and strength. The American Academy of Pediatrics (2011) suggests that backpacks be kept at less than 20 percent of a child's total body weight to prevent injury, so this standard is suggested to be used with other weighted items.

Purchase the needed fabric for the weight bag casing. The case should be a very sturdy fabric, such as good quality cotton sheeting, in order to hold the filling.

Materials

- Fabric
- Old clothes
- Webbing for handles at each end
- Sewing machine
- Needles, scissors and thread
- Measuring tape
- Ceiling hanger for weight bag (see fitness section of department stores)
- Carabineer

Instructions for Sewing

1. To make the weight bag, fold a sheet or use a baby quilt.
2. Sew webbing handles at each end lengthwise
3. Cut a matching piece of fabric, pin and sew around 3 edges and then mark the bag evenly into lengthwise channels about 5 inches across.
4. Gather soft material scraps (old t-shirts, towels, etc., work great). Remove any fasteners and rip into pieces. Stuff the channels using a long stick to poke the fabric down into the tubes. Try to fill each channel equally (not too full or you won't be able to sew widthwise to keep the filling from shifting).

5. Sew across the top edge to seal in place. Finish the fourth side – hem by hand or top stitch on a machine. Put a carabineer in the handles and hang from the ceiling when in use. Store it flat and hang it up from opposite ends to prevent the fabric from shifting down to the bottom side.

Weighted Lap Snake or Lap Animal

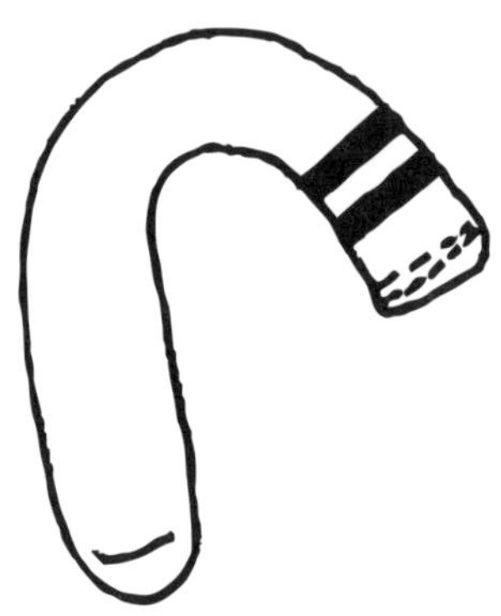

Many children with ASD find sitting still for any reason very difficult due to their sensory needs. Extra weight provides deep pressure touch and calming proprioceptive input. Many children cannot tolerate a weighted vest, but may tolerate a less intrusive "lap snake" or a favorite stuffed toy that has been weighted. This is a easy way to try the concept and see how the child responds.

Sew one or several snakes and introduce them when the child is sitting, calm and happy. Place one or more in the child's lap or drape it over their shoulders. Observe if the child is less restless upon receiving it. Some teachers use such items as a calming influence when they cannot stay right beside the child.

Instructions for Sewing

1. Find a long tube socks, one for each "snake." Alternatively, use thick tights or stockings and cut them off about 18" from the toe; serge or whip stitch the cut edges.

2. Fill each sock with four cups of rice or other similar small items such as plastic pellets, pinto beans or split peas.

3. Close up the end of the tube sock by hand or machine, sewing the opening with small, sturdy stitches.

4. If desired, draw a simple face on the sewn side of the sock, making the seam the "mouth."

5. When adding weight to a stuffed toy, examine the toy to see if the fabric is dense and strong and if there are no seams that are easy to open. Determine and weigh your filling. Carefully open the seam and add filling gradually, then carefully hand or machine sew the access point closed.

Platform Swing

Materials:

- good-quality plywood - 4' long x 2.5' wide
- good quality rope (amount depends on the height of your ceiling)
- pipe insulation (approx. 14' to go around the edge of the swing)
- vinyl (approx. 14' to cover the pipe insulation)
- clamps (8)
- staples
- D ring (to hang the swing) *swing is hung from a beam in the ceiling

Have a contractor inspect the beams of your ceiling to ensure strength. The eye bolt inserted into the beam should be welded to prevent stretching of the bolt. A rotation device is recommended to prevent the ropes from twisting over each other.

Complete instructions regarding installation of a swing and equipment is available from Southpaw Enterprises; please see *Resources*.

Instructions:

1. Round edges of the plywood and drill two holes in each corner for the rope.
2. Cut your rope into four equal pieces and string through the holes at each corner.
3. Clamp the ropes (Figure 1).

4. At the other end of the ropes, make a loop and clamp it. Ensure that each rope is exactly the same length (Figure 2).

5. Staple the pipe insulation around the perimeter of the swing (Figure 3).

6. Staple the vinyl over top the pipe insulation (Figure 3).

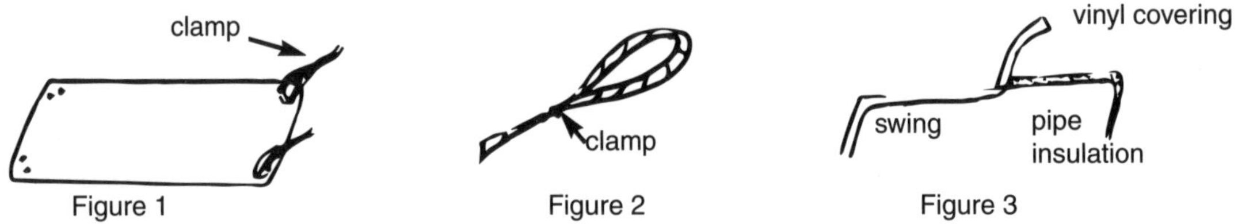

Figure 1 Figure 2 Figure 3

Scooterboard

Materials:

- good-quality plywood (2' x 1' or from child's armpit to mid-thigh for length)
- padding (carpet underpad works well)
- vinyl to cover
- staples
- 4 castors (good quality, multi-directional castors)

Instructions:

1. Cut the plywood and round front corners (Figure 4).

2. Staple the padding onto the board.

3. Staple the vinyl covering over the board.

4. Add the castors underneath (ensure that your screws are not longer than the width of your plywood) (Figure 5).

Instruct your children on the safety of the scooterboard. It is for sitting, kneeling and lying on tummy or back. **NEVER STAND ON YOUR SCOOTERBOARD.**

During activities which can be fast, a helmet is recommended. Always supervise your child on the scooterboard. See the visual cues in chapter eight for ideas on different scooterboard activities.

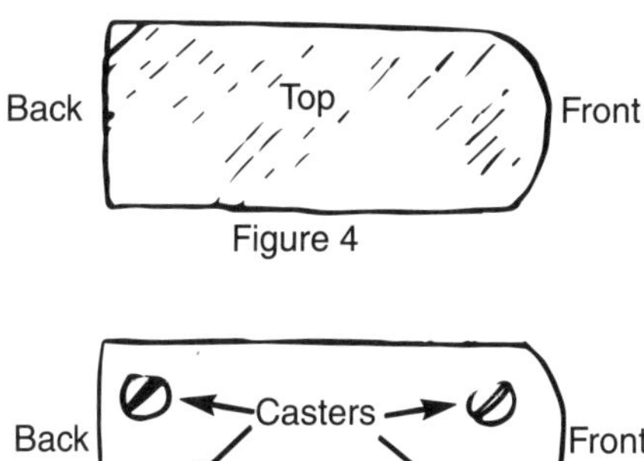

Figure 4

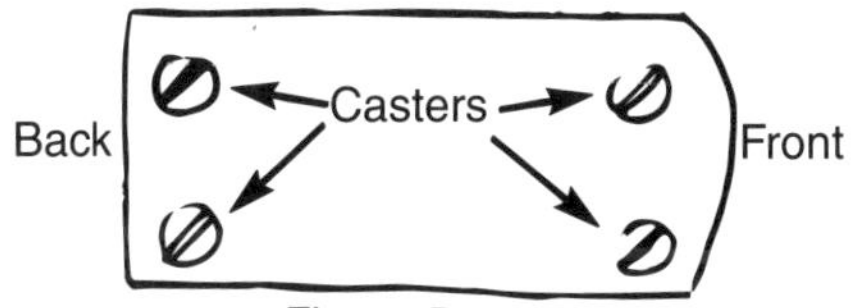

Figure 5

Stretchy Hammocks – no-sew method!

This type of hammock provides total body pressure touch, which is well tolerated by almost all children with ASD. The soft, stretchy fabric gives resistance and provides heavy work load on the muscles and joints to build body awareness, strength and coordination. Moving between layers makes it especially fun as a hideout.

Supplies (4-point suspension style)

- Four pieces of strong yet thin rope – 2 feet long per corner piece
- Four golf balls
- Multiple layers in different colors of the heaviest weight lycra/spandex
- Ceiling suspension system, carabineers optional

Assembly

1. Fold/cut the stretchy fabric into layers which suits your child's size and your suspension system.
2. Secure all 4 corners of the fabric to the ropes with the golf ball method.
3. Place the golf ball under all layers of fabric - gather up the fabric around the ball and secure it with the folded rope in a slipknot; this tightens as weight is put on the fabric and stretched out.
4. Hook the four corner ropes to the suspension hooks and remember to do a weight test!

5. Your ropes must be short enough that the child will not "bottom out" or fall out while in the hammock! Try various configurations until the child lies at a comfortable angle.

6. You can pop out the golf ball corners and ropes when you need to put the lycra in the washing machine.

Stress Balloon Fidget Tool

As part of a sensory diet or sensory activity program, many children need extra touch input. This balloon tool is squeezable, which provides the child a chance to use calming deep pressure touch while using the tool. The tool is very quiet, which means it can be used during school, church or other environments where noise can be disruptive. The resistance of the balloon is excellent for learning to squeeze and release as in many progressive relaxation training programs.

The stress tool can be kept in a pocket, fanny pack or fidget basket, which can be made readily available to the child when there is down time or when waiting more than a minute or two is required. It can also be used as a sensory preparation toy which a child squeezes and releases several times to build awareness of finger position before doing a fine motor task such as drawing.

CAUTION: Balloons, if eaten, can be very dangerous for young children. Latex allergies may prevent the presence of any balloons in the classroom. If the child uses the stress balloon near their mouth, look for a more appropriate and safe mouth tool. Do not use balloons if the child is allergic to latex.

Supplies:

- 2 (or 3) 9" helium quality balloons
- filling—flour, corn starch, lentils, bird seed or coffee (for added sensory smell input), rice, pinto beans, split peas, or other non-toxic substance
- plastic water bottle
- tiny elastics or fine thread

Instructions:

1. Pour about 1/3 cup of filling in a plastic pop bottle.
2. Inflate a 9" balloon to about the size of a fist, pinch the neck, and stretch the neck of the balloon securely over the neck of the bottle.
3. Turn the bottle over. The contents of the bottle should be displaced by the air from the balloon and should pour easily into the balloon. If it does not, gently squeeze the bottle.
4. Remove balloon from the bottle, squeeze out the excess air and secure the neck with a tiny elastic or piece of thread. If desired, snip the "lips" of the balloon off first.
5. Cut the neck off a second balloon and stretch it over the first balloon, inserting the sealed end in first. It's like putting on a bathing cap.

If you wish a three-layer balloon, repeat with a third balloon.

Low-Cost Indoor Sensory Equipment Ideas

Many children with ASD have a strong need to move. Movement helps them stay focused, adaptable and skillful. Movement opportunities are essential components of sensory diets. Unfortunately, many schools have greatly reduced their indoor and outdoor playground equipment to reduce costs and safety risks. However, there are many ways to provide sensory input that children with ASD love and enjoy with little cost.

How do you use Indoor Equipment?

Many ideas have already been discussed in chapter five—Strategies for Challenging Behavior, as we explored the link between behavior and strong sensory needs, especially for vestibular (movement) and proprioceptive (body position sense). This list gives more suggestions for equipment not already discussed.

Equipment Ideas:

- cardboard boxes for rolling, tunnels, climbing, stepping in/out and making hideouts
- buckets from the dollar store for hauling and pouring
- blankets and hammocks for swinging, hiding and rolling
- lycra fabric/bungee cords to play various push/pull games
- swivel chairs for spinning (remember to ask the child to direct the activity!)
- old mattresses/air mattresses, pillows, water beds for jumping and crashing
- blow up/plastic wading pools as sensory bins to fill with rice, beans or pillows
- a smooth, thin board 8 to 10 inches wide and several feet long to make an indoor slide by placing it on steps or making a bridge by putting it across a few books, or make a teeter-totter over a flat stool
- broomsticks or dowels to do chin-ups or floor pulls
- beach ball – fill with small amount of water to make a "wacky ball" that won't run away because the water weighs it down
- old bicycle inner tubes for stretching and playing tug of war
- plastic water or soda bottles filled with water for a bowling game
- laundry baskets to sit and climb in and out of (good symbolic play – train or bus ride)
- zoomball – a great two person game for upper-body coordination and visual tracking and convergence. Many children with ASD love this toy because it's highly visual. Attach one set of the handles up high on a hook and let them send the buoy' up, or try it lying down, kneeling, or on the tummy. For preschool children, the dollar store version is fine, as the strings are shorter.

Fidget Bag Tools

As discussed in chapter five, the Sensory Diet, many children with ASD find sensory experiences to be soothing and organizing. As adults, we all fidget with pens, coins, jewelry, etc. Children often need more intense input for the same sensory benefits of keeping awake and alert and being able to listen. The use of fidget tools supports self-regulation and can lead to immediate changes in attention and organization.

These tools can also be used to ease transitions, prepare for upcoming stressful events and contribute to a child's independence in maintaining self-regulation.

When children have fewer meltdowns, they feel better about themselves and their ability to be in control. Parents and teachers appreciate the chance to go to church, shopping malls or restaurants without worrying about tantrums or other disruptive behaviors. Waiting times and long car or bus rides may be made easier if the child can be happily fidgeting.

Often a basket or bin is kept handy at school or a fanny pack is used for outings. Items need to be changed frequently, as the sensory systems adapt and sensory diets are enriched by new sensory experiences.

Considerations for Classroom Use

- set clear rules about the use of the fidget tool
- keep tools in hand or on the lap, preferably at midline.
- use one tool at a time
- consider individual needs and interests
- include soundless tools
- incorporate repetitive, rhythmic actions
- include tools whose actions do not require vision
- include tools that have no goal or end product
- involve provision of resistance (proprioceptive input)
- consider the limited emotional appeal
- return all fidgets tools to the bag or basket. Consult with your occupational therapist for other ideas for mouth and tactile activities, all of which can be included in a fidget bag. Of course, if children are still putting things in their mouths, you'll need to screen the items for safety

What should go in a fidget bag? The child's sensory likes and dislikes should be considered as well as the sensory goals and specific sensory diet. A combination of mouth, tactile and small finger toys for manipulation is generally preferred. Highly visual toys are not recommended if the fidgets are for group time; they'll be too distracting for the other children. Here are some favorites:

- scrub brushes
- massager (spiky roller)
- stress balls or flour balloon
- therapy putty, silly putty or other "slime"
- hair elastics or rubber bands
- key ring
- bungee cord, rainbow loom, vanity bracelets
- jewelry (watch bands with Velcro closures, rings, (fidget necklaces)
- transformers or other tiny toys which have parts that move
- stretch toys
- koosh balls
- fabric swatches
- bendables (such as small rubber toys, certain hair curlers, pipe cleaners or twist ties)
- puzzles (such as a Rubic's cube)
- fidget for your digit, spin ring

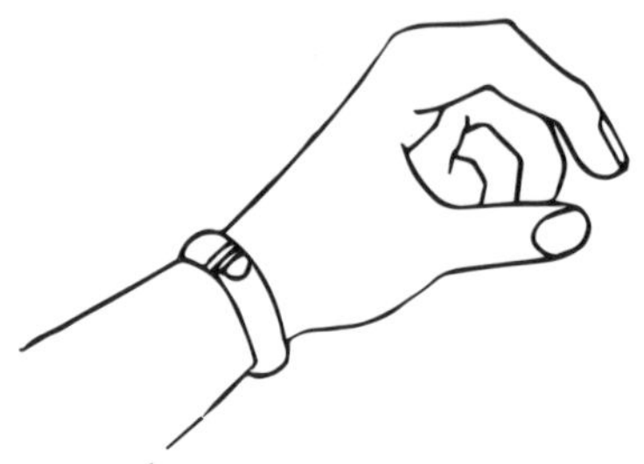

Equipment Suppliers

Canadian

Autism Awareness Centre

Book supplier and workshop organizer in Canada and the UK

Calgary Alberta Canada

www.autismawarenesscentre.com

FDMT

Therapy and educational supplier, manufacturer of therapeutic equipment

Quebec Canada

www.fdmt.ca

Flaghouse

Special needs equipment

235 Yorkland Blvd, Suite 300 North York, Ontario. Canada M2S 4Y8

www.flaghouse.ca

School Specialty Canada

Therapy and school supplies

www.schoolspecialty.ca

Spectrum Educational

Special education and therapy supplier

www.education.spectrum-nasco.ca

SticKids™

Software and activity kit that supplies user-friendly therapeutic strategies to support sensory processing, sensory integration and motor disorders, 2005

Cochrane Alberta

www.stickids.ca

International Equipment Suppliers

Flaghouse USA

www.flaghouse.com

1-800-743-7900

Mealtimes

A resource for oral-motor, feeding and mealtime programs

www.new-vis.com

ENASCO

Special education and therapy supplier

www.enasco.com/specialeducation

Fun and Function

Sensory equipment, toys

http://funandfunction.com

1-800-231-6329 or 1-215-876-8500

Lace and Fabric

Sensory swings, lycra sheets, lycra tunnels

www.laceandfabric.com

Limikids

Home gym equipment for kids. Indoor home playground for complex sports exercises.

www.limikids.com

PDP Products and Professional Development Programs

Courses and material on topics related to sensory integration. visual processing and integrated listening systems

www.pdppro.com

Sportime Abiliations

Also carries the School Specialty Line and manufactures sensory equipment

www.abilitations.com

Pocketful of Therapy, Inc.

Therapeutic toys, books and therapy supplies for children. Newsletter, Twitter, Facebook and blog.

www.pfot.com

732-462-4474

ShoeboxTasks

Educational Tools for Autistic Students, distributes and manufactures TEACCH work tasks

www.shoeboxtasks.com

Southpaw Enterprises

Professional equipment used in sensory integration treatment including many types of suspended equipment, sensory rooms, weighted and other fine and gross motor equipment, books and videos, toys and therapy supplies.

www.southpawenterprises.com

1-800-228-1698

Therapro Inc.

Toys and equipment used in sensory integration treatment and home and school programming; fine and gross motor activities.

www.therapro.com

1-508-872-9494

TFH Special Needs Toys UK, USA and Canada

Equipment company for use in sensory programs and environments

www.tfhuk.com or www.tfhusa.com

Websites:

American Occupational Therapy Assocation, Inc. (AOTA)
www.aota.org resources
Resources, journals, continuing education for OTs

Autism Speaks
www.autismspeaks.org
Resources for visuals

Cincinnati Children's Hospital Medical Center—Evidence Based Care
www.cincinnatichildrens.org/service/j/anderson-center/evidence-based-care/recommendations/specialty-discipline/

CSRI Canadian Self-Regulation Initiative
www.self-regulation.ca/#

Developmental Delay Directory Resources
www.devdelay.org
Resources on holistic and conventional treatment

Diana Henry Occupational Therapy Service
www.ateachabout.com
Handbooks, workshops. videos

Future Horizons
www.fhautim.com
Books, conferences, relating to special needs

Linda Hodgdon
www.usevisualstrategies.com/about-linda-hodgdon/
Speech-Language Pathologist, Visual Strategy Communication videos, books, workshops

OT Plan
www.otplan.com
Occupational Therapy Plan—an activity idea search engine for pediatric occupational therapy activities. Match skills you want to work on with materials you have.

OTA Waterton
www.otawatertown.com
Resources for OTs

Parentbooks
www.parentbooks.ca
Toronto bookstore that carries all special needs topics PDP

Paula Kluth
www.paulakluth.com
Inclusive classrooms and communities, books, blog, articles

Sensory Comfort
www.sensorycomfort.com
Wide-ranging links to many resources

Sensory Integration Global Network
www.siglobalnetwork.org
An organization committed to supporting research and disseminating information about the work of Dr. J. Ayres in sensory integration theory

Sensory Integration UK
www.sensoryintegration.co.uk

Sensory Processing Disorder Foundation
www.spdfoundation.net
The SPD Foundation is a world leader in research, education, and advocacy for Sensory Processing Disorder, a neurological condition that disrupts the daily lives of many children and adults.

Sensory World
www.sensoryworld.com
Books, DVDs, conferences, and *Sensory Focus* Magazine

Tasks Galore Publishing Inc.
www.tasksgalore.com
Book on structured teaching, independent work tasks, activities

TEACCH (Treatment and Education of Autistic and Related Communication Handicapped Children)
www.TEACCH.com
State-funded program in North Carolina, USA, with unique teaching strategies

Vital Links
www.vitallinks.net
Therapeutic Listening and Astronaut Training

Your Therapy Source
www.yourtherapysource.com
ebooks for pediatric therapy, social media (Blogs, Facebook and Pinterest)

Zero to Three
www.zerotothreee.org

Sensory-Friendly Clothing Websites

www.kozieclothes.com

www.nonetz.com

www.smartknitkids.com

www.softclothing.net

http://worldssoftest.com/thinSoftclothing.net

Recommended DVDs

Getting Kids in Sync DVD: Sensory-Motor Activities to Help Children Develop Body Awareness and Integrate Their Senses. DVD, Carol Kranowitz

Self-Regulation in Children: Keeping the Body, Mind & Emotions on Task. DVD, Theresa Garland

Sensory Processing Disorder: Practical Solutions that Work. DVD, Rodalyn Varney Whitney

OT for Children with Autism, DVD. Britt Collins

Sensory Issues in Learning & Behavior. DVD. Carol Kranowitz, (Updated and re-titled version of the DVD, "The Out-of-Sync Child.")

Sensory Strategies to Improve Communication, Social Skills and Behavior, DVD. Paula Aquilla

Tablet Applications

It is impossible to print an up-to-date list of current apps, as new are apps published daily. These are just a few OT favorites, used when working with individuals with Autism and sensory processing issues. For up-to-date listing of apps related to Autism, an app called Autism Apps is available that reviews new apps weekly.

Autism General

1. ASD Tools
2. First Then
3. Time Timer
4. First Then Board
5. Emotions
6. iFollowRoutine
7. ABA FlashCards
8. Daily Tasks
9. Autism Apps
10. Memory (PCS)
11. Autism iHelp (language concepts)
12. Bitsboard

Auditory Skills

1. Sounds of the House
2. Nature Scene
3. Nature Scapes
4. Podcasts
5. Alarm Clock HD Free

Music/Auditory Skills

1. Music Sparkle
2. Piano Free
3. Sounds of the House

Communication Skills

1. Bitsboard (can choose games based on themes to develop literacy etc.)

Executive Function

1. Flower Garden
2. What's Next
3. Your Fantastic Elastic Brain
4. Mirta the Super Fly Lite - Brainy Fables i

Sensory Diet/Self Regulation

1. Brain Works
2. Zones of Regulation

Breathing/Relax

1. Relax M.P. HD
2. Breathe, Think, Do with Sesame gallery
3. Breathing Zone $4
4. Duckie Deck Huff n' Puff (blow into microphone, bit hard)
5. Breathe2Relax – free (i/a)
6. Sleep Time- Alarm Clock (i/a)
7. Relax Melodies (i/a),
8. Breathe, Think, Do with Sesame
9. Mindshift

Print/Write/Type

1. Typing JR
2. PaperPort Notes
3. Audio Note
4. Letter School
5. Writing Wizard

Reference List

Books

Aud Sonders, S. (2003). *Giggle Time, Establishing the Social Connection: A Program to Develop Communication Skills of Children with Autism, Asperger Syndrome and PDD.* London: Jessica Kingsley Publishers.

Ayres, A.J. (1972). *Sensory Integration and Learning Disabilities.* Los Angeles: Western Psychological Services.

Ayres, A.J. (1979). *Sensory Integration and Learning Disabilities.* Los Angeles: Western Psychological Services.

Ayres, A.J. (1995). *Sensory Integration and Learning Disabilities.* Los Angeles: Western Psychological Services.

Bialer, D.S. & Miller, L.J. (2011). *No Longer a Secret: Unique Common Sense Strategies for Children with Sensory or Motor Challenges.* Arlington: Sensory World.

Biel, L. & Peske, N. (2005). *Raising a Sensory Smart Child.* New York: Penguin.

Blanche, E., Botticelli, T., & Hallaway, M. (1995). *Combining Neurodevelopmental Treatment and Sensory Integration Principles.* Tuscon: Therapy Skill Builders.

Bogdashina, O. (2003). *Sensory Perceptual Issues in Autism and Asperger Syndrome.* London: Jessica Kingsley Publishers.

Boon, M. (2001). *Helping Children with Dyspraxia.* London: Jessica Kingsley Publishers.

DeGangi, G. (2000). *Pediatric Disorders of Regulation in Affect and Behavior.* San Diego: Academic Press.

Dunn-Buron, K. & Curtis, M (2003). *The Incredible 5-Point Scale.* Shawnee Mission, KS:AAPC.

Grandin, T. & Scariano. (1986). *Emergence: Labeled Autistic.* Novato: Arena Press.

Grandin, T. (1996) *Thinking in Pictures: and Other Reports from My Life with Autism.* New York: Vintage Books.

Goddard-Blythe, S. (2011). *The Genius of Natural Childhood.* Gloucestershire: Hawthorn Press.

Hannaford, C. (2005). *Smart Moves: Why Learning Is Not All In Your Head.* Second Edition. Salt Lake City: Great River Books.

Heller, S. (2002). *Too Loud Too Bright Too Fast Too Tight: What to Do if You are Sensory Defensive in an Over-Stimulating World.* New York: Harper Collins Publishers.

Higashida, N., & Mitchel, D. (2013). *The Reason I Jump: The Inner Voice of a Thirteen-Year-Old Boy with Autism.* United States of America: Alfred A. Knopf Canada.

Kawar, M., Frick, S. & Frick, R. (2000). *Astronaut Training: A Sound Activated Vestibular-Visual Protocol.* PDP Products.

Kranowitz, C. (1998) *The Out -of-Sync Child.* New York: Perigee.

Kranowitz, C. (2000). *Answers to Questions Teachers Ask about Sensory Integration.* Las Vegas: Sensory Resources.

Kranowitz, C. (2004). *The Out of Sync Child has Fun: Activities for Kids with Sensory Integration Dysfunction.* Las Vegas: Sensory Resources.

Kuypers, L. (2011) *The Zones of Regulation: A Curriculum Designed to Foster Self-Regulation and Emotional Control.* San Jose, California: Social Thinking Publishing.

Kurtz, L. (2008). *Understanding Motor Skills in Children with Dyspraxia, ADHD, Autism, and Other Learning Disabilities.* London: Jessica Kingsley Publishers.

Lane, K.A. (2005). *Developing Ocular Motor and Visual Perceptual Skills: An Activity Workbook.* Thorofare: SLACK Incorporated.

Lashno, M. (2010). *Mixed Signals. Understanding and Treating Your Child's Sensory Processing Issues.* Maryland: Woodbine House.

Leary, M.R. & Donnellan, A.M., (2012). *Autism: Sensory-Movement Differences and Diversity.* Cambridge: Cambridge Book Review Press.

Moyes, R. (2010). *Building Sensory Friendly Classrooms: To Support Children with Challenging Behaviors.* Arlington: Sensory World.

Mukhopadhyay, T.J. (2008). *How Can I Talk if My Lips Don't Move?: Inside My Autistic Mind.* New York: Arcade Publishing.

Oetter, P., Richter, E. & Frick, S. (1988). *M.O.R.E.: Integrating the Mouth with Sensory and Postural Functions.* Hugo: PDP Press.

Ostovar, R. (2009). *The Ultimate Guide to Sensory Processing Disorder. Easy, Everyday Solutions to Sensory Challenges.* Arlington: Sensory World.

Platt, G. (2011). *Beating Dyspraxia: with a Hop, Skip and a Jump.* London: Jessica Kingsley Publishers.

Ratey, J. (2008). *Spark: The Revolutionary New Science of Exercise.* New York: Little Brown.

Reaven, J., et al. (2011). *Facing Your Fears.* Baltimore, Maryland: Paul H. Brookes Pub. Co.

Rotz, R. & Wright, S., D. (2005). *Fidget to Focus: Outwit Your Boredom: Sensory Strategies for Living with ADD.* Bloomington: iUniverse.

Sangirardi Ganz, J. (2005). *Including SI for Parents Sensory Integration Strategies at Home and School.* Prospect: Biographical Publishing Company.

Shanker, S. (2013). *Calm, Alert, and Learning: Classroom Strategies for Self-Regulation.* Don Mills: Pearson Canada Inc.

Smith, K. and Gouze, K. (2004). *The Sensory Sensitive Child: Practical Solutions for Out-of-Bounds Behavior.* New York: Harper Collins Publishers.

Smith Myles, B., Tapscott Cook, K., Miller, N., Rinner, L. & Robbins, L. (2000). *Asperger Syndrome and Sensory Issues: Practical Solutions for Making Sense of the World.* Shawnee Mission: Autism Asperger Publishing Co.

Smith Roley, S., Imperatore Blanche, E. & Schaaf. R. (2001). *Understanding the Nature of Sensory Integration with Diverse Populations.* Tucson: Therapy Skill Builders.

Wieder, S. & Wachs, H. (2012). *Visual/Spatial Portals of Thinking, Feeling and Movement: Advancing Competencies and Emotional Development in Children with Learning and Autism Spectrum Disorders.* Mendham: Profectum Foundation.

Williams, D. (1992). *Nobody Nowhere: The Extraordinary Biography of an Autistic.* Toronto: Doubleday Canada.

Wilbarger, P. & Wilbarger, J. (1991) *Sensory Defensiveness in Children Aged 2-12: An Intervention Guide for Parents and Other Caretakers.* Stillwater: PDP Press.

Williams, M. & Shellenberger, S. (1994) *"How Does Your Engine Run?": A Leader's Guide to the Alert Program for Self-Regulation.* Stillwater: PDP Press.

Williams, M. & Shellenberger, S. (2001). *Staying Alert at Home and School.* Albuquerque: Therapy Works Inc.

Williamson, G. & Anzalone, M. (2001). *Sensory Integration and Self-Regulation in Infants and Toddlers: Helping Very Young Children Interact with Their Environment.* Arlington: Zero to Three.

Yack, E., Sutton, S. & Aquilla, P. (1998) *Building Bridges Through Sensory Integration: Occupational Therapy for Children with Autism/PDD.* Toronto: Print Three.

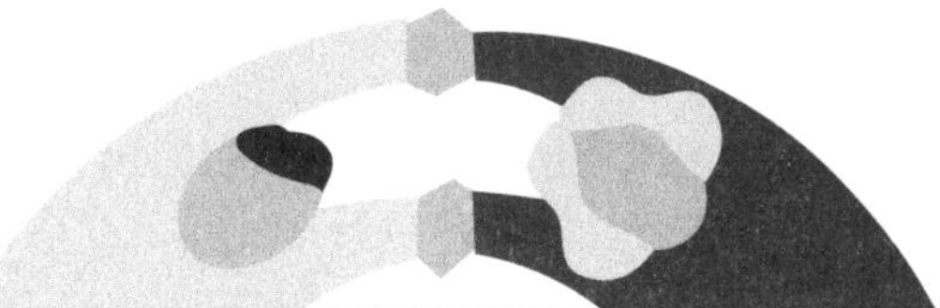

REFERENCES

Books

Alderson, J. (2011). *Challenging the Myths of Autism.* Toronto, Ontario: Collins.

American Psychiatric Association. (2013). *Diagnositic and Statistical Manual* (5th Edition). Washington, DC: APA.

Aron, E. (2002). *The Highly Sensitive Child.* New York: Broadway Books.

Aspy, R. & Grossman, B. (2007). *The Ziggurat Model: A Framwork for Designing Comprehensive Interventions for Individuals with High-Functioning Autism and Asperger Syndrome.* Shawnee Mission, Kansas: Autism Asperger Publishing Company.

Auer, C (2006). *Parenting a Child with Sensory Processing Disorder.* Oakland, CA: New Harbinger Pub.

Aud Sonders, S. (2003). Giggle Time, *Establishing the Social Connection: A Program to Develop Communication Skills of Children with Autism, Asperger Syndrome and PDD.* London: Jessica Kingsley Publishers.

Ayres, A.J. (1972). *Sensory Integration and Learning Disabilities.* Los Angeles: Western Psychological Services.

Ayres, A.J. (1979). *Sensory Integration and Learning Disabilities.* Los Angeles: Western Psychological Services.

Ayres, A.J. (1995). *Sensory Integration and Learning Disabilities.* Los Angeles: Western Psychological Services.

Bialer, D.S. & Miller, L.J. (2011). *No Longer a Secret: Unique Common Sense Strategies for Children with Sensory or Motor Challenges.* Arlington: Sensory World.

Biel, L. & Peske, N. (2005). *Raising a Sensory Smart Child.* New York: Penguin.

Blackman, L. (1999). *Lucy's Story: Autism and Other Adventures.* London: Jessica Kingsley Publishers.

Blanche, E., Botticelli, T., & Hallaway, M. (1995). *Combining Neurodevelopmental Treatment and Sensory Integration Principles.* Tuscon: Therapy Skill Builders.

Bogdashina, O. (2003). *Sensory Perceptual Issues in Autism and Asperger Syndrome.* London: Jessica Kingsley Publishers.

Boon, M. (2001). *Helping Children with Dyspraxia.* London: Jessica Kingsley Publishers.

Bundy, A., Lane, S. & Murray, E. (2002). *Sensory Integration Theory and Practice.* Philadelphia: F. A. Davis Co.

Caldwell, P. (2008). *Using Intensive Interaction and Sensory Integration: A Handbook for Those Who Support People with Severe Autistic Disorder.* London: Jessica Kingsley Publishers.

Connell, G. & McCarthy, C. (2014). *A Moving Child is Learning Child: How the Body Teaches the Brain to Think.* Minneapolis, MN: Free Spirit Publishing.

Culp, S. (2011). *A Buffer of Sensory Interventions: Solutions for Middle and High School Students with Autism Spectrum Disorders.* Shawnee Mission, Kansas: AAPC Publshing.

DeGangi, G. (2000). *Pediatric Disorders of Regulation in Affect and Behavior.* San Diego: Academic Press.

Dunn-Buron, K. & Curtis, M (2003). *The Incredible 5-Point Scale.* Shawnee Mission, KS:AAPC.

Elder Robinson, J. (2011). *My Adventures with Asperger's and My Advice for Fellow Aspergians, Misfits, Families, and Teachers.* Toronto, Ontario: Anchor Canada.

Fleishmann, C. (2012). *Carly's Voice: Breaking Through Autism.* New York: Touchstone Books.

Frick, S. & Kawar, M. (2005). *Core Concepts in Action.* Madison, WI: Vital Links.

Frick, S., Kawar, M. & Young, S. (2006). *Listening with the Whole Body.* Madison, WI: Vital Links.

Frick, S. & Young, S. (2009). *Listening with the Whole Body: Clinical Concepts and Treatment Guidelines for Therapeutic Listening.* Madison, Wisconsin: Vital Links.

Gans, J.S., (2005). *Including SI for Parents: Sensory Integration Strategies at Home and School.* Prospect, Connecticut: Biographical Publshing Company.

Garland, T. (2014). *Self-Regulation Intervention and Strategies: Keeping the Body, Mind & Emotions on Task in Children with Autism, ADHD or Sensory Disorders.* Wisconsin: PESI Publishing and Media.

Grandin, T. & Scariano, M. (1986). *Emergence: Labeled Autistic.* Novato: Arena Press.

Grandin, T. (1996) *Thinking in Pictures: and Other Reports from My Life with Autism.* New York: Vintage Books.

Goddard-Blythe, S. (2011). *The Genius of Natural Childhood.* Gloucestershire: Hawthorn Press.

Greenspan, S. & Wieder, S. (1998) *The Child with Special Needs: Encouraging Intellectual and Emotional Growth.* Reading. Mass:Addison-Wesley

Greenspan, S. & Wieder, S. (2006). *Engaging Autism.* Cambridge, MA: Da Capo Lifelong Books.

Greenspan, S. & Tippy, G. (2011). *Respecting Autsim: The Rebecca School DIR Casebook for Parents and Professionals.* New York, NY: Vantage Press.

Hannaford, C. (2005). *Smart Moves: Why Learning Is Not All in Your Head.* Second Edition. Salt Lake City: Great River Books.

Heller, S. (2002). *Too Loud Too Bright Too Fast Too Tight: What to Do if You Are Sensory Defensive in an Over-Stimulating World.* New York: Harper Collins Publishers.

Higashida, N., & Mitchel, D. (2013). *The Reason I Jump: The Inner Voice of a Thirteen-Year-Old Boy with Autism.* United States of America: Alfred A. Knopf Canada.

Huebner, R. (2001). *Autism: A Sensorimotor Approach to Management.* Gaithersburg, Maryland: Aspen Publishers Inc.

Hyche, K. & Maertz, V. (2014). *Classroom Strategies for Children with ADHD, Autism & Sensory Processing Disorders: Solutions for Behavior, Attention and Emotional Regulation.* Eau Claire, WI: PESI Publishing and Media.

Kashman, N. & Mora, J. (2005). *The Sensory Connection: An OT and SLP Team Approach.* Las Vegas, Nevada: Sensory Resources.

Kawar, M., Frick, S. & Frick, R. (2000). *Astronaut Training: A Sound Activated Vestibular-Visual Protocol.* PDP Products.

Kluth, P. (2009). *The Autism Checklist: A Practical Reference for Parents and Teachers.* San Francisco, CA: Jossey-Bass.

Kranowitz, C. (1998) *The Out-of-Sync Child.* New York: Perigee.

Kranwowitz, C. (2000). *Answers to Questions Teachers Ask about Sensory Integration.* Las Vegas: Sensory Resources.

Kranowitz, C. (2004). *The Out of Sync Child has Fun: Activities for Kids with Sensory Integration Dysfunction.* Las Vegas: Sensory Resources.

REFERENCES

Kuypers, L. (2011) *The Zones of Regulation: A Curriculum Designed to Foster Self-Regulation and Emotional Control.* San Jose, California: Social Thinking Publishing.

Kurtz, L. (2008). *Understanding Motor Skills in Children with Dyspraxia, ADHD, Autism, and Other Learning Disabilities.* London: Jessica Kingsley Publishers.

Lane, K.A. (2005). *Developing Ocular Motor and Visual Perceptual Skills: An Activity Workbook.* Thorofare: SLACK Incorporated.

Lashno, M. (2010). *Mixed Signals: Understanding and Treating Your Child's Sensory Processing Issues.* Maryland: Woodbine House.

Lears, L. (1998). *Ian's Walk: A Story about Autism.* Chicago, IL: Albert Whitman & Co.

Leary, M., R. & Donnellan, A. M., (2012). *Autism: Sensory-Movement Differences and Diversity.* Cambridge: Cambridge Book Review Press.

Mauro, T. (2006). *The Everything Parent's Guide to Sensory Integration Disorder.* Avon: F+W Inc.

Miller-Kuhaneck, H. (2004). *Autism: A Comprehensive Occupational Therapy Approach.* Bethesda, Maryland: AOTA Inc.

Miller, L.J. (2006). *Sensational Kids: Hope and Help for Children with Sensory Processing Disorder.* New York: G.P. Putnam's Sons.

Moor, J. (2008). *Playing, Laughing and Learning with Children on the Autism Spectrum: A Practical Resouce of Play Ideas for Parents and Carers.* London, England: Jessica Kingsley Publishers.

Moyes, R. (2010). *Building Sensory Friendly Classrooms to Support Children with Challenging Behaviors.* Arlington, Texas: Sensory World.

Mucklow, N. (2008). *The Sensory Team Handbook.* Kingston, Ontario: Michael Grass House.

Mukhopadhyay, T. (2003). *The Mind Tree.* New York, NY: Arcade.

Mukhopadhyay, T. J. (2008). *How Can I Talk if My Lips Don't Move?: Inside My Autistic Mind.* New York: Arcade Publishing.

Murray-Slutsky, C. & Paris, B. (2005). *Is It Sensory or Behavior.* San Antonio, TX: PsychCorp.

Oetter, P., Richter, E. & Frick, S. (1988). *M.O.R.E.: Integrating the Mouth with Sensory and Postural Functions.* Hugo: PDP Press.

Ostovar, R. (2009). *The Ultimate Guide to Sensory Processing Disorder.* Arlington: Sensory World.

Peete Robinson, H. (2010). *My Brother Charlie.* Danbury, CT: Scholastic Books.

Platt, G. (2011). *Beating Dyspraxia: With a Hop, Skip and a Jump.* London: Jessica Kingsley Publishers.

Prizant, B., Wetherby, A., Rubin, E., Rydell, P., & Laurent, C. (2006). *The SCERTS Model: A Comprehensive Educational Approach for Children with ASD.* Baltimore: Brookes.

Ratey, J. (2008). *Spark: The Revolutionary New Science of Exercise.* New York: Little Brown.

Reaven, J. et al. (2011). *Facing Your Fears.* Baltimore, Maryland: Paul H. Brookes Pub. Co.

Rogers, S. & Dawson, G. (2010) *Early Start Denver Model for Young Children with Autism: Promoting Language, Learning and Engagement.* New York, New York: The Guilford Press.

Rotz, R. & Wright, S.D. (2005). *Fidget to Focus: Outwit Your Boredom: Sensory Strategies for Living with ADD.* Bloomington: Universe.

Sangirardi Ganz, J. (2005). *Including SI for Parents Sensory Integration Strategies at Home and School.* Prospect: Biographical Publishing Company.

Shanker, S. (2013). *Calm, Alert, and Learning: Classroom Strategies for Self-Regulation.* Don Mills: Pearson Canada Inc.

Shapiro, O. (2009). *Autism and Me: Sibling Stories.* Chicago, IL: Albert Whitman & Co.

Sicile-Kira, C. & Sicile-Kira J. (2012). *A Full Life with Autism: From Learning to Forming Relationships to Achieving Independence.* New York, NY: Palgrave Macmillan

Smith, K. & Gouze, K. (2004). *The Sensory Sensitive Child: Practical Solutions for Out-of-Bounds Behaviour.* New York: Harper Collins Publishers.

Smith Myles, B., Tapscott Cook, K., Miller, N., Rinner, L. & Robbins, L. (2000). *Asperger Syndrome and Sensory Issues: Practical Solutions for Making Sense of the World.* Shawnee Mission: Autism Asperger Publishing Co.

Smith Roley, S., Imperatore Blanche, E. & Schaaf. R. (2001). *Understanding the Nature of Sensory Integration with Diverse Populations.* Tuscon: Therapy Skill Builders.

Tourville, A. (2010). *My Friend Has Autism.* Mankato, MN: Capstone Press.

Wieder, S., & Wachs, H. (2012). *Visual/Spatial Portals of Thinking, Feeling and Movement: Advancing Competencies and Emotional Development in Children with Learning and Autism Spectrum Disorders.* Mendham: Profectum Foundation.

Willey, L.H. (1999). *Pretending to be Normal.* London: Jessica Kingsley Publishers

Williams, D. (1992). *Nobody Nowhere: The Extraordinary Biography of an Autistic.* Toronto: Doubleday Canada.

Williams, D. (1999). *Somebody Somewhere: Breaking Free from the World of Autism.* London, England: Jessica Kingsley Publishers.

Williams, D. (1999). *Autism and Sensing: The Unlost Instinct.* London, England: Jessica Kingsley Publishers.

Wilbarger, P. & Wilbarger, J. (1991) *Sensory Defensiveness in Children Aged 2-12: An Intervention Guide for Parents and Other Caretakers.* Stillwater: PDP Press.

Williams, M. & Shellenberger, S. (1994) *"How Does Your Engine Run?": A Leader's Guide to The Alert Program for Self-Regulation.* Stillwater: PDP Press.

Williams, M. & Shellenberger, S. (2001). *Staying Alert at Home and School.* Albuquerque: Therapy Works Inc.

Williamson, G. & Anzalone, M. (2001). *Sensory Integration and Self-Regulation in Infants and Toddlers: Helping Very Young Children Interact with Their Environment.* Arlington: Zero to Three.

Books for Children

Griffin, M. (2010). *Picky, Picky Pete.* Arlington, TX: Sensory World.

Harding, J. (2011). *Ellie Bean the Drama Queen.* Arlington, TX: Sensory World.

Kranowitz, C. (2004). *The Goodenoughs Get in Sync.* Las Vegas, NV: Sensory Resources.

Laird, C. (2009) *I'm Not Weird, I Have SPD.* Denver, CO: Outskirts.

Lynch, C. (2012). *Totally Chill: My Complete Guide to Staying Cool.* Shawnee Mission, KS: AAPC.

Roth-Fisch, M. (2009). *Sensitive Sam.* Arlington, TX: Sensory World.

Steiner, H. (2012). *This is Gabriel Making Sense of School.* Arlington, TX: Sensory World.

Veenendall, J. (2008). *Arnie and His School Tools: Simple Sensory Solutions That Build Success.* Shawnee Mission, KS: AAPC.

Veenendall, J. (2009). *Why Does Izzy Cover Her Ears? Dealing with Sensory Overload.* Shawnee Mission, KS: AAPC.

Wilson, L. F. (2009). *Squirmy Wormy.* Arlington, TX: Sensory World

Reference Articles

Baltazar, A. (2004). Writing social stories for the child with sensory integration dysfunction: An introductory resource and guide for therapists, teachers and parents. *SISIS*, 27, 1, 1-4.

Bhat, A., Landa, R. & Galloway, C. (2011). Current perspectives on motor functioning in infants, children and adults with Autism Spectrum Disorders, *Physical Therapy*, 91, 1-14.

Bloomer, M. & Rose, C. (1989). Frames of reference: guiding treatment for children with autism. *Developmental Disabilities: A Handbook for Occupational Therapists*, 12-26.

Case-Smith, J. & Arbesman, B. (2008). Evidence-based review of interventions for autism used in or of relevance to occupational therapy. *American Journal of Occupational Therapy*, 62(4), 416-429.

Cohn, E. (2001). Parent perspectives of occupational therapy using a sensory integration approach. *AJOT*, 55, 285-293.

Cool, S. (1990, Dec.). Use of a surgical brush in treatment of sensory defensiveness: Commentary and exploration. *Sensory Integration Special Interest Newsletter.* 4-6.

Dunn, W., Smith Myles, B. & Orr, W. (2002). Sensory processing issues associated with Asperger Syndrome: A preliminary investigation. *American Journal of Occupational Therapy.* 56(1), 97-102.

Dunn, W., Saiter, J. & Rinner, L. (2002). Asperger Syndrome and sensory processing: a conceptual model and guidance for intervention planning. *Focus on Autism and Other Developmental Disabilities.*

Duzik, M. et al. (2007). Dyspraxia in autism: association with motor, social, and communicative deficits. *Developmental Medicine & Child Neurology.* 49, 734-739.

Freret Schoener, R. et al. (2008). You can know me now if you listen: sensory, motor and communication issues in a non-verbal person with autism. *AJOT*, 62, 5, 547-553.

Gal, E., Ben Meir, A. & Katz, N. (2013). Development and reliability of the autism work skills questionnaire (AWSQ). *AJOT*, 67, 61-65.

Gowan, E. & Hamilton, A. (2012). Motor abilities in autism: A review using a computational context. *Journal of Autism and Developmental Disorders*, eScholarID:164739 | PMID:22723127 | DOI:10.1007/s10803-012-1574-0

Law, M. (2006). Autism Spectrum Disorders and Occupational Therapy, CAOT Briefing to the Senate Standing Committee on Social Affairs, Science and Technology. Canadian Association of Occupational Therapists.

Miller, L.J. & Lane, S. (2000). Toward a consensus in terminology in sensory integration theory and practice. Part 1 and 2, *Sensory Integration Special Interest Section Quarterly.*

Parham et al. (2007). Fidelity in sensory integration intervention research. *AJOT*, 61, 216-227.

Talay-Ongan, A. & Wood, K. (2000). Unusual sensory sensitivities in autism: a possible crossroads. *International Journal of Disability, Development and Education*, 47, 2, 201-211.

Research Articles

Ashburner, J. et al (2008). Sensory Processing and classroom emotional, behavioral, and educational outcomes in children with autism spectrum disorders., *AJOT*, 62,5, 564-573.

Ahn, R., Miller, L.J. & McIntosh, D (2004). Prevalence of parent's perceptions of sensory processing disorders among kindergarten children. *AJOT*, 56, 287-302.

Ayres, A. J. & Tickle, L. (1980). Hyper-responsivity to touch and vestibular stimuli as a predictor of positive response to sensory integration procedures by autistic children. *AJOT*, 34, 375-381.

Ayres, A.J. & Mailloux, Z. (1983). Possible pubertal effect on therapeutic gains in an autistic girl. *American Journal of Occupational Therapy*, 34, 375-381.

Bagatell et al. (2010). Effectiveness of therapy ball chairs on classroom participation in children with autism spectrum disorders. *AJOT*, 64, 895-903.

Baranek, G. & Berkson, G. (1994). Tactile defensiveness in children with developmental disabilities: responsiveness and habituation. *Journal of Autism and Developmental Disorders*. Vol. 24, No. 4, 457-472.

Baranek, et al. (2002). Sensory processing correlates of occupational performance in children with Fragile X syndrome: Preliminary findings. *AJOT*, 63, 538-546.

Baranek, G., Boyd, B., Pe, M., David, F. & Watson, L. (2007). Hyperresponsive sensory patterns in young children with autism, developmental delay, and typical development. *American Jounal of Mental Retardation*, 112, 233-245.

Ben-Sasson et al. (2007). Extreme sensory modulation behaviors in toddlers with Autism Spectrum Disorders, *AJOT*, 61-5, 584-592.

Bundy, A. (2007). How does sensory processing affect play? *AJOT*, 61, 2, 2001-207.

Case-Smith, J. & Bryan, T. (1999). The effects of occupational therapy with sensory integration emphasis on preschool-age children with autism. *American Journal of Occupational Therapy*. 33, 489-497.

Cohn, E, Miller, L.J., & Tickle-Degnen, L. (2000). Parental hopes for therapy outcomes: Children with sensory modulation disorder. *AJOT*, 54, 36-43.

Collins, A. & Dworkin, R. (2011). Pilot study of the effect of weighted vests. *AJOT*, 65, 688-694.

Dickie, V. et al. (2009). Parent reports of sensory experiences of preschool children with and without autism: A qualitative study. *AJOT*, 63, 2, 172-181.

Dunn, W. & Bennet D. (2002). Patterns of sensory processing in children with attention deficit hyperactivity disorder. *Occupational Therapy Journal of Research*, 22, 4-15.

Dunn, W., Smith Myles, B. & Orr, W. (2002). Sensory processing issues associated with Asperger Syndrome: A preliminary investigation. *American Journal of Occupational Therapy*. 56(1), 97-102.

Dunn, W., Saiter, J. & Rinner, L. (2002). Asperger Syndrome and sensory processing: A conceptual model and guidance for intervention planning. *Focus on Autism and Other Developmental Disabilities*. 17(3). 172-185.

Fertel-Daly, D., Bedell, G., Hinjosa, J. (2001). The effects of a weighted vest on attention to task and self-stimulatory behaviors in preschoolers with pervasive developmental disorders. *AJOT*, November/December, 629-640.

Goin-Kochel, R., MacIntosh, V & Myers, B. (2009). Parental reports of the efficacy of treatments and therapies for their children with autism spectrum disorders. *Research in Autism Spectrum Disorders*, 3(2), 528-537.

Green, V., Pituch, K., Itchon, J., Choi, A. O'Reilly, M. & Sigafoos, J. (2006). Internet survey of treatments used by parents of children with autism. *Research in Developmental Disabilities*, 27(1). 70-84.

Hilton, C., Graver. K., & LaVesser, P. (2007). Relationship between social competence and sensory processing in children with high functioning autism spectrum disorders. *Research in Autism Spectrum Disorders*, 1, 164- 173.

Hilton, C., et al. (2010). Sensory responsiveness as a predictor of social severity in children with high functioning autism spectrum disorders (HFASD). *Research in Autism Spectrum Disorders*, 4(4), 746-754.

Koizel, L., Budding, D., & Chidekel, D. (2011). Sensory integration: Sensory processing, and sensory modulation disorder: Putative functional neuroanatomic underpinnings. *Cerebellum*, DOI, 10.1007.

Inamura, K. N., Wiss, T. & Parham, D. (1990). The effects of hug machine usage on the behavioral organization of children with autism and autistic-like characteristics. Part I. *Sensory Integration Quarterly*, XVII.

Inamura, K.N., Wiss, T. & Parham. D. (1990). The effects of hug machine usage on the behavioral organization of children with autism and autistic-like characteristics. Part 2. *Sensory Integration Quarterly*, XVIII.

Iwasaki, K. & Holm. M. (1989). Sensory treatment for the reduction of stereotypic behaviors in person with severe multiple disabilities. *Occupational Therapy Journal Of Research*, 9, 170-183.

Kientz, M. & Dunn, W. (1997). A comparison of children with autism and typical children using the Sensory Profile. *American Journal of Occupational Therapy*, 51, 530-537.

Lane, A.E. et al. (2010). Sensory processing subtypes in autism: Association with adaptive behavior. *Journal of Autism and Developmental Disorders*, 40(1), 112-122.

Mailloux, et al. (2011). Verification and clarification of patterns of sensory integrative dysfunction. *AJOT*, 65, 143-151.

McIntosh, D., Miller, L.J., Shyu, V. & Hagerman, R. (1999). Sensory modulation disruption, electrodermal responses, and functional behaviors. *Developmental Medicine & Child Neurology*, 41, 608-615.

Miller, L.J., Coll, J.R. & Schoen, S. (2007). A randomized controlled pilot study of the effectiveness of occupational therapy for children with sensory modulation disorder. *AJOT*, 61(2), 228-238.

Miller, L.J., Schoen, S., James, K. & Scaaf, R. (2007). Lessons learned: A pilot study on occupational therapy effectiveness for children with sensory modulation disorder. *AJOT*, 61,161-169.

Miller-Kuhanek, Henry, D., Glennon, T. & Mu, K. (2007). Development of the sensory processing measure-school: initial studies of reliability and validity. *AJOT*, 61,170-175.ckc./

Owen, J., Marco, E., Desai, S., Fourie, E., Harris, J., Hill, S., Arnett, A. & Mukherjee, P. (2013). Abnormal white matter microstructure in children with sensory processing disorders. *NeuroImage: Clinical* 2, 844-853.

Parham et al. (2011). Development of a fidelity measure for research on the effectiveness of the Ayres Sensory Integration® intervention. *AJOT*, 65, 133-142.

Pfeiffer, B. et al. (2008). Effectiveness of disc'o'sit cushions on attention to task in second-grade students with attention difficulties. *AJOT*, 62,3,274-281.

Pfeiffer, B. et al. (2005). Sensory modulation and affective disorders in children and adolescents with Asperger's Disorder, *AJOT*, 59,3. 335-345.

Parham, L., Cohn, E., Spitzer, S., Koomar, J., Miller, L.J., Burke, J., et al. (2007). Fidelity in sensory integration intervention research. *AJOT*, 61, 216-227.

Pfeiffer, B., Koeneg, K., Kinnealey, M., Sheppard, M. & Henderson, L. (2011). Effectiveness of sensory integration interventions in children with autism spectrum disorders: A pilot study. *AJOT*, 65-1, 76-85.

Polatajko, H. & Cantin, N. (2010). Exploring the effectiveness of occupational therapy interventions, other than the sensory integration approach, with children and adolescents experiencing difficulty processing and integrating sensory information, *AJOT*, 64:415-429.

Schaaf, R., Miller, L.J., Seawell, D. & O'Keefe, S. (2003). Children with disturbances in sensory processing: A pilot study examining the role of the parasympathetic nervous system. *AJOT*, 57, 442.

Schaaf, R. and McKeon Nightlinger, K. (2007). Occupational therapy using a sensory integrative approach: A case study of effectiveness. *American Journal of Occupational Therapy*, 6.

Schaff, R. C., et al. (2011). The everyday routines of families of children with autism examining the impact of sensory processing difficulties on the family. *Autism*, 15(3), 373-389.

Schaaf, R. (2011). Interventions that address sensory dysfunction for individuals with autism spectrum disorders: Preliminary evidence for the superiority of sensory integration compared to other sensory approaches. In E. P. Reichow, D. V.Cicchetti, & F.R. Volkmar (Eds). *Evidence-Based Practices and Treatments for Children with Autism*. New York: Springer Sciences + Business Media.

Schaff, R., C. et al. (2012a). Occupational therapy and sensory integration for children with autism: a feasibility, safety, acceptability and fidelity study. *Autism: The International Journal of Research and Practice*, Doi:10.1177/1362361311435157.

Schaaf, R. & Imperatore Blanche, E. (2012). Emerging as leaders in autism research and practice: using the data-driven intervention process. *American Journal of Occupational Therapy*, 66,503-505.

Schaaf, R., Hunt, J. & Benevides, T. (2012). Occupational therapy using sensory integration to improve participation of a child with autism: A case report. *American Journal of Occupational Therapy*, 66, 5, 547-555.

Schaaf, R., Benevides, T., Maillouz, Z., Faller, P., Hunt, J., van Hooydonk, E., Freeman, R., Leiby, B., Sendecki, J. & Kelly, D. (2013). An intervention for sensory difficulties in children with autism: A randomized trial. *Journal of Autism and Developmental Disorders*, DOI.1007/s10803-013-1983-8.

Schilling, D., Washington, K., Billingsley, F., & Deitz, J. (2003) Classroom seating for children with attention deficit hyperactivity disorder: Therapy balls versus chairs. *AJOT*, 57, 534-541.

Schilling, D. & Schwartz, I. (2004). Alternative seating for young children with autism spectrum disorder: Effects of classroom behavior. *Journal of Autism and Developmental Disorders*, 34, 423-432.

Schoen, S., Miller, L.J. & Green, K. (2008). Pilot study of the sensory over-responsivity scales: assessment and inventory. *AJOT*, 62, 393- 406.

Schoen, S., Miller, L., Brett-Green, B. & Nielsen, D. (2009). Physiological and behavioiural differences in sensory processing: a comparison of children with ASD and AMD. *Frontiers in Integrative Neuroscience*. 3, 1-11.

Shields Bagby, M., Dickie, V. & Baranek, G. (2012). How sensory ecperiences of children with and without autism affect family occupations. *AJOT*, 66, 1, 78-86.

Silva, L. & Schalock, M. (2012). Sense and self-regulation checklist, a measure of comorbid autism symptoms: Initial psychometric evidence. *AJOT*, 66, 2, 177-186.

Sinclair, S., Press, B., Koenig, K. & Kinnealey, M. (2005). Effects of sensory integration intervention on self-stimulating and self-injurious behaviors. *AJOT*, 59(4), 418-425.

Smith Roley, S., Mailloux, A., Parham, D., Schaaf, R. Lane, C. & Cermak, S. (2104). Sensory integration and praxis patterns in children. *AJOT*, 69 (1),

Umeda, C. & Dietz, J. (2011). Effects of therapy cushions on classroom behaviours on children with autism spectrum disorder. *AJOT*, 65, 2-159.

VandenBerg, N. (2001) The use of a weighted vest to increase on-task behavior in children with attention difficulties, *AJOT*, November/ December 621-628

Watling, R. & Deitz, J. (2007). Immediate effect of Ayres's sensory integration based occupational therapy intervention on children with autism spectrum disorders. *AJOT*, 67, 574-583.

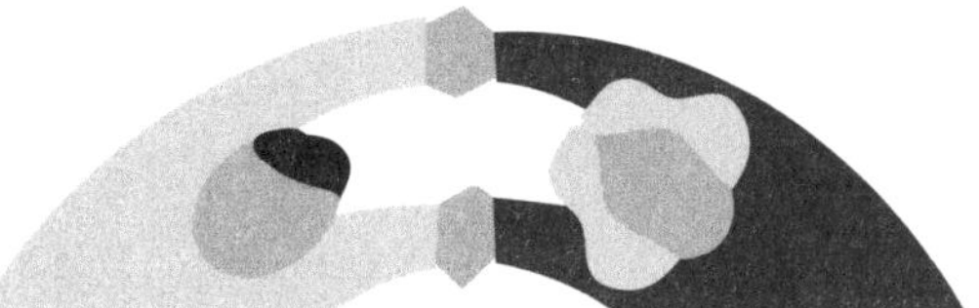

ABOUT THE AUTHORS

Ellen Yack, MEd, BSc, OT

Ellen Yack has practiced as an occupational therapist since 1979 and has a Masters Degree in Education. She is the Director of Ellen Yack and Associates, a private agency providing occupational therapy and speech therapy services to children and adolescents and their families. Her areas of expertise include sensory integration, autism spectrum disorders, self-regulation and motor development. Ellen conducts a variety of workshops and presentations for parents and professionals and has published in her field. Ellen provides a variety of consultation services to individuals and organizations. She was the occupational therapy consultant at the Geneva Centre for Autism for 15 years and currently consults for the autism programs at the Toronto District Catholic School Board and Aisling Discoveries Child and Family Centre. Ellen also works with adults with sensory processing challenges and consults for the Redpath Centre for Social and Emotional Development. Ellen lives in Toronto with her husband Irv Marks and their children Lia, Michael and Robbie.

Paula Aquilla, BSc, OT, DOMP

Paula Aquilla lives in Toronto with her husband Mark and daughters Katie and Ella. Paula is an occupational therapist (since 1986) and an osteopathic manual practitioner (since 2011). She works with adults and children in clinical, educational, home, and community- based settings. She founded the YES I CAN! INTEGRATED NURSERY SCHOOL, YES I CAN! SUMMER CAMP and the I LOVE MY BABY PROGRAM in Toronto and served as the director for six years. Paula was also the founding executive director of GIANT STEPS, a private school for children with autism, at the Toronto location. She runs a private practice serving children with special needs and their families. Paula has given many workshops on the use of sensory integration internationally She created the occupational therapy program at Aptus Treatment Centers where she continues to consult. Her practice is an approved placement for students from the University of Toronto's occupational therapy department, where Paula is also a guest lecturer. She is a professor at the Canadian College of Osteopathy. Paula is also a consultant to the MacMaster University Occupational Therapy students. Paula brings warmth and enthusiasm to her work with children.

Shirley Sutton, BSc, OT

Shirley Sutton has worked as an occupational therapist with children and adults with special needs since 1976. She has practiced in a variety of settings, including hospitals, schools and other community settings. She recently retired from providing OT to Early Intervention Services in Simcoe County. She owns and manages her own private practice specializing in consultations and sensory equipment. Shirley offers travelling clinics across Ontario and provides workshops across Canada. She has written various articles since the initial publication of Building Bridges and is respected for her creative and practical strategies that are easy to implement at home and school. Shirley's practice is located by the shores of beautiful Georgian Bay in ski country, Collingwood Ontario. Shirley lives in Collingwood with her husband Eric. She is proud to have graduated by becoming a grandmother.

INDEX

Note: an *f* denotes a figure.

A

Activities, 193–243
- backyard and mini trampoline games, 218–219
- blowing, 205–206
- chewing, 206–207
- drooling, prevention, 208–209
- edible dough, fine motor fun, 213–215
- fine motor, 209–210
- fingers, learning to feel with, 196–198
- gross motor, 215–217
- hands, heavy work for, 211
- mouth business, 207–208
- oral motor, 204–205
- proprioceptive, 202–203
- sensory diets, 195–196
- silly putty, 215
- swimming games, 217–218
- tactile play recipes, 199–200
- two-handed (bilateral) tasks, 212–213
- vestibular, 200–202
- visual cues and strategies for gross motor activities, 220–243

Adaptation of settings, 151–191
- communication between home and school, 188–190
- consistency in environment, 151–152
- equipment, 156–158
- fine motor work, 178–181
- generalization of learning, 151
- home accommodations, 153–156
- manipulatives, 169–170
- music, 177–178
- physical education/exercise time, 167–169
- preparation for school years ahead, 183–184
- problem-solving worksheet for students with sensory processing disorder, 184–187
- school and daycare accommodations, 158–164
- sensory activities, 171–172
- sensory activity transitions and preparation, 152
- sitting and staying in a circle, 165–167
- snack time, 174–177
- social, 181–183
- washroom time, 173–174

Alerting techniques, 103–104

Animal walks, 221, 228–231

Arousal states, regulation of, 59

Attention deficit, 56–57

Auditory checklists
- dressing, 77
- eating, 79–80
- play, 87
- school/work, 83–84
- self-care, 73
- sensory, 70
- social skills, 89–90

Auditory sensitivity behavior strategies, 113

Autism spectrum disorder classifications, 3–4
- new classification system, 4
- previous labels, 3

Autobiographical reports, 6–7

Autopsy studies, 5–6

B

Backyard and mini trampoline games, 218–219
Behavior strategies, 91–120
    alerting techniques, 103–104
    calming techniques, 102–103
    organizing techniques, 103
    relaxation technique, 114–120
    sensory avoidant behaviors, 110–113
    sensory diet, 96–101
    sensory seeking behavior strategies, 104–110
    Wilbarger therapressure for sensory defensiveness, 92–96
Big ball exercises, 221–222, 231–236
Biting and grinding teeth behavior strategies, 105
Blowing activities, 205–206
Brain injury, 4–5

C

Calming techniques, 102–103
Car rides, swings, or any imposed movement, avoiding, behavior strategies, 111–112
Checklists
    dressing checklist, 75–77
    eating checklist, 78–80
    play checklist, 85–87
    school/work checklist, 81–84
    self-care checklist, 72–74
    sensory screening checklist, 69–71
    social skills checklist, 88–90
Chewing activities, 206–207
Communication between home and school, 158–161, 188–190
Consistency in environment, importance of, 151–152
Crashing, bumping, and clinging behavior strategies, 106

D

Defensiveness, 50–51
Diagnostic and Statistical Manual V (DSM V), 3, 12
Discrimination, 51–52
Dressing checklist, 75–77
    auditory, 77
    proprioception, 75–76
    smell/taste, 77
    tactile, 75
    vestibular, 76
    visual, 76–77
Dressing, self-care skills development, 126–130
    auditory, 128
    other, 128–130
    proprioceptive, 126–127
    smell, 128
    tactile, 127–128
    vestibular, 127
    vision, 128
Drooling, prevention activities, 208–209
Dunn Model of SPD, 35

E

Eating checklist, 78–80
    auditory, 79–80
    proprioception, 78–79
    smell/taste, 80
    touch, 78
    vestibular, 79
    visual, 79
Eating, self-care skills development, 142–146
    auditory, 144–145
    other strategies, 145–146
    proprioception, 142–143
    smell/taste, 145

tactile, 144
vestibular, 143–144
vision, 144
Edible dough, fine motor fun activities, 213–215
Equipment for adaptation of settings, 156–158
Equipment suppliers, 260–264
Eye contact, avoiding, behavior strategies, 110–111

F

Face, hands, and body washing, self-care skills development, 131–133
auditory, 133
other strategies, 133
proprioception, 131–132
smell, 133
tactile, 132
taste, 133
vestibular, 132
visual, 133
Fidget bag tools, 258–260
Fight, fright, or flight, 55
Fine motor activities, 209–210
Fine motor work adaptation of settings, 178–181
auditory, 179
other strategies, 180–181
proprioception, 178–179
smell/taste, 180
tactile, 179
vestibular, 179
visual, 179
Fingers, learning to feel with activities, 196–198
Flapping behavior strategies, 107

G

Generalization of learning, 151
Grandin, Temple, 6, 246
Grooming, self-care skills development, 130–131
Gross motor activities, 215–217

H

Hair brushing, self-care skills development, 136–138
other strategies, 137–138
proprioception, 136–137
smells, 137
tactile, 137
vestibular, 137
visual, 137
Hair cutting, self-care skills development, 140–142
auditory, 141
other strategies, 141–142
proprioception, 140
smell, 141
tactile, 140–141
vestibular, 140
visual, 141
Handling sensory material, avoiding, behavior strategies, 112
Hands, avoiding use, behavior strategies, 113
Hands, heavy work activities, 211
History, autism spectrum disorders and sensory integration, 4–7
autobiographical reports, 6–7
autopsy studies, 5–6
brain injury, 4–5
hyper-/hypo-reactions to sensory input, 5
neurological impairment, 4
perceptual difficulties, 4
sensory integration impairment, 5
Hitting slapping, pinching, squeezing, grabbing, and pulling behavior strategies, 106

Home accommodations adaptation of settings, 153–156
auditory, 155
other strategies, 155–156
proprioception, 153
smell/taste, 155
tactile, 154
vestibular, 153
visual, 154
Hyper-/hypo-reactions to sensory input, 5

I

Identification of sensory integration problems, 65–90
definition, 65–66
dressing checklist, 75–77
published questionnaires, 67–68
self-care checklist, 72–74
sensory screening checklist, 69–71
sensory history and profiles, 66–67
Interpretation, 19–20

L

Low-cost indoor sensory equipment ideas, 257–258

M

Make-it-yourself equipment, 245–264
fidget bag tools, 258–260
low-cost indoor sensory equipment ideas, 257–258
platform swing, 253–254
scooterboard, 254–255
stress balloon fidget tool, 256–257
stretchy hammock, 255–244
suppliers, 260–264
weighted blanket or punching bag, 249–252
weighted lap snake or lap animal, 252–253
weighted products, 246–247
weighted vest, 247–249
Manipulatives adaptation of settings, 169–170
auditory, 170
other strategies, 170
proprioception, 169
smell/taste, 170
tactile, 169
vestibular, 169
visual, 170
Masturbation behavior strategies, 109
Miller taxonomy of SPD, 36–37
Mouth business activities, 207–208
Mouth hypersensitivity reduction, 96
Music adaptation of settings, 177–178
auditory, 177–178
other strategies, 178
proprioception, 177
smell/taste, 178
tactile, 177
vestibular, 177
visual, 177

N

Neurological impairment, 4
New classification system, 4

O

Occupational therapists, 8–10
consultation, 10
definition, 8
education, 8
Wilbarger therapressure for sensory defensiveness, role in, 94
Occupational therapy, 7–10

abilities, 9
and children with ASD, 10–12
environmental factors, 9
sensory integration theory as framework, 10–11
service delivery, 12
skills, 9
Oral motor activities, 204–205
Organization of response, 22
Organizing techniques, 103
Orientation, 18–19
Over-responsivity
examples, 17
regulation of, 59
vestibular, 55–56

P

Perceptual difficulties, 4
Physical education/exercise time adaptation of settings, 167–169
auditory, 168
other strategies, 168–169
proprioception, 167
smell/taste, 168
tactile, 168
vestibular, 167–168
visual, 168
Pica behavior strategies, 109–110
Platform swing, 253–254
Play checklist, 85–87
auditory, 87
proprioception, 85–86
smell/taste, 87
touch, 85
vestibular, 86
visual, 86–87
Play, self-care skills development, 146–149
auditory, 148
other strategies, 148–149
proprioception, 146–147
smell/taste, 148
tactile, 147–148
vestibular, 147
visual, 148
Preparation for school years ahead, 183–184
Preservative play behavior strategies, 108
Previous labels for autism, 3
Problem-solving worksheet for students with sensory processing disorder, 184–187
Process of sensory integration, 16–23
execution of response, 23
interpretation, 19–20
organization of response, 22
orientation, 18–19
sensory registration, 16–18
Progressive relaxation exercises, sensory diet, 77, 98–100
Proprioception checklists
dressing, 75–76
eating, 78–79
play, 85–86
school/work, 81–82
self-care, 72
sensory, 69–70
social skills, 88
Proprioceptive activities, 202–203
Proprioceptive system, 58–62
definition, 58
dysfunction, 60–62
overresponsivity, regulation of, 59
regulation of arousal states, 59
Proprioceptive system dysfunction, 60–62

R

Relaxation technique, 114–120
instructions, 115–120
progressive relaxation, 114
types, 114
Roughhousing, 221, 223–227
Running, spinning, or movement seeking behavior strategies, 105

S

Saliva, playing with behavior strategies, 107
School and daycare accommodations for adaptation of settings, 158–164
auditory, 163
general strategies, 164–165
multi-sensory, 161
proprioception, 161–162
smell/taste, 164
tactile, 162–163
vestibular, 162
visual, 163
School/work checklist, 81–84
auditory, 83–84
proprioception, 81–82
smell/taste, 84
touch, 81
vestibular, 82
visual, 82–83
Scooterboard, 254–255
Scooterboard activities, 222, 236–239
Self-care checklist, 72–74
auditory, 73
emotional/behavioral, 74
general observations, 74
proprioception, 72
smell/taste, 73–74
tactile, 72
vestibular, 72–73
visual, 73
Self-care skills development, 121–149
dressing, 126–130
eating, 142–146
face, hands, and body washing, 131–133
grooming, 130–131
hair brushing, 136–138
hair cutting, 140–142
play, 146–149
sleep, 122–126
teeth brushing, 138–140
toilet training, 134–136
wake up time, 126
Self-regulation, 25–28
Sensory activities adaptation of settings, 171–172
auditory, 172
other strategies, 172
proprioception, 171
smell/taste, 172
tactile, 171
vestibular, 171
visual, 172
Sensory activity transitions and preparation, 152
Sensory avoidant behaviors strategies, 110–113
auditory sensitivity, 113
car rides, swings, or any imposed movement, avoiding, 111–112
eye contact, avoiding, 110–111
handling sensory material, avoiding, 112
hands, avoiding use, 113
taking off clothes, 110
Sensory defensive behaviors, 21–22, 94–96

Sensory diet, 96–101, 195–196
accommodations, 98
activities, 195–196
aims, 97
definition, 97
implementation, 98
progressive relaxation exercises, 77, 98–100
results, 101
sitting/circle time, 101
tactile activities, 100
Wilbarger therapressure, incorporation of, 94
Sensory gifts vs. sensory challenges, 25
Sensory integration
additional differences in sensory experiences, 24
definition, 13
development of theory, 14
dysfunction, 35–37
dyspraxia, 31–35
as foundation for learning, 13f
impairment, 5
motor planning, 29–31
process, 16–23
self-regulation, 25–28
sensory gifts vs. sensory challenges, 25
and sensory processing, 14
Sensory integration theory
as framework for occupational therapy, 10–11
intervention, guidance for, 39–40
limitations, 43
parent and professional assistance, 41–43
research, 43–45
understanding, increase in, 39
Sensory processing
definition, 14
interpretation, 19–20
organization of response, 22
orientation, 18–19
sensory registration, 16–18
Sensory processing disorder (SPD), 35–38
Dunn Model of SPD, 35
incidence and cause, 38
Miller taxonomy of SPD, 36–37
signs, 37
Sensory registration, 16–18
Sensory screening checklist, 69–71
auditory, 70
olfactory/gustatory, 70–71
proprioceptive, 69–70
tactile, 69
vestibular, 69
visual, 70
Sensory seeking behavior strategies, 104–110
biting and grinding teeth, 105
crashing, bumping, and clinging, 106
flapping, 107
hitting slapping, pinching, squeezing, grabbing, and pulling, 106
masturbation, 109
pica, 109–110
preservative play, 108
running, spinning, or movement seeking, 105
saliva, playing with, 107
smelling behaviors, 108
Sensory systems, 47–62
proprioceptive system, 58–62
tactile system, 47–52
vestibular system, 52–58
Silly putty activities, 215
Sitting and staying in a circle adaptation of settings, 165–167

auditory, 16
other strategies, 166–167
proprioception, 165
smell/taste, 166
tactile, 165–166
vestibular, 165
visual, 166
Sitting/circle time, sensory diet, 101
Sleep, self-care skills development, 122–126
auditory, 125
other strategies, 125
proprioception, 123–124
smell, 125
tactile, 124
vestibular, 124
vision, 124–125
Smelling behaviors behavior strategies, 108
Smell/taste checklists
dressing, 77
eating, 80
play, 87
school/work, 84
self-care, 73–74
sensory, 70–71
social skills, 90
Snack time adaptation of settings, 174–177
auditory, 176
other strategies, 176–177
proprioception, 175
smell/taste, 176
tactile, 175–176
vestibular, 175
visual, 176
Social adaptation of settings, 181–183
auditory, 182
other strategies, 182–183
proprioception, 181
smell/taste, 182
tactile, 181–182
vestibular, 181
visual, 182
Social skills checklist, 88–90
auditory, 89–90
proprioception, 88
smell/taste, 90
touch, 88
vestibular, 88–89
visual, 89
Stress balloon fidget tool, 256–257
Stretchy hammock, 255–244
Swimming games, 217–218

T

Tactile activities, sensory diet, 100
Tactile checklists
dressing, 75
eating, 79–80
play, 85
school/work, 83–84
self-care, 72
sensory, 69
social skills, 88
Tactile play recipes, 199–200
Tactile system, 47–52
definition, 47–48
discriminative system, 49
dysfunction, 49–52
protective system, 48–49
Tactile system dysfunction, 49–52
defensiveness, 50–51

discrimination, 51–52
underresponsivity, 51
Taking off clothes, behavior strategies, 110
Teeth brushing, self-care skills development, 138–140
auditory, 139
general strategies, 139–140
proprioception, 138
smell/taste, 139
tactile, 138–139
vision, 139
Temple Grandin (HBO), 6
Toilet training, self-care skills development, 134–136
auditory, 136
other strategies, 136
proprioceptive, 134
smell, 136
tactile, 135
vestibular, 134–135
visual, 135
Two-handed (bilateral) tasks, 212–213

U

Under-responsivity
examples, 17–18
touch, 51
vestibular, 57–58

V

Vestibular activities, 200–202
Vestibular checklists
dressing, 76
eating, 79
play, 86
school/work, 82
self-care, 72–73
sensory, 69
social skills, 88–89
Vestibular system, 52–58
definition, 52–53
dysfunction, 55–58
role in modulation of other systems, 53–54
Vestibular system dysfunction, 55–58
attention deficit, 56–57
fight, fright, or flight, 55
over-responsiveness, 55–56
underresponsivity, 57–58
Visual checklists
dressing, 76–77
eating, 79
play, 86–87
school/work, 82–83
self-care, 73
sensory, 70
social skills, 89
Visual cues and strategies for gross motor activities, 220–243
animal walks, 221, 228–231
big ball exercises, 221–222, 231–236
roughhousing, 221, 223–227
scooter board activities, 222, 236–239
yoga activities, 222, 240–243

W

Wake up time skills development, 126
Washroom time adaptation of settings, 173–174
auditory, 174
other strategies, 174
proprioception, 173
smell/taste, 174
tactile, 173

vestibular, 173

visual, 174

Weighted blanket or punching bag, 249–252

Weighted lap snake or lap animal, 252–253

Weighted products, 246–247

Weighted vest, 247–249

Wilbarger therapressure for sensory defensiveness, 92–96

anecdotal reporting, 93

mouth hypersensitivity reduction, 96

occupational therapist, role in, 94

origins, 92

routine

sensory defensiveness, 94–96

sensory diet schedule, incorporation in, 94

Williams, Donna, 6, 246

Yoga activities, 222, 240–243